W9-BOA-171

DC PUBLIC LIBRARY

3 1172 06034 2037

THE NPR
CLASSICAL MUSIC
COMPANION

The

NPR

CLASSICAL MUSIC
COMPANION

*An Essential Guide
for Enlightened Listening*

MILES HOFFMAN

Houghton Mifflin Company

BOSTON   NEW YORK

Copyright © 1997 by Miles Hoffman and National Public Radio
All rights reserved

For information about permission to reproduce selections from
this book, write to Permissions, Houghton Mifflin Company,
215 Park Avenue South, New York, New York 10003.

Visit our Web site: www.houghtonmifflinbooks.com.

Library of Congress Cataloging-in-Publication Data

Hoffman, Miles.
    The NPR classical music companion : an essential guide for
enlightened listening / Miles Hoffman.
        p.   cm.
    Includes index.
    ISBN-13: 978-0-618-61945-0 (pbk.)
    ISBN-10: 0-618-61945-3 (pbk.)
    1. Music — Dictionaries. 2. Music — Terminology — Popular works.
I. National Public Radio (U.S.) II. Title.
    ML108.H64   1997   97-10479
    780'.3 — dc21   97-10479   CIP

Printed in the United States of America

MP 10 9 8 7 6 5 4 3 2 1

Book design by Melodie Wertelet

National Public Radio, NPR, Performance Today, and Morning Edition
are registered service marks of National Public Radio, Inc.

MUS,
REF,
780.3
H 711

FOR SUSAN

ACKNOWLEDGMENTS

The staff of NPR®'s *Performance Today*® is a collection of ex-traordinarily talented, dedicated, and congenial individuals, and I consider myself very fortunate to be associated with them. I would like to thank in particular Don Lee, the executive producer of *Performance Today,* who has supported my on-air efforts since the beginning, and who asked me to write this book; *PT* host Martin Goldsmith, who has been an inspiring colleague and a good friend, and who is quite simply the best in the business; Penny Hain, assistant producer, who has improved my "Coming to Terms" commentaries every week for years with her judicious and highly skilled editing; and Benjamin Roe, NPR's senior pro-ducer for music and special projects, who personally produced some 250 installments of "Coming to Terms." Ben's broad knowl-edge, intellectual vigor, love of music, and love of radio spurred me to expand my interests and sharpen my thinking, and to explore in great depth questions that in some cases I hadn't pre-viously considered at all.

Many of my musical friends and associates were kind enough to share their time and expertise with me as I wrote this book. I'm indebted to them all, and I hope they will forgive me for not listing them individually: it would be a very long list. Often my colleagues provided insights and information that I could have found nowhere else. I would especially like to thank Elisabeth Adkins, associate concertmaster of the National Symphony Or-chestra and my colleague in the American Chamber Players, who read the manuscript and made many helpful suggestions.

At Houghton Mifflin, my editor is Wendy Holt, and I'm deeply grateful to her. I appreciate not only her remarkably astute and sympathetic editing, but also her enthusiasm and her patience, neither of which ever flagged, and both of which helped sustain my spirits during the many months of writing. She did a terrific job. I'm grateful as well to Jayne Yaffe for her careful and thorough manuscript editing.

Finally, and with all my heart, I thank my wife, Susan. Her gifts of eye, ear, and insight are uncanny, and there's not a page of this book that is not the better for her contributions — just as there's not a day of my life that is not the better and more joyful for her presence in it.

AUTHOR'S NOTE

"It is likewise to be observed that this society hath a peculiar cant
and jargon of their own, that no other mortal can understand . . ."

— Jonathan Swift, *Gulliver's Travels*

～

"Jargonbusters" was the name Martin Goldsmith had in mind
when he asked me, in the fall of 1989, if I'd be interested in doing
a regular feature for National Public Radio®'s *Performance Today*.
Martin was about to take over as host of the program, and he had
an idea for a weekly feature that would include "listener-friendly"
explanations of some of the many foreign words and technical
terms peculiar to the world of classical music. Martin's estimate of
my radio skills (and listener-friendliness potential) was based almost entirely on a series of public radio programs I had written
eight years before called *Classics Illustrated: Great Music and Conversations with People Who Know More Than You Do.* The velvet-
voiced straight man for those programs was my friend Glen
Howard, a brilliant (and very funny) lawyer and former rock-and-
roll disk jockey, and my role was to impersonate such luminaries
as Bubba Offanonanoff, famous Russian emigré ocarina virtuoso;
Sugar Ray Gupta Gesh, "the André Previn of the Subcontinent";
and Waldo Sprout, expert on self-improvement through musically treated vegetables. Martin, then the program director of
WETA-FM in Washington, D.C., actually put these shows on
the air.

At any rate, I thought Martin's idea for a new *Performance Today* feature was wonderful: the tangle of foreign terms and technical jargon surrounding classical music often forms an unfortunate

barrier, distancing or discomforting people unnecessarily, and to chip away at that barrier seemed a very good thing. I agreed to give it a try. And as I recall, my enthusiasm was considerably heightened by Martin's willingness to drop "Jargonbusters" as a title and accept "Coming to Terms" in its place. We weren't sure how it would turn out, but as I write these words almost eight years later, Martin and I are still "coming to terms" together every week on *PT*.

The NPR Classical Music Companion is a natural offspring of "Coming to Terms." I make no claims to have written an exhaustive reference work — that wasn't my goal. I've tried, rather, to discuss the terms that "ordinary listeners" and music lovers are most likely to hear on the radio or come across in concert programs, program notes, newspaper reviews, and CD booklets. And I've tried to examine the kinds of subjects that people most often wonder about: "What does a conductor really do?" for example, or "What does it mean for a piece of music to be in a key, and why does a composer choose one key instead of another?" "Why does so much modern music sound like gobbledygook — or worse?" I like to think that the countless questions I've received at NPR via phone, mail, and E-mail, in addition to years of conversations with concert audiences all over the country, have given me a pretty good sense of what's on listeners' minds.

Above all, I've tried to write a reference book that's readable; one that, while providing important basic definitions, also provides helpful background material, interesting perspectives (including, at times, the specific perspective of a performing musician), and even a little humor. Like "Coming to Terms," *The NPR Classical Music Companion* is intended for people who enjoy classical music and are curious about it, whether or not they've had any previous musical education or training. And like "Coming to Terms," this book reflects my belief that the world of classical music is a world of beauty and pleasure, to be explored not with apprehension or anxiety, but with delight.

THE NPR
CLASSICAL MUSIC
COMPANION

A CAPPELLA

"The choir performed a cappella." "The piece was for mixed chorus and soloists a cappella." When applied to choral music or its performance, the term *a cappella* means "without instrumental accompaniment." In Italian, the literal meaning of *a cappella* is "as in the chapel," or "in the style of the chapel," and, indeed, the term was first used to describe the unaccompanied vocal music that the Italian composer Giovanni Pierluigi da Palestrina (ca. 1525–1594) and his sixteenth-century colleagues composed for the Church. Today, however, the term is accepted in the domain of the secular as well as the sacred, or wherever instruments are not invited.

ABSOLUTE PITCH

Absolute pitch, also known as **PERFECT PITCH**, is the ability to hear a note or sound and identify its exact pitch, that is, the name of the note, without using any external reference such as an instrument or tuning device [see PITCH]. A person who has absolute pitch simply hears a note and knows what it is — B-flat, C-sharp, E-natural — as if the note had traveled through the air with its name attached. If the note B-flat is sounded, for example, what a person without absolute pitch hears is a note. What a person *with* absolute pitch hears is a B-flat.

Are people born with absolute pitch, or do they learn it? This is a classic "nature-nurture" question, with no definitive answer. The ear can certainly be trained through practice, exercises, and drills (ear training courses are a staple in music schools and conservatories), and there are those who claim to have devised methods "guaranteed" to develop absolute pitch. It also seems clear that early childhood training and musical exposure contribute to the development of pitch sensitivity. It seems just as clear, however, that nature plays a role. Even among equally well trained musicians and members of the same household — and among famous composers, for that matter — some people have absolute pitch and some don't. There are different degrees and gradations of absolute pitch, too. Some people, for example, can identify a note if it's played on the piano but not on another instrument, while others can immediately identify any sound at all — a steam whistle, a car horn, a wolf's howl — by pitch. Simply put, some people have "better ears" than others. Perhaps the fairest conclusion is that if people aren't necessarily born having absolute pitch, then at the very least some have a greater innate capacity to develop it.

But how important is it for a musician to have absolute pitch, anyway? Some musicians who have it downplay its value, partly from modesty or politeness, but it's doubtful they would give it up if they could, and in any case those who have it can't conceive of what it would be like *not* to have it. Some musicians who don't have it downplay its value, partly from envy, but it's probable that most would prefer to have it, if they had a choice. On the one hand, it's a way to know more about what you hear, and is therefore intrinsically desirable. And from a practical standpoint, it can come in quite handy. Absolute pitch can make it easier to "hear" music just by looking at printed notes on a page, for example, and it can be very helpful in memorizing pieces for performance, playing or singing pieces for the first time (sight-reading), and recognizing musical cues — or mistakes — when playing with others. For a conductor, absolute pitch can make it easier to keep track of who's playing what and to locate problems quickly. On the other hand, absolute pitch guarantees neither musical creativity nor beautiful performances, and is not an indispensable ingredient for either.

An ingredient that *is* indispensable to composing and to all good musicianship is RELATIVE PITCH. Relative pitch is the ability to determine pitch from a known starting point, the ability, in other words, to perceive intervals, which are the distances in pitch *between* notes. With relative pitch you hear first if a note is higher or lower than another (or the same), and the better or more refined your relative pitch, the more precisely you can tell *how much* higher or lower. If a person without absolute pitch but with good relative pitch hears a note that he somehow knows to be a C-sharp, for example, he can then determine the identity of subsequent notes by relating them to the C-sharp, and to one another.

Relative pitch doesn't carry guarantees of accomplishment any more than absolute pitch does. But since the pitch relationships between and among notes form the basis for all melody and harmony, good relative pitch is essential for composing. And since hearing those relationships is the basis for playing or singing notes correctly, *in tune,* both alone and with others, good relative pitch is essential for performing. It's also important for listening to music, for recognizing and appreciating musical patterns, phrases, and gestures. Just as with absolute pitch, there are gradations of relative pitch. Highly trained musicians may be particularly discerning, but anybody who can carry a tune or recognize a tune has relative pitch.

❧

Absolute pitch and relative pitch are faculties of sound perception, not sound production. There are many people with "great ears" who can neither sing nor whistle in tune, and it's either because they simply can't sing or whistle, or because they don't have a well-developed aural-oral connection. In the same way, a musically trained ear doesn't necessarily lead to a facility for mimicking accents or speaking foreign languages. It's not just the ear that counts, it's the mouth as well, and the mysterious pathways between the two. A musician must make sure not just that his ears are working, but that he's applying what he hears and making the connection to the hands, fingers, lips, or vocal cords.

An accompaniment is music that supports other music being played or sung at the same time. It's the part in a composition that provides the musical context, or background, for a more prominent part. At any given moment, the principal part of a musical composition usually features a melody or theme of some kind, and the accompaniment may consist of another melody or melodies, a rhythmic pulse or underpinning, a structure of chords or harmonies, or a combination of any or all of these elements. In a painting or photograph, the choice of setting has an enormous influence on how the principal subject appears to the viewer and on how it affects the viewer. It's the same in music: context is crucial to meaning and emotional effect. The goal of an accompaniment is to marry the elements of melody, rhythm, and harmony to the principal musical material in such a way as to make that material more beautiful, more compelling, or simply more interesting. [See MELODY; RHYTHM; HARMONY~CHORD.]

An accompaniment may be provided by a single instrument or voice, by a combination of instruments or voices, or by a combination of instruments *and* voices. A pianist may accompany a flutist, for example, or three string players may accompany a fourth, or a chorus and orchestra may accompany a vocal soloist. On keyboard instruments like the piano and organ, or on the harp, it's common for one hand to play a melody while the other plays an accompaniment. In the course of any one piece, however, instruments or voices — or left and right hands — often switch roles, with one first carrying the melody, then participating in the accompaniment. This role-switching occurs in all kinds of pieces, from vocal duets to choral works, from sonatas to string quartets to symphonies. Even in concertos, where the music that the orchestra plays is called the orchestral accompaniment, the orchestra doesn't always accompany: sometimes it comes to the fore to play the principal musical material while the soloist is either silent or just "noodling" along with decorative — i.e., accompanimental — passages [see CONCERTO]. In any kind of musical collaboration, it's very important for performers to recognize and adjust to different musical material, to know when to accompany discreetly and when to "bring out" a melody or thematic passage.

And now, a word on behalf of pianists: With two hands and ten fingers at their disposal, pianists can play melodies and chords at the same time. The piano can thus provide the elements of harmony, melody, and rhythm simultaneously, which makes it the ideal accompanying instrument. And indeed, for two centuries composers have found the piano indispensable for accompanying singers and solo instrumentalists. (Before the invention of the piano, its older keyboard cousins the organ, harpsichord, and clavichord filled the bill. The lute and the guitar can also play melodies and chords simultaneously, which is why they too have been extremely popular accompanying instruments. See KEYBOARD INSTRUMENTS; GUITAR; LUTE.)

It is a common misconception, however, that when a pianist plays with one other performer the pianist is always "just" accompanying. For example, while it's true that in songs, arias, and sonatas throughout the 1600s and 1700s, accompanying keyboard instruments were generally subordinate to the voice or solo instrument, it's also true that in sonatas of the late eighteenth century the piano was often considered the dominant participant [see SONATA]. Many of Mozart's sonatas (and some of Beethoven's), for instance, were published with such titles as Sonata for Pianoforte with the Accompaniment of the Violin. (This publishing practice was actually more than a little unfair to the violin, or to whatever "other" instrument was involved, but it had its roots in the historical notion that certain kinds of sonatas were created by "adding" another instrument to the piano sonata.) Also, in the early nineteenth century, Franz Schubert (1797–1828) significantly changed the nature of vocal accompaniments by writing songs whose piano parts were of independent dramatic and musical character: the piano and the voice became equal partners. Many later song composers followed Schubert's example, and a large percentage of both sonatas and songs from Schubert's time onward are properly considered true duos, rather than pieces for soloist with piano accompaniment. In general, then, it's only right to call the people who play the piano in song or sonata recitals *pianists,* not accompanists.

[See ARIA; ART SONG; INNER VOICES.]

ACOUSTICS

Acoustics is the science of sound. More specifically, it's the branch of physics that deals with sound waves and their properties: how sound waves are generated, how they behave in various circumstances, how they interact. Applied to music, acoustics is the basis for understanding the functioning of all musical instruments and of the voice; the nature of musical tones or notes, their relationships to each other, and why they sound the way they do in different combinations; and the differences in quality of musical sounds, from differences in volume to differences in timbre, or "tone color" [see TIMBRE].

Most of the time, however, when we encounter the word *acoustics* in the world of music it has a very different sense. It usually has an adjective attached, as in "excellent acoustics" or "terrible acoustics," and generally refers to the qualities and characteristics of a room, concert hall, auditorium, or theater. To ask "What are the acoustics like?" in a specific room is to ask what that room is like for listening to music. How does the space itself affect sound?

The list of adjectives used to describe room acoustics is a long and interesting one, and covers gradations much more subtle and descriptive than just "excellent" or "terrible." Acoustics can be dry, warm, reverberant, rich, clear, harsh, brilliant, live, or dead. They can be honest or deceptive, accurate, flattering, or fuzzy. They can also be brilliant but harsh, clear but dry, dry but honest, or some other combination of qualities that is either positive or problematic. In general, the best acoustics for listening to music usually involve a healthy balance of resonance and richness of sound with clarity, or accuracy, of sound. There is no one set of acoustics that is perfect for everything, however. Different kinds of music may be better served by different acoustics, and it's important that the selection suit the setting, and vice versa. A piece for solo cello or a work of medieval vocal music, for example, might sound wonderful in the richly reverberant acoustics of a cavernous church, while a string quartet or sonata for violin and piano in the same space would sound like mush.

Absolutely everything in the design and construction of a room contributes to its acoustics, from the shape and size of the room, to the construction and finishing materials, to the seating configuration and stage design, to the seemingly insignificant decorative details. It's therefore next to impossible to say exactly why the acoustics are better in one room (or concert hall, or auditorium) than in another. Some things are predictable — if two rooms are the same size and shape, but the walls of one are naked stone and the walls of the other are covered with thick drapes, the room with the drapes will be the "deader" of the two. (Stone tends to reflect sound, drapes tend to absorb it. When sound is absorbed, it "dies.") But how often are rooms exactly the same except for one simple variable? The effects of each variable in a room are not precisely predictable because the variables never operate independently; they overlap and interact. Yes, stone tends to reflect sound, wood tends to vibrate with sound, and fabric tends to absorb sound. But a curved stone wall reflects sound differently from a straight stone wall, and wood vibrates differently depending on what it's attached to, how it's attached, and how far it is from the source of the sound, and fabric seat covers might soften a harsh auditorium sound just enough while heavy curtains at the back and sides of a stage might stifle the sound . . . and so on. The number of people in a room affects the acoustics, too, and so does the weather, since the quality of the air affects how sound travels through it. It's the "total package" that counts, the sum of interactions among all factors that can affect the way sound waves are projected, reflected, bounced around, or absorbed.

While the acoustics of a concert hall or auditorium naturally affect the quality of the listener's experience, what's sometimes overlooked is that the acoustics determine how the music sounds to the *performer,* as well, while he or she is performing. What's more, the acoustics onstage are often very different from the acoustics "out in the hall." This can have a very significant influence on the quality of the performance. When the acoustics are lovely onstage, a performer sounds good to himself, feels encouraged, and finds it easier to perform beautifully. In cases where the acoustics onstage are extremely dry, that is, lacking all resonance, or where the performer feels he's playing into a dead hall, it's harder for him to play naturally and comfortably because of the feeling that no matter what he does the sound won't be beautiful. Some stages have live spots and dead spots, and on some stages it's simply hard to hear from one spot to another, even if it's only a matter of a few feet. When the musicians performing together have a hard time hearing one another — and unfortunately this is not at all uncommon — it's naturally harder to maintain cohesiveness and clarity. Musicians talk about halls and stages that "give something back," that add something to a performance and make it a delightful experience, and about other halls where "you're on your own," forced to rely upon craft, experience, and a sense of professional responsibility to give a good performance despite the surroundings.

Principles of acoustical design based on the nature of sound waves and the properties of materials have been known since Greek and Roman times. Nonetheless, there has always been something mysterious about why one space turns out sounding radiant and another dull, something that seems to have to do as much with art as with science. Nowadays specialists called acoustical engineers are hired to design the interiors of concert halls. Using sophisticated instruments, highly accurate measurements, and the latest in modern materials and architectural elements, they sometimes achieve wonderful results. They also sometimes demonstrate that the people who built concert halls in the "old days" knew what they were doing.

ADAGIO

[See TEMPO MARKINGS.]

ALLEGRO

[See TEMPO MARKINGS.]

ANDANTE

[See TEMPO MARKINGS.]

ARIA

Arias are the pieces for solo voice with instrumental accompaniment that are found in operas, oratorios, and cantatas. They're songs, in a sense, but they tend to be more musically elaborate and vocally demanding than the kinds of pieces usually *called* songs.

The original and still primary meaning of the Italian word *aria* is "air," as in the air we breathe, but this meaning has nothing to do with the evolution of the term in its musical sense. The etymological paths are long and twisted, but by the 1400s *aria* had also come to mean "a musical setting of poetry." The first arias, in fact, were merely simple tunes into which any poems having the right rhythmic structure could be "plugged." By the 1500s the English and the French had borrowed the term, but the English *ayre* or *air,* and the French *air,* both went on to develop along different, and generally less complex, lines than the Italian *aria.*

The development of opera in Italy in the 1600s is what brought the aria to glory. The dominant style in the earliest operas had been a kind of dramatic declamation, more like musical reciting than what we now think of as operatic singing. As opera evolved, however, arias became much more melodious and musically interesting, and a division of labor developed: reciting style, or *recitative,* became "drier" and faster and was used mostly to impart information and advance the action, while the aria became the vehicle for emotional response, for the expression of passion [see RECITATIVE]. By the mid-1600s, the aria was already by far the most important element of opera; beautiful arias were what audiences came to hear.

For about one hundred years, roughly from 1650 to 1750, the principal type of aria in opera, and also in the oratorios and cantatas of composers like Johann Sebastian Bach (1685–1750) and George Frideric Handel (1685–1759), was the *da capo* aria. *Da capo* is Italian for "from the beginning." A *da capo* aria has three sections — an opening section, a contrasting second section, and a repeat, "from the beginning," of the first section. In actual practice, however, the third section was never a literal repeat of the first. It was the section in which singers would use the opening material as a kind of skeleton, to be fleshed out with all sorts of musical embellishments.

The reign of the *da capo* aria coincided with the reign of the *castrati* as the stars of opera [see CASTRATI]. These singers, men who had been castrated as boys, were famous for their powerful high voices and technical virtuosity, and they made the *da capo* aria — especially its repeated section — into a vehicle not just for passionate expression, but for fabulous self-display. Eventually, though, the virtuoso showing-off degenerated into pure excess, which came at the expense of emotional expression and dramatic realism. This led to a reaction against the *da capo* form, and to a decline in its popularity.

Christoph Willibald Gluck (1714–1787), a German-Bohemian composer of French and Italian opera, stripped the aria of frills and led the movement back toward what he took to be realism and honest emotional expression in opera. After 1750 the aria developed in many directions, but in its various structures and styles it continued to thrive. It's no exaggeration, in fact, to say that the aria has been one of the most successful and durable forms in the history of Western music: with a detour for the later operas of Richard Wagner (1813–1883), who abandoned arias and other set pieces in favor of a continuous vocal-orchestral texture, the aria has remained an absolutely vital feature of operatic composition from the 1600s to this day.

[See OPERA; CANTATA; ORATORIO.]

ARPEGGIO

A *chord* is three or more notes played (or sung) simultaneously. To play an arpeggio is to play the notes of a chord *consecutively,* usually in quick succession. An arpeggio can be major or minor, ascending or descending in pitch, and it can cover the span of more than one octave. Musicians often talk about a "two-octave arpeggio," or a "three-octave arpeggio," where the sequence of notes remains the same in each octave [see OCTAVE; PITCH].

Since the notes of a C-major chord, for example, are C, E, and G, a two-octave C-major arpeggio, ascending and descending, may be pictured as:

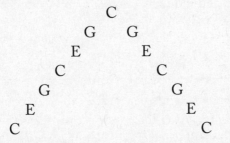

Note that each span from C to C is an octave, hence each direction covers two octaves, and the sequence on the way down is an exact mirror of the sequence on the way up. An arpeggio may be thought of as *skipping* up and down the scale, rather than going step by step.

Chords are the structural units of harmony: a C-major chord defines the harmony of C major. It *is* C major. The same is true of a C-major arpeggio. Arpeggios define harmonies just as surely as chords do because they're simply stretched-out versions of chords.

[See HARMONY~CHORD.]

All musicians, singers as well as instrumentalists, practice arpeggios, for the same reasons that they practice scales: it's good for developing and maintaining precise intonation, technical facility, evenness and beauty of sound, and good rhythm.

[See SCALE.]

⤵

To "arpeggiate" a chord is to take a chord that is in fact notated as a chord, with the notes stacked up on one another, and play it as an arpeggio. Pianists call this "rolling" a chord. A roll can be a matter of personal discretion (or necessity, if the pianist's hands aren't big enough to play all the notes of a chord at once), but often a composer specifically calls for it. It's usually indicated in the music by a wavy vertical line to the left of the chord.

⤵

The word *arpeggio* comes from the Italian *arpeggiare,* "to play the harp." (*Arpa* is Italian for harp.) Arpeggios do come quite naturally on the harp, but for the record, harpists can also play chords, scales, and individual notes in any sequence required.

ARRANGEMENT

To make an arrangement of a musical composition is to rewrite the composition for a new set of musical forces, vocal or instrumental. Beethoven's Fifth Symphony may be arranged for balalaika ensemble, for example, or, along more traditional lines, a Schubert song for voice and piano may be arranged for violin and piano.

In the process of arrangement, a piece may be shortened, lengthened, simplified, or made more complicated. The melodies, harmonies, and rhythms may all be subject to alterations of one kind or another, and the piece may be completely transposed, that is, shifted to a different key [see KEY~TONALITY]. An arrangement does not involve a complete change of identity, however: the original composition always remains recognizable.

The reasons for making arrangements are most often practical ones. A junior high school orchestra might need a simplified arrangement of a difficult work, for example, a pop singer might need songs arranged for his particular backup group, a composer might feel that in an arrangement calling for fewer musicians a piece will be performed more often, a violinist might feel that an arrangement of a Schubert song would make a perfect encore piece . . . or a balalaika ensemble might feel the need to make a splash. In some cases, an arrangement may actually represent an improvement, a sprucing up of a work that frankly needs it. And when the original forces are not available, an arrangement may be the only way to hear a piece at all.

Arrangements are often made by composers themselves, or by **ARRANGERS,** musicians who have specialized experience and training but who don't necessarily compose original works. Arranging is by no means just a mechanical task: it can be done sensitively, ingeniously, and beautifully, and it can also be done badly. The best arrangements, while not intended to replace the original, are always *interesting.* They bring a welcome variety, and can prompt us to listen to a piece with fresh ears — to hear things in it that we may not have noticed before, or to hear the whole piece in a different way. The violinist Samuel Dushkin (1891–1976) collaborated with the composer Igor Stravinsky (1882–1971) on a number of arrangements for violin and piano of works that Stravinsky had originally written for orchestra. Dushkin wrote, "There are two ways of approaching the problem of making arrangements. One is to make playable music for the desired instrument. The other is to go back to the essence of the music and rewrite or recreate the music in the spirit of the new instrument." Stravinsky, according to Dushkin, "was interested only in the latter."

TRANSCRIPTION is another word for arrangement. The repertoire of pieces for solo viola, for example, is not as extensive as the solo cello repertoire, therefore violists often play cello works that have been "transcribed" for viola. A **REDUCTION** is also an arrangement, but of a specific kind: a work for large musical forces is "reduced" to a version for smaller forces. In practice, *reduction* almost always refers to a "piano reduction," an arrangement for piano of music originally written for orchestra or instrumental ensemble. Again, the reasons for making such arrangements are practical: many pieces, whether concertos or works with vocal soloists and/or chorus, involve the accompaniment of an orchestra, and it's a lot easier to schedule — and pay for — a pianist to rehearse a piece than a full orchestra. You don't need as big a room, either. In the days before phonographs and radios, piano reductions were also the only way people could become familiar, in their homes, with many chamber music works and with the great works of the symphonic and operatic literature. The piano as a "home entertainment system" in middle-class families exploded in popularity in the nineteenth century, and music publishers did big business in reductions for piano and for piano, four-hands (two players).

An ORCHESTRATION is the opposite of a reduction: to orchestrate a piece is to arrange it for orchestra. Some composers write mostly at the piano. Their music starts out in a version for piano (or with piano accompaniment instead of orchestra), and they either orchestrate it later themselves or hire someone (an arranger) to orchestrate it. The use of such arrangers is most common in the fields of popular music, film music, and Broadway musicals. [See ORCHESTRATION.]

ART SONG

Art song is a general term that refers to the kinds of songs written by classically trained composers for classically trained singers, usually songs for solo voice with piano accompaniment. It's not an entirely *necessary* term, really — composers themselves don't talk about writing "art songs," they simply say "songs," as do most people most of the time. But it can be a useful term for distinguishing songs in the classical music tradition from folk songs and pop songs. In German, art songs are called *Lieder* (pronounced "leader"; the singular is *Lied*), a word frequently used by non-German speakers, too, especially when referring to songs with German texts. In French the word for popular song is *chanson*, but for art song it's *mélodie*.

An art song is a poem set to music. When the marriage of poetry and music is a healthy one, the poetic images inspire and inform the musical language, while the music illuminates and intensifies the emotional expression of the words. The art song as we know it today is a product of the nineteenth-century movement known as Romanticism, whose ideals included a close connection between literature and music and the glorification of the expression of intense individual feelings [see ROMANTICISM]. It is also, incidentally, primarily a creation of German-speaking composers. Italian composers had long been famous for their talent in setting words to music, but since the 1600s they had channeled that talent into opera, and specifically into the development of the aria [see ARIA].

The composer most closely identified with the growth of the art song into an important and independent musical form is Franz Schubert (1797–1828). From the age of fourteen until his death at age thirty-one, Schubert wrote approximately six hundred songs, single-handedly creating a huge repertoire and demonstrating the art song's remarkable potential for variety of subject matter and range of emotional expression. Schubert's gifts for "translating" poetry into music and for creating beautiful melody and harmony can only be described as genius, and he also changed the nature of piano accompaniments, elevating the piano from what had been a mostly subordinate position to the role of an independent, fully equal dramatic and poetic partner to the voice. In fairness, other composers had written art songs before Schubert. Mozart, for example, wrote beautiful songs, and Beethoven composed a number of extraordinary, innovative works that undoubtedly influenced Schubert. But songs were more or less incidental to the work of Mozart and Beethoven. Schubert's impact on the history of the art song was on a different scale, consistent with his complete devotion to the form, the infinite beauties of his songs, and the immensity of his output.

Of the many *Lieder* composers who followed Schubert in the nineteenth century and who inevitably felt his influence, the greatest and most important were Robert Schumann (1810–1856), who expanded the role of the piano even further; Johannes Brahms (1833–1897); and Hugo Wolf (1860–1903). Gustav Mahler (1860–1911) and Richard Strauss (1864–1949) carried the tradition through the end of the nineteenth century into the twentieth. In France, the first important composer to write art songs was Hector Berlioz (1803–1869). Later luminaries of the *mélodie* included Charles Gounod (1818–1893), Jules Massenet (1842–1912), Gabriel Fauré (1845–1924), Henri Duparc (1848–1933), Claude Debussy (1862–1918), and Francis Poulenc (1899–1963). Modest Mussorgsky (1839–1881), Peter Ilyich Tchaikovsky (1840–1893), and Sergei Rachmaninoff (1873–1943) wrote many wonderful Russian songs, and the twentieth-century Americans Charles Ives (1874–1954), Aaron Copland (1900–1990), and Samuel Barber (1910–1981), along with Englishman Benjamin Britten (1913–1976), all made important contributions to the literature of art songs in English. Fine contemporary composers continue to write fine art songs: though musical styles change all the time, expressing emotion through song is not something that ever goes out of style, and the art song is not a form that is ever likely to be obsolete.

In theory, an art song is an art song and a pop song is a pop song, and although the difference may be hard to articulate, usually it's not hard to discern. In some cases, however, the lines can blur with the passage of time. For example, can the songs of George Gershwin (1898–1937) be considered art songs even though they started out as show tunes? Perhaps, perhaps not, but many singers include Gershwin on "classical" vocal recitals these days. The poetic — or at least rhyming — texts, mostly by Ira Gershwin (1896–1983), are always clever and often touching, and the musical settings are undeniably sophisticated and compelling. Lasting value has a way of asserting itself, and while distinctions can be very important — to avoid them is to risk devaluing genuine accomplishment — in the end, quality is undoubtedly more persuasive than pedigree.

[See ACCOMPANIMENT; SONG CYCLE.]

Atonality and dissonance are often linked in listeners' minds — and not without reason — but they're not the same thing.

DISSONANCE is the simultaneous sounding of two or more notes to produce a jarring, harsh, or disagreeable result, an effect of clashing or unease. It's from the Latin words for "sounding" and "apart," and its opposite is *consonance,* a pleasing sound, a "sounding together."

ATONALITY is the absence of *tonality,* which is the musical framework of major and minor keys, with chords and harmonies that are built on the notes of major and minor scales and that follow each other according to certain established principles [see KEY~TONALITY; HARMONY~CHORD]. Atonal music, in other words, is music that isn't written in a key and that doesn't follow the rules of *tonal harmony* as practiced since about 1600. Atonality figures prominently in the work of many twentieth-century composers.

It is true that atonal music generally incorporates lots of dissonance. But tonal music, the music of Bach, Mozart, Beethoven, *et al.,* contains plenty of dissonance, too, dissonance that can be every bit as harsh as that found in atonal music. (The opening chord of the last movement of Beethoven's Ninth Symphony, for example, is glaringly dissonant.) The difference is that in tonal music dissonances are considered "unstable" harmonies that must be "resolved" to something more solid — they must lead to consonances. The crucial dynamic of tonal harmony is that dissonance creates dramatic tension, and consonance provides the satisfaction of resolution, including the ultimate resolution of return to the home key. (A piece in C major may wander far afield harmonically, but in the end it always returns to C major.) We don't think of tonal music as dissonant because even its harshest dissonances are heard in an overall context of consonance.

Atonal music provides no such context. Consonant harmonies

are not necessarily used as structural pillars, and they're not considered any more stable than dissonant ones; therefore dissonances don't need to be resolved. A dissonance may be "left hanging," or one dissonance may follow another, or there may be groups of dissonances, or a whole piece may consist of nothing but dissonances. In the absence of a theoretical or structural justification for the importance of consonance, many composers of atonal music have felt free, or even compelled, to abandon consonance entirely. Under these circumstances, it's only natural that many people have come to equate atonality with dissonance.

On the other hand, there's no reason that atonal music can't include whole strings of consonances, as well as — or instead of — dissonances. The term *atonal* tells us what a piece isn't, but it doesn't tell us what it *is*. Many different styles and musical languages, whether harsh, lush, bland, intense, cool, ugly, or beautiful, can be accurately described as atonal. The real pioneers of atonal music, in fact, were composers like Richard Wagner (1813–1883) and Claude Debussy (1862–1918). They both left plenty of unresolved dissonances in their wake, and in other ways their harmonic progressions didn't follow the "rules" or principles of traditional tonal harmony. But the adjective *dissonant* would certainly not be the first choice to describe their music. The "twelve-tone" atonal music of Arnold Schoenberg (1874–1951) tends to be quite strongly and consistently dissonant, and a difficult pill for many to swallow, but Schoenberg's pupil Alban Berg (1885–1935) mixed atonality and dissonance with traditional harmonies and melodies to create a richly expressive personal style [see TWELVE-TONE MUSIC]. Leoš Janáček, Ernest Bloch, Béla Bartók, Igor Stravinsky, Bohuslav Martinů, Sergei Prokofiev, Darius Milhaud, Paul Hindemith, Aaron Copland, Dmitri Shostakovich, Olivier Messiaen, Samuel Barber, Benjamin Britten, Alberto Ginastera — these are among the many twentieth-century composers of widely divergent styles who have made use of atonality to a greater or lesser degree.

Tonal music has a built-in logic, a logic established by centuries of development. Any composer writing in a musical language that is *not* tonal must create his or her own logic, and this is extremely difficult. Some do it well, some don't. When it's done badly, the results sound random, unsatisfying, or just plain ugly, and no volume of detailed program notes or explanatory essays will be of any help. When it's done well, the logic makes itself understood, and the musical language, though perhaps unfamiliar, unusual, or highly spiced with dissonance, is comprehensible and convincing. Notes, harmonies, and rhythms follow one another in patterns that make sense, that are compelling rather than seemingly arbitrary. At any given moment, the musical material we're hearing sounds as if it should indeed have followed what came before, and what came before makes sense in light of what we're hearing now. Narrative, drama, emotional impact — all are possible.

Nonetheless, there seems to be something basic to human nature about the perception of what constitutes "pleasing sounds." Theoreticians have labored to come up with technical definitions of consonance based on acoustical physics, but when all is said and done consonances are consonances because to most people they sound good. We abandon them, and the structural framework they provide, at great risk. It's entirely possible, in fact, that the best is already past; that the system of tonality that flowered in the eighteenth and nineteenth centuries represents the absolute summit of human accomplishment in music, and that all our attempts to find successors or substitutes for tonality will turn out to have been efforts along a downhill slope. Civilizations rise and fall, after all, and from the distance of centuries we can often say when certain cultural or political developments reached their peaks.

But it's also true that in this century, especially over the last forty-five years or so, many composers seem to have lost sight of the reasons most people listen to music. They've somehow either misunderstood or ignored our need for emotional journeys, for narrative, drama, meaning, for *perceivable* logic and coherence, and their music has reflected this. Certain fashionable academic and critical trends have at times provided philosophical ammunition and have exacerbated the problem.

Therefore, while atonality itself often takes the blame for the unpopularity of much contemporary music, it's not necessarily atonality's fault. It is more the fault of composers who write bad music. To a certain extent, the negative reaction to atonality is understandable. Whereas bad tonal music is usually at worst silly or boring, bad atonal music can be excruciating. The beatless "screech-bloop" type of atonal music comes quickly to mind, unfortunately. But atonal music is by no means all "screech-bloop." Good composers write good music, no matter the style or musical language, and it is just as much a mistake to equate *atonal* with *ugly* as to assume that *tonal* always means *beautiful*. We may well be on a slippery slope, but there's plenty of good atonal music, and plenty more still to be written.

B

BARITONE

[See VOICE TYPES.]

BAROQUE

The Baroque era in Western music extends from about 1600 to 1750. It is preceded by the Renaissance and followed, after a transitional period of approximately a quarter century, by the Classical era, the era of Haydn, Mozart, and Beethoven.

The end of the sixteenth century saw the birth, in Florence, Italy, of a new art form, one that rejected the multivoice, or *polyphonic,* style that had prevailed in music for the previous century and a half and replaced it with a modern style of music that featured solo voice with instrumental accompaniment [see COUNTERPOINT~POLYPHONY; RENAISSANCE]. The new art form was none other than opera, and the modern style of vocal writing, which we now call "monody," was the style that ushered in the Baroque era [see MONODY]. The earliest surviving opera was written in the year 1600. The year 1750 serves as a convenient closing point for the era because it marks the death of Johann Sebastian Bach (1685–1750), the greatest of all Baroque composers.

Many of the most important forms of Western music — forms that are still at the center of our performing repertoire — were developed during the Baroque era. In addition to opera and its primary components, recitative and aria, the Baroque era gave rise to the sonata, concerto, suite, prelude, fugue, overture, oratorio, and cantata. Even the symphony has its roots in the Baroque.

Given the remarkable fertility of the period, it is no surprise that there is no such thing as a single Baroque style consistent from country to country, composer to composer, or form to form. It's good to remember, in fact, that terms like *Renaissance, Baroque, Classical,* and *Romantic* are terms of convenience. They're useful for organizing time lines and for describing broad trends, but musical and historical realities are always fluid and diverse, and resistant to labeling.

That being said, there are various features and principles that may be considered characteristic of Baroque music, even if they're by no means universally applicable. They include the following:

- ✧ the style, derived from monody, of a single high voice or high instrument carrying a melody, accompanied by *basso continuo* (also just called *continuo:* a continuous bass line plus chords and "filler"). The accompanied duet style — *two* high parts and continuo — is also typical. Both these styles are examples of what is known generally as "melody and accompaniment."
- ✧ solidification of the system of writing music in clearly defined major and minor keys
- ✧ rhythmic regularity and continuity
- ✧ emphasis on the importance of sharp contrasts within pieces, whether in tempo (fast vs. slow), dynamics (loud vs. soft), musical forces (large groups vs. small groups or vs. individuals), or tonality (major vs. minor keys). The principle of contrast between large forces and small is the underlying principle of the concerto.
- ✧ continuation, despite the rise of melody and accompaniment style, of the polyphonic, or *contrapuntal,* tradition, in keyboard music especially, but also in other instrumental music and choral music; in particular, the development and "perfection" of the fugue
- ✧ emphasis on the contrast between free, improvisatory style and orderly, usually contrapuntal style, as in the juxtaposition

of prelude and fugue; exploration of the dramatic and expressive potential inherent in the search for freedom *within* orderly processes, as in the fugue itself

◇ emphasis on emotional expression. Baroque composers, especially in Germany, were influenced by a contemporary theory known as the Doctrine of the Affections, which asserted that (1) it was the composer's duty to touch the "affections," or emotions, of the listener, (2) it was possible to express, in music, any number of specific, idealized emotions, recognizable to the listener, and (3) each piece or section of a piece should be devoted to the expression of only one of these specific emotions. In reality neither the expressive content of music nor listeners' emotional responses can be so neatly pigeonholed or controlled (the psyche, or soul, doesn't stick to the rules very well), but it's interesting to think about the goals that many Baroque composers may have had in mind as they composed.

In addition to Bach, the two greatest figures of Baroque composition were George Frideric Handel (1685–1759), who, like Bach, was a prolific genius, at home in virtually all Baroque forms, and Claudio Monteverdi (1567–1643), the most important of the early opera composers, who made the transition from master of Renaissance style to pioneer of the Baroque. Other major composers of the Baroque era include Giuseppe Torelli (1658–1709), Henry Purcell (1659–1695), Alessandro Scarlatti (1660–1725), Antonio Vivaldi (ca. 1675–1741), Georg Philipp Telemann (1681–1767), Jean-Philippe Rameau (1683–1764), and Domenico Scarlatti (1685–1757), to name just a few. For more detailed information about musical forms and practices associated with the Baroque era, see the following individual entries: ARIA; BEL CANTO; CANTATA; CASTRATI; CONCERTO; CONTINUO; COUNTERPOINT~POLYPHONY; DYNAMICS; FUGUE; INTERMEZZO; KEY~TONALITY; KEYBOARD INSTRUMENTS; MASS; OPERA; ORATORIO; OVERTURE; PRELUDE; RECITATIVE; SONATA; SUITE; SYMPHONY; TOCCATA.

The word *baroque* is thought to derive from a Portuguese word, *barroco,* meaning "misshapen pearl." Writers of the mid-to-late eighteenth century — including the French philosopher Jean-Jacques Rousseau, in his *Dictionnaire de musique* (1768) — applied the label "baroque" disparagingly; they felt that Baroque music was overly ornate and "worked out," confused, bizarre, and distorted by an excessive intensity of emotional expression. Later listeners and theorists have felt differently.

BASS

[See VIOLIN FAMILY; VOICE TYPES.]

BASS CLARINET

[See REED INSTRUMENTS; WOODWIND INSTRUMENTS.]

BASS DRUM

[See PERCUSSION INSTRUMENTS.]

BASSO CONTINUO

[See CONTINUO.]

BASSOON

[See REED INSTRUMENTS; WOODWIND INSTRUMENTS.]

In music, time is measured in beats. A beat, then, is a unit of time. But *beat* is also the word for the rhythmic impulse — whether felt, understood, or indicated with a physical gesture from a hand, foot, or conductor's baton — that marks the start of each unit of time. It can also be the word for the physical gesture itself, as in, "That conductor has a very clear beat."

A beat is a regular, repeated impulse, like a pulse, but like a pulse it's also variable: fast music has a fast beat — the time intervals between the impulses are short — and slow music has a slow beat. Beats are grouped into measures, so that one speaks of "three beats to the measure," for example, or "four beats to the measure." In any given piece, a note value such as the eighth note, quarter note, or half note is assigned as the value of the beat. For example, "2/4 time" means that there are two beats per measure and that the value of the beat is a quarter note (indicated by the "4"). And "6/8 time" means that the beat is an eighth note and there are six beats per measure. [See METER; NOTATION.]

The double meaning of *beat* — impulse and duration — can sometimes lead to confusion. To start at the beginning of a measure and "hold a note for three beats" means to hold the note for the length of time covered by three complete beats. To hold a note "*until* the third beat" is another way of saying to hold it for *two* complete beats.

Here are a few common terms that have to do with beat:

ON THE BEAT: When a note or sound coincides with a beat, that is, with the beginning of a beat, it is said to be "on the beat."

DOWNBEAT: The downbeat is the first beat of a measure. It is also the strongest beat, where the greatest "weight" or rhythmic emphasis normally falls — although music may be written in such a way as to shift that emphasis. A downbeat, like any other beat, may be "empty," meaning empty of sound, while the beat itself is still counted and felt.

The word *downbeat* may also refer to the gesture that a conductor gives on the downbeat of a measure.

UPBEAT: An upbeat is a beat that occurs just before a downbeat, but the term is used primarily when the beat in question has a preparatory function, when it "belongs," in a sense, to the following downbeat. In "The Star-Spangled Banner," for example, the opening word, "Oh," comes on the upbeat to the first measure, and "say" comes on the downbeat. The word *upbeat* may refer either to a beat or to an actual note or group of notes. If a certain note comes on the upbeat, in other words, then it's also correct to say that that note *is* an upbeat. Musicians very often use the colloquial term *pickup* to describe such a note (or group of notes), as in, "Do you have a pickup to the third measure, or do you start right on the downbeat?"

The word *upbeat* may also refer to the gesture that a conductor makes on the upbeat of a measure, usually as a preparatory signal for the orchestra.

OFFBEAT: In the most general sense, an offbeat is any beat that is not the downbeat of a measure. It implies a "weak," or unstressed beat, often a beat that occurs between two stronger beats. (Like *upbeat*, the term *offbeat* may refer either to the beat itself or to a note that occurs on the offbeat.) Think of a pattern like "*Boom*-chick, *Boom*-chick, *Boom*-chick." The "chicks" are offbeats. To thicken the plot, however, if the "boom-chicks" are grouped two to a measure, "*Boom*-chick, boom-chick/*Boom*-chick, boom-chick/*Boom*-chick, boom-chick," then the lowercase booms, while "on" the second beat of each measure, are also offbeats, because the second beats are weaker than the downbeats. Similarly, in the pattern "*Oom*-pah-pah, *Oom*-pah-pah, *Oom*-pah-pah," the "pah"s are all offbeats. When a composer chooses to place an unexpected stress on the offbeat, the result is called syncopation [see SYNCOPATION].

[See RHYTHM; CONDUCTOR.]

Bel canto is Italian for "beautiful singing," as in, "Last night's recital by Ms. Spruzzicabuzzi was a wonderful example of true bel canto." Today the term is most often associated with certain early-nineteenth-century Italian operas and with the florid, virtuoso singing style they require. Gioacchino Rossini (1792–1868), Gaetano Donizetti (1797–1848), and Vincenzo Bellini (1801–1835) are three of the most famous composers of "bel canto opera."

The foundation of bel canto is proper technique, which results in "vocal freedom," the production of beautiful tone with minimum effort. Free, effortless tone production is what makes possible great flexibility and range of the voice, beautiful transitions from one part of the range to another, and great resonance, or power. Although bel canto style certainly puts a premium on singing that's fast, flashy, and high, it begins with the ability to sing a simple melodic line beautifully and to pass from one sustained note to another in a lovely, easy way.

The term *bel canto* has been around for a very long time. It was originally applied to the vocal technique of the *castrati,* the great stars of Italian opera in the 1600s and 1700s [see CASTRATI]. It's interesting, though, that for the last three hundred years, virtually every generation has lamented that the previous generation had the secret of the "true" bel canto style and that the current style was now corrupted, the secret lost. It does take work to maintain the tradition — singers must learn to sing and composers must learn to write for the voice — but although times, tastes, and styles change, the truth is that bel canto has survived every generation in one way or another and is still perfectly alive and well today. Singers like Joan Sutherland, Marilyn Horne, Cecilia Bartoli, and Thomas Hampson, for example, would be standouts in any era.

A stick of wood, a few small metal parts, and some horsehair: it may sound humble, but the bow is what string players use to draw life from their instruments. Like a singer's breath passing over the vocal cords and setting them in motion, the bow touches the strings and causes them to vibrate and produce sound. And the *kind* of sound depends on how the bow is used — what the brush is for the painter, the bow is for the string player. The quality of bows ranges from bad to great, and the best are worth far more than their weight in gold.

Bows are used to play the violin, viola, cello, and double bass. Each of these instruments has its own specialized bow: the bows are all similar in basic design, but they differ in length, thickness, and weight. The larger the instrument, the heavier and thicker the bow. Violin bows are the lightest (about two ounces), with the narrowest sticks, and double bass bows are the heaviest (about five ounces), with the thickest sticks. Length doesn't follow quite the same logic: the viola bow is the longest, at about 29.3 inches, followed by the just slightly shorter violin bow. The bass bow is shorter still, and the cello bow is the shortest, over an inch shorter than the viola bow. By convention and tradition, the bow is held with the right hand, the instrument with the left. (The members of the viol family are also bowed. See VIOL.)

A fact that is sometimes overlooked is that the bow does not come with the instrument. Bow making is a completely separate art from violin making: violin makers don't make bows, and bow makers don't make instruments. The father of the modern bow was the Frenchman François Tourte (1747–1835), who standardized the design and made bows of outstanding quality. While many of the finest violin makers have been Italian — starting with such illustrious figures as Nicolò Amati, Antonio Stradivari, and Giuseppe Guarneri — most of the great bow makers, especially in the nineteenth and early twentieth centuries, have been French or English. Like fine old violins, fine old bows appreciate in value enormously, and the bows made by Tourte and his successors can be worth many thousands of dollars. Professional musicians routinely use bows that are worth anywhere from $2,500, for excellent modern bows, to $10,000 to $25,000 or more, for bows by the nineteenth-century masters. Museum-quality Tourtes have been known to bring over $100,000 at auction.

What makes a good bow? A good bow feels well balanced and comfortable, and responds easily to the manipulations of the player in all kinds of musical passages. Above all, however, a bow is judged on the clarity, volume, warmth, and overall beauty of the sound it draws from an instrument. Differences among fine bows may be extremely subtle, but the difference in sound between a fine bow and a run-of-the-mill bow is usually very great, easily detected in direct comparison even by those who claim to have uneducated ears. And the *same* bow will draw different sounds from different instruments. A particular violin bow, for example, will suit some violins better than others. That's why, when buying a bow, a string player takes great pains to choose one that's not just good, but that's also a good match for his or her own instrument.

The stick is by far the most important — and most valuable — part of the bow. Light, slender, flexible, and yet remarkably strong, it's hand-carved from a single piece of wood and bent by heat to provide its characteristic curve inward toward the hair. (Up until the mid-eighteenth century, sticks were generally curved outward from the hair, a weaker configuration.) Since the time of Tourte, the sticks of all fine bows have been made from just one kind of wood, a brazilwood called *pernambuco*, named for the state in northeastern Brazil where it's found. Pernambuco is an extremely dense wood, so dense that it doesn't float. If in fact for some reason a block of pernambuco *does* float, it's not suitable for making bows, because it's the very density of the wood (along with a characteristic interlocking grain) that allows it to remain strong even when it's carved into long, slender sticks. Today, however, with the depletion of the forests of Pernambuco, pernambuco wood is becoming increasingly rare. A number of bow makers have experimented with carbon fiber materials for their sticks, and in some cases the results have been quite impressive. It's possible that in the not too distant future, most bow sticks will be made of synthetic materials.

And the hair? It is indeed from the tails of horses, male horses primarily, with the best hair coming from horses in cold regions such as Siberia, Manchuria, southern Argentina, and in some cases Canada and Poland. It is stuck into the head of the bow with a small wedge of wood and attached in the same way to a slender carved block (usually of ebony or tortoiseshell) called, of all things, the *frog,* that sits on the stick toward the bottom. The frog is free to slide back and forth on the stick a bit, and the hair is tightened and loosened by pulling and releasing the frog with a screw that fits into the end of the bow. Before playing, the string player tightens the hair and rubs it with sticky rosin powder (from a cake of hard rosin) that enables the hair to grip the strings well enough to set them vibrating. Since there are some two hundred hairs in the hank fitted to the bow, it's not critical if a few break now and then; when hairs break during a performance, the player simply pulls off the dangling ends and discards them. Over time, bow hair stretches out and gets brittle and "tired," not holding rosin well and not drawing the best possible sound. Every few months or so, therefore, professionals have their bows "rehaired": all the hair is removed from the bow and replaced with fresh hair.

BOWING refers to the various ways the bow is used to play a stringed instrument.

String players move their bows in two directions: "up" and "down." When the player's bow hand is moving away from his body, the stroke is called a "down-bow," and when the hand moves toward the body, it's an "up-bow." The symbol ⊓ placed over a note indicates a down-bow, while the symbol V indicates an up-bow. When two or more consecutive notes are to be played without changing the direction of the bow, a curved line called a "slur" is drawn either above or below them, and the notes are described as "slurred." (A slur usually indicates that notes are to be played *legato,* or smoothly connected, but sometimes notes can be articulated separately within a slur. See LEGATO.) String players talk about the "bowing" or "bowings" for a passage when they're referring to where the up-bows and down-bows will be and which notes will be slurred.

The names for different kinds of bow strokes are usually Italian or French — or both — and can be quite picturesque. There's the Italian *saltando,* for example, or *sautillé,* in French, which means "jumping"; *jeté,* which means "thrown"; *flautato,* for "like a flute"; and *martellato,* or *martelé,* which means "hammered." A basic back-and-forth stroke with the bow remaining "on the string" (that is, not bouncing) is called a *détaché,* French for "detached," or "separate." The generic term for a bouncing bow stroke, on the other hand, is *spiccato,* which is an Italian word that *also* means "detached" [see SPICCATO]. *Staccato* is yet another word for "detached," but when used as the name for a bow stroke, it denotes a stroke that's on the string, with a series of sharply articulated notes played all in one up-bow or down-bow [see STACCATO]. A "flying staccato" is a very rapid staccato in which the bow is allowed to bounce off the string. *Col legno* means to strike the strings "with the wood" of the bow, instead of playing with the hair, and *sul ponticello* means to play "on the bridge," or very near the bridge, a technique that produces a strange, whistling, icy sound [see COL LEGNO].

Composers frequently indicate the specific kinds of bow strokes they want, using either symbols (such as dots or dashes over the notes) or words. They can't indicate every possible shade and nuance, though, nor do they try. They know that, ultimately, most of the fine details of bowings and bow strokes are the responsibility of the person using the bow. When string players play with other string players, whether in a chamber music group or in an orchestra, they usually take special care to match bow strokes. Matching strokes doesn't mean just keeping the bows going up and down at the same time, although that can be important (especially visually). It also means matching types of strokes, often to the point of using the same part of the bow, moving the bow at the same speed, and applying the same kind of pressure to the strings. Matching bow strokes is essential for creating a unified sound, and is a critical element in shaping a convincing musical interpretation.

[See STRADIVARIUS; VIOLIN FAMILY.]

BRASS INSTRUMENTS

The principal brass instruments of the modern symphony orchestra are the FRENCH HORN (also called HORN), TRUMPET, TROMBONE, and TUBA.

Brass instruments are wind instruments, and although they may be coiled or bent into different shapes, all brass instruments consist essentially of a very long metal tube [see WIND INSTRUMENTS]. If you straightened out all the tubing on a French horn, for example, it would be about seventeen feet long. The trumpet would be four to five and a half feet, the trombone nine to thirteen feet, and the tuba sixteen to twenty-six feet. A mouthpiece is inserted in one end of the tube; the other end of the tube flares outward and is called the "bell." All modern brass instruments use a cup-shaped mouthpiece, the specific configuration of the cup varying with each instrument. The brass player doesn't simply blow into the mouthpiece, however, he *buzzes,* compressing his lips and forcing air through them so that they vibrate together. The vibrations of the lips, focused and amplified by the mouthpiece and directed into the tube, cause the column of air inside the tube to vibrate, and as in all wind instruments, the vibrating air column produces the sound of the instrument.

There are two ways to play different notes (that is, to vary the pitch of notes) on a brass instrument. One is to change the length of the tube, and thus the length of the vibrating air column. This can be done using either valves — as on the French horn, trumpet, and tuba — or a slide, as on the trombone. The longer the tube, the lower the frequency at which the air column vibrates and the lower the note; the shorter the tube, the higher the frequency and the higher the note [see PITCH]. The other way is to increase (to varying degrees) the tension of the lips and the pressure of the breath. This is called "overblowing." Overblowing changes the pressure of the air column within the tube, causing it to vibrate in partial lengths, at higher frequencies. A player can also combine the two methods: any single length of tubing can produce a series of higher notes depending on the degree of overblowing, and each different length of tubing produces a *different* series of notes. (French hornists have yet another technique available, although it's one that's almost never used with modern instruments. It's called "hand-stopping," and it requires partially closing off the bell with the right hand.)

Not all brass instruments are made of brass. Many French horns, for example, are made of nickel silver, an alloy of copper, zinc, and nickel (it's silver in name and color only), and some are made of nickel bronze, an alloy of copper, tin, and nickel. (Brass itself is an alloy of copper and zinc.) Many brass instruments are silver-plated (sterling silver on brass), and some are gold-plated.

The FRENCH HORN is called "French" only in English. Nobody is entirely sure *why* it's called French, especially since the French themselves simply call it *cor* ("horn"); the Italians, *corno;* and the Germans, *Horn*. A likely theory is that the English originally called the instrument the French horn (in the 1600s) for the simple reason that it came from France. And even in English, the French horn is often just called the "horn." A concerto for French horn and orchestra, for example, is called a "horn concerto"; a quintet for French horn and string quartet is a "horn quintet"; and if a musician says "I play the horn," he means that he plays the French horn. There are many horn players, in fact, who would like to see the "French" dropped altogether. (The *English* horn is a member of the oboe family. See WOODWIND INSTRUMENTS.)

The immediate ancestors of the modern horn were sixteenth- and seventeenth-century hunting horns, brass hoops (with flared bells) that were played slung over the shoulder, sometimes on horseback. By the end of the seventeenth century, refined versions of the hunting horn had made their way out of the fields, off the shoulder, and into the orchestra, and by the mid-eighteenth century most orchestras included a pair of horns. It was not until the early nineteenth century, however, that horns with valves ("valve horns") were invented. Before that, all horns were "natural horns." To produce a series of different notes on a natural horn, the player must rely entirely on lip technique (overblowing) and hand-stopping. It's possible to change the length of the entire tube on a natural horn, but only by adding lengths of tubing called "crooks," or by switching one crook for another. The problem with adding or switching crooks is that it can't be done while playing. On valve horns, however, different crooks are built into the instrument, and the (three) valves make it possible to engage the crooks while playing, greatly expanding the range of notes available at any one time. For a variety of technical reasons, it also allows for a more consistent sound and generally more reliable pitch.

Haydn's horn concerto, Mozart's four horn concertos, and Beethoven's sonata for horn and piano were all written for natural horn, although they're usually played today on valve horn. The first orchestral music calling specifically for valve horns dates from 1835, and the first important solo work for valve horn was Robert Schumann's Adagio and Allegro for horn and piano, written in 1849. Schumann also wrote a *Konzertstück* (*Concert Piece*) for four horns and orchestra later that same year. Other major works for solo horn include the two concertos for horn and orchestra by Richard Strauss (the first from 1883, the second from 1942), and Benjamin Britten's Serenade for tenor (voice), horn, and strings (1943). Among the chamber music works that feature the French horn, the two best known and best loved are undoubt-edly the Mozart Horn Quintet (1782) and the Brahms Horn Trio (trio for horn, violin, and piano, 1865).

The TRUMPET is the highest-pitched and most brilliant member of the brass family. Like early horns, early trumpets were "natural" instruments, without valves. The earliest trumpets, used as signaling or ceremonial instruments in many ancient cultures, were *very* natural: they were made of such things as ram's horns, ox horns, seashells, and elephant tusks. Metal trumpets (silver, bronze, brass) of the Middle Ages were generally long straight tubes with flared bells; it wasn't until the fifteenth century that instrument makers learned to bend brass tubes, which allowed them to make the instruments more compact. The first bent trumpets were in the shape of a flattened S-curve, but they were soon made obsolete by trumpets whose tubing was fashioned into an elongated oval coil. Instrument makers of the time also invented a trumpet with a sliding, telescoping tube extension. This "slide trumpet" survived in specialized roles for several centuries, but it's mainly remembered now as the precursor of the trombone [see next page]. With various modifications, the oval coil has remained the basic shape of the trumpet to this day.

Throughout the Middle Ages (pre-1430) and Renaissance (ca. 1430–1600), trumpets retained their traditional military and ceremonial functions: they were used mainly for signals and fanfares. In the 1600s, however, opera composers began including trumpets among the instruments of the orchestra, where they were often paired with kettledrums (timpani) to provide festive or martial effects. Trumpet players during the Baroque period (ca. 1600–1750) also developed a type of extremely high, melodic solo playing called *clarino* style. J. S. Bach's Second Brandenburg Concerto (ca. 1721) includes a part for solo trumpet in this style. Clarino playing, which demanded a very specialized, virtuoso technique, began to disappear as the Baroque waned, however, and by the time of Haydn and Mozart it was already considered something of a lost art. (When modern trumpeters play the Second Brandenburg Concerto they use different instruments from the kind used in Bach's day, and the technique is not the same as that required for the original clarino style.) During the Classical era (ca. 1775–1820), composers employed trumpets mainly to add brilliance and power to the orchestra, usually in the traditional combination with timpani. Two important solo works nonetheless date from the Classical era: Joseph Haydn's Concerto in E-flat for trumpet and orchestra (1796) and Johann Nepomuk Hummel's Concerto, also in E-flat (1803).

The new technology of the early 1800s that produced the valve horn also made possible the valve trumpet. As on the horn, the valves (usually either two or three) provided added range and reliability. With the availability of greatly improved instruments — and players who had learned to use them — orchestral composers of the nineteenth century began to exploit the melodic potential and expressive range of the trumpet much more extensively. Twentieth-century orchestral composers certainly followed suit, but despite all the interesting, intricate, and even intimate music that's been written for trumpet over the last century and a half, the trumpet has never lost its age-old character as a signaling instrument, an instrument that can call people to attention in a powerful and dramatic way.

The TROMBONE (also sometimes called SLIDE TROMBONE) has remained largely unchanged for over five centuries. *Trombone* is Italian for "big trumpet": instrument makers in the fifteenth century created the trombone as a bigger, lower-pitched, and improved version of the slide trumpet. Up until the eighteenth century, the lovely English name for trombone was *sackbut*, a word of Old French or possibly Spanish derivation.

During the Renaissance, musicians played the trombone in town bands, royal ceremonial bands, and in mixed ensembles with string and keyboard instruments and voices. At the time, the trombone was a more refined instrument than either the trumpet or the horn. It was better suited for blending with other instruments and voices, and because of the slide, better able to play real melodies, as opposed to simple fanfares. The trombone was also used in Renaissance church music, usually to reinforce lower voice parts; later, during the Baroque period, Handel and Bach occasionally used it for the same purpose. It was not until the late 1700s that the trombone was employed in the opera orchestra with any regularity, and then its primary function was to evoke feelings of awe in scenes involving the spiritual or the supernatural. Mozart used trombones for this purpose in his operas *The Magic Flute* and *Don Giovanni*, and he included a prominent trombone solo in his *Requiem*. Beethoven was the first to include trombones in symphonic music, introducing them to great dramatic effect in the last movement of his Fifth Symphony (1808). The trombones have been regular members of the orchestra since.

Trombones come in various sizes. The standard orchestral trombone is known as the tenor trombone. Much orchestral music of the nineteenth and twentieth centuries also calls for bass trombone, but since the true bass trombone is a very long, very unwieldy instrument, most bass trombone parts are played today on a hybrid instrument called the tenor-bass trombone. The tenor-bass trombone is approximately the size of a tenor trombone, but for notes in the low register — the bass trombone register — it has an extra length of coiled tubing that can be engaged by pressing a valve. There are relatively few solo compositions for trombone, and the trombone is rarely featured in chamber music, although the French composer Francis Poulenc wrote an excellent trio for trombone, trumpet, and horn (1922).

The TUBA is the biggest, heaviest, widest, and lowest-pitched of the brass instruments, the true bass of the family. It's also by far the youngest member. It was invented in Germany in the 1830s and has never been a "natural" instrument — it has always had valves. Like the trombone, the tuba comes in several different sizes. The size most commonly used in the orchestra is called the contrabass-tuba, or double-bass tuba. Solo opportunities for tuba players outside the orchestra are few, although the English composer Ralph (pronounced "Rafe") Vaughan Williams wrote a fine concerto for tuba and orchestra (1954). It's not surprising, in view of his many innovations in orchestral instrumentation and sonority, that Hector Berlioz (1803–1869) was the first important composer to write for the tuba.

⌐

Although the chamber music repertoire for brass instruments in combination with other types of instruments is not extensive, there is a large and very interesting repertoire of music for brass quintet. Some of this music is original, but much of it is music that was written for other instrumental combinations and later

arranged for brass quintet. A brass quintet consists of two trumpets, horn, trombone, and tuba.

[See ORCHESTRA; ROMANTICISM; see also MUTE.]

B W V

[See OPUS NUMBER.]

C

CADENCE ∼ CADENZA

A cadence is a sequence of notes or chords that brings a musical piece, section, or phrase to a conclusion, or to a temporary stop. Most cadences conform to one of several easily recognized patterns or formulas, and the familiarity of these formulas is what reinforces their "closing" function. The two chords to which the word *amen* is usually sung at the end of a hymn, for example, constitute a cadence, as do the chords that accompany the words "home of the brave" at the end of "The Star-Spangled Banner" [see HARMONY∼CHORD].

The word *cadence* derives from the Latin *cadere,* "to fall": in most early church music, melodies descended or "fell" in pitch to their final note. The famous verse from Shakespeare's *Twelfth Night* that begins with the words "If music be the food of love, play on," also includes the line, "That strain again! It had a dying fall."

∽

The words *cadence* and *cadenza* are closely related. In Italian, in fact, they're the same word — *cadenza.* (In French they're both *cadence,* and in German, *Kadenz.*) The reason for the linguistic overlap is that originally cadenzas were simply embellishments of cadences: the earliest cadenzas were flashy, improvised passages that singers of seventeenth- and eighteenth-century Italian opera inserted just before the final cadences of their arias. Composers of instrumental music later borrowed the idea, and the cadenzas we're now most familiar with are brilliant display passages in concertos, passages in which the soloist puts on a show while the orchestra remains silent. Concerto cadenzas usually occur toward the ends of movements, especially first movements.

[See CONCERTO.]

CANON

A canon is a composition with two or more voices, or "parts," in which a melody is first stated in one voice and then restated, or *imitated,* in the other(s). The voices of a canon are individual musical lines; they may be sung, or they may be played on an instrument or instruments. Canons have a staggered start, which is to say that each voice enters in its turn shortly after the other. As the voices enter, the statements of the melody overlap, but they never "line up." Instead, the voices fit together to create an interesting overall sound and a satisfying progression of harmonies. In technical terms, the canon is a form of *imitative counterpoint* [see COUNTERPOINT~POLYPHONY; FUGUE].

Canons often close with a short *coda,* in which the voices join together without imitation after they've all finished the melody [see CODA]. In one kind of canon, however, the voices return to the beginning of the melody each time they reach the end of it, which means that the imitation, and the canon, can continue indefinitely. The formal name for this kind of canon is "perpetual canon." The more common but equally correct name is ROUND. Three of the best-known rounds are "Row, Row, Row Your Boat," "Frère Jacques," and "Three Blind Mice."

The canon is a very old form: the earliest surviving canon is an English round called "Sumer is icumen in" ("Summer is coming in"), which dates back to the thirteenth century. During the Renaissance period (ca. 1430–1600), the canon became a very popular and important means of musical expression in both religious and secular composition, and Renaissance composers such as Guillaume Dufay (ca. 1400–1474), Johannes Ockeghem (1430–1495), Josquin des Prez (ca. 1450–1521), and Giovanni Pierluigi da Palestrina (ca. 1525–1594) wrote canons that were often very complicated and sophisticated [see RENAISSANCE]. In these canons, melodies aren't merely imitated "strictly"; they're imitated backward, upside down, upside down *and* backward, and with rhythmic variations. (Backward means going from the last note to the first instead of from the first to the last. Upside down means that wherever the original melody goes up by a certain interval, the imitation goes down by that same interval, and where the original goes down the imitation goes up.) J. S. Bach (1685–1750) continued the tradition of canonic writing during the Baroque period, reaching great heights of technical accomplishment and emotional expression, and in the second half of the eighteenth century Haydn (1732–1809) and Mozart (1756–1791) also mastered the canon and employed it frequently.

In England during the sixteenth, seventeenth, and eighteenth centuries, a type of round called the *catch* was especially popular. Catches, always for three or more male voices, were cleverly constructed so that the words of the individual parts overlapped to create humorous juxtapositions. "Humorous" isn't quite a complete description: the chief appeal of many catches was that they were, frankly, obscene. ("Three Blind Mice," which on first glance doesn't seem particularly salacious, was first published in a collection of catches in 1609.) The popularity of these musical amusements in England was so great that, in the 1700s especially, a number of private societies formed for the specific purpose of singing catches.

⌐

Is there a difference between a canon and a fugue? Yes. The primary difference is that a fugue consists of more than just overlapping statements of a melody. In the fugue there's a melody, called the "subject," which is imitated in the various voices, but there's also at least one secondary melody, called a "countersubject," which is passed from voice to voice, and there are passages called "episodes" in which the melody isn't heard at all.

The word *cantata* comes from the Italian *cantare,* "to sing." A cantata is an extended composition for voice, or voices, with instrumental accompaniment; when the term is used today it usually refers to a multisection piece made up of arias, recitatives, duets, and choruses [see ARIA; RECITATIVE]. The main factors that distinguish a cantata from an *oratorio* are that an oratorio usually has a more substantial and continuous story line than a cantata, and a cantata is considerably shorter. The average cantata might last twenty or thirty minutes, while a good-sized oratorio can easily go two or three hours [see ORATORIO].

The cantata was one of the most important vocal forms of the Baroque period (ca. 1600–1750), and like most other Baroque forms, it developed in Italy. Italian cantatas of the seventeenth century were mostly *solo cantatas,* for just one voice and continuo. The continuo part, which consisted of a bass line, chords, and various improvised embellishments, was played by a keyboard instrument like the harpsichord or organ plus a bass instrument like the cello or viola da gamba [see CONTINUO]. Solo cantatas were generally secular in nature, with dramatic or pastoral subjects, and they typically consisted of several arias strung together with recitatives. Although they weren't staged, they were virtually identical in musical style to early Italian opera. Cantata is one of those umbrella terms, however, under which fit many variations in style, structure, and substance. The first "cantatas" appeared around 1620, but through the latter part of the seventeenth century and the early eighteenth century the form evolved. Sacred subjects were introduced, instrumentation became more elaborate, choruses made their appearance, and regional variations developed as the French, Germans, and English all borrowed the form and treated it in their own way. In Italy, the solo cantata remained very popular. In addition to 115 operas and 150 oratorios, for example, Alessandro Scarlatti (1660–1725) alone wrote well over 600 solo cantatas.

The history of the cantata is particularly fascinating because in the early 1700s the form was essentially usurped by one man — Johann Sebastian Bach (1685–1750). Bach's combination of religious devotion and creative genius found a perfect vehicle in the cantata, and his achievements are of such scope and magnitude that for many people the term *cantata* is now virtually synonymous with *Bach cantata*.

A Bach cantata is a church cantata, more specifically a German Protestant, or Lutheran, cantata, and, technically speaking, a "chorale cantata." A chorale is a Lutheran hymn, with words in German. Some chorales were simply German versions of old Latin hymns, but many were newly composed, including a large number composed by Martin Luther himself. Many chorales also took the form of popular tunes specially fitted with religious texts, so that one might find the sixteenth-century German equivalent of "Baby, Won't You Rock Me All Night," for example, recast as "O Lord, Thou Art My Rock."

In Germany the cantata developed primarily as a religious form, and German composers introduced the use of well-known chorales as the basis for both music and text. The Germans were also innovative in their use of choruses and sizable orchestras to complement vocal soloists. When Bach came along he built on the German tradition that had already been established, but transformed that tradition by his endless inventiveness and by the depth and beauty of his musical expression. In Bach's case, "endless inventiveness" is no cliché: while he was cantor, or director of music, for the St. Thomas Church in Leipzig (1723–1750), it was his responsibility — along with teaching music and Latin and composing Masses, passions, music for festivals, special services, weddings, and funerals — to have a cantata ready for every Sunday of the year. During the course of his career he very likely composed more than three hundred cantatas, of which about two hundred survive. (A humorous musical scholar once said, "Among the two hundred or so Bach cantatas is some of the greatest music ever written, but every once in a while there's something not quite up to his usual standards, and you can almost hear the old man saying, 'Oh shoot, it's Thursday night and I have to have this ready by Sunday.'")

Bach didn't compose according to formulas, and his cantatas take many different shapes. As a general rule, however, a Bach cantata usually opens with an elaborate, freely embellished version of a chorale, for chorus and orchestra, and closes with a very simple but powerful setting of the same chorale. In the closing chorale setting, the orchestra "doubles" the chorus, meaning it plays the same notes the chorus sings, and only those notes. In between the opening and closing sections is some sequence of arias, recitatives, and choruses, with vocal duets and vocal-instrumental duets also common. These interior sections always include instrumental accompaniment, and are often somehow based on the text or tune of the chorale. Bach wrote a number of secular cantatas, too, but only a handful survive.

CAPRICCIO ~ CAPRICE

Caprice is the French (and English) version of the Italian word *capriccio*, which is from the Latin *caper*, meaning "goat." Goats — some goats, anyway — have a reputation for leaping and "capering" about wherever and however it suits their fancy. In music, since the sixteenth century or so, *capriccio* has been used as a title for pieces that don't fit neatly in a category — lively pieces, usually, in which composers follow their imaginations, their whims, rather than strict rules.

In the nineteenth century, *capriccio* was one of the many names composers gave to the kinds of short, highly personal, and evocative pieces for solo piano known generically as "character pieces" [see CHARACTER PIECE]. These were pieces based specifically on the idea that the composer should allow his moods or feelings to dictate the musical form. Among the most famous nineteenth-century capriccios, however, are the twenty-four capriccios for solo *violin* by Niccolò Paganini (1782–1840). These capriccios (almost always referred to in English as *caprices*) are actually a set of extremely challenging concert études, pieces that Paganini used to show off both his astonishing violin technique and his highly imaginative compositional technique [see ETUDE].

Some nineteenth-century composers also used the word *capriccio* in titles for orchestra pieces — usually popular medleys or foreign-flavored suites [see SUITE]. Tchaikovsky wrote a *Capriccio Italien* and Nikolay Rimsky-Korsakov wrote a *Capriccio Espagnol,* for example. Why both composers paired the French form of the adjective with the Italian form of the noun is a good question. At the very least, the choice seems somewhat . . . capricious.

CASTRATI

The definition, accurate if not delicate: singing eunuchs. *Castrati* is the plural form of *castrato,* Italian for "castrated," or "one who is castrated," and yes it *is* true that if a boy is castrated before puberty, his voice will always remain high-pitched. For better or for worse, it's also true that the singers known as castrati played a central role in the development of opera, and by extension, in the history of Western music.

The practice of castration for musical purposes was peculiar to Italy, and to some extent Germany, and documents show that castrati were regularly employed as chapel singers in those two countries as early as the 1500s. The Catholic Church had for centuries banned women from singing during services, and had depended on boy sopranos or "falsettists" — men singing with falsetto voices — to sing high vocal parts. As religious music became more complex and demanding, the advantage of castrati was that they could sing naturally in the range of a boy soprano with the power and stamina of a man.

With the birth of opera around 1600, a new field opened for the castrati. Castrati performed in Jacopo Peri's *Euridice* (1600) and in Claudio Monteverdi's *Orfeo* (1607) — generally considered the first great Italian opera — and after that their popularity, along with opera's, increased steadily and enormously. Women in the seventeenth century were still largely forbidden from taking part in public performances (especially in areas under papal control), and throughout the 1600s almost all roles in Italian serious opera *(opera seria)*, female and male, were written for castrati. Up until about 1750, in fact — even after women had begun to take the stage — castrati remained the stars of Italian serious opera.

Why? They were virtuosos. Castrati were renowned for their vocal range, agility, and power, and their lung capacity was legendary. Their voices were known as "white voices," less warm and expressive than women's voices, but, to seventeenth- and eighteenth-century listeners, at least, more impressive. The most spectacular of the castrati, such as Carlo Broschi (1705–1782), known as Farinelli, and Francesco Bernardi (1680–1750), known as Senesino, had spectacular careers, becoming as rich and famous in their time as rock stars in ours. Some of the castrati were also well-known ladies' men. It's a common misconception that these men were impotent. Sterile, yes, but impotent, no. (Even in the absence of the sex glands, the adrenal glands produce male hormones in sufficient quantity to preserve potency.)

Unfortunately, in the areas of both virtuosity and ego, the star castrati tended to lack restraint, and this led to musical abuses. In the hands of the castrati, the aria, originally intended to carry the dramatic and emotional weight in opera, became merely a vehicle for showing off. Singers inserted endless flashy cadenzas in their arias wherever they wished, and the result was that operas lost their form and their musical-dramatic coherence [see ARIA; CADENCE-CADENZA]. By the mid-1700s a reform movement had begun. This movement, led by the composer Christoph Willibald Gluck (1714–1787) and his librettist, Ranieri de Calzabigi (1714–1795), pushed serious opera in a different direction: the link between musical expression and dramatic action took on renewed importance, and the "pointless" vocal display of the castrati fell into disrepute.

The castrati didn't suddenly disappear from the musical scene, however. Composers of the late eighteenth century (including

Mozart) still wrote occasional operatic roles for castrati, and Gioacchino Rossini (1792–1868), the last to do so, wrote castrato roles into the 1820s. Also, although Church authorities had long officially forbidden the practice of castration, they continued to tolerate the results, and castrati sang in Italian chapels throughout the nineteenth century. The last known castrato, Alessandro Moreschi, a singer in the choir of the Vatican's Sistine Chapel, died in 1922. Moreschi made phonograph recordings in the first years of the century, but whether it was his fault or the recordings', their quality is poor, and they undoubtedly do not give a fair idea of what the great castrati sounded like in their prime.

One final note: while castration before puberty guarantees a high voice, it doesn't, alas, guarantee a beautiful one. In towns all through Italy in the seventeenth and eighteenth centuries, impoverished parents offered their young sons for castration in the hopes that they would eventually reap great rewards. But many of these boys grew up, in the words of the eighteenth-century English traveler and musicologist Dr. Charles Burney, "without any voice at all, or at least without one sufficient to compensate for such a loss."

[See BEL CANTO; OPERA; VIRTUOSO; VOICE TYPES.]

CELESTA

[See PERCUSSION INSTRUMENTS.]

CELLO

[See VIOLIN FAMILY.]

The chaconne and the passacaglia (pronounced "pahssa-cahlya") are musical forms that were popular with composers during the Baroque era (ca. 1600–1750). They're both derived from dance forms, probably Spanish dances (although the chaconne may have originated in Mexico).

The two forms are difficult to distinguish from each other. In fact, Baroque composers *didn't* distinguish between them — they used the terms *chaconne* and *passacaglia* more or less interchangeably. Both forms are moderately slow, with three beats to the measure, and both are "variation" forms, featuring the combination of what might be called a constant musical factor with a changing musical factor. The constant factor is either a continuously repeated bass line called a *basso ostinato* (also called "ground bass") or a continuously repeated series of harmonies. The changing factor — where the composer lets his fancy run free — is a series of melodic and rhythmic variations unfolding in the upper musical lines [see OSTINATO].

The chaconne and the passacaglia are forms that depend on the dynamic equilibrium, central to music of the Baroque, between structural order and expressive freedom. The most famous of all chaconnes, the one found in Johann Sebastian Bach's Partita in D Minor for solo violin, offers a brilliant and moving example of this equilibrium. Bach's *Chaconne* also demonstrates very clearly the principle that pieces derived from dance forms are not necessarily meant for dancing.

[See BAROQUE; DANCE.]

CHAMBER MUSIC

Chamber music is music for small formations — from as few as two musicians to as many as nine or ten. The term originated, most likely in the 1500s, as a designation for music that was meant to be performed in a room, or chamber, of a private residence, as

opposed to music intended for the church or theater. (The word
chamber is from the Latin *camera*. In Italian, chamber music is
musica da camera; in French, *musique de chambre;* and in German,
Kammermusik.)

The term *chamber music* most often refers to instrumental
music, but chamber music pieces occasionally include a singer or
singers. What they almost never include, or require, is a conductor. An important distinction between chamber music and orchestral music is that in an orchestra a number of people play the
same part — all the first violins play the first violin part, for instance, and all the cellos play the cello part — whereas in chamber
music each part is played by only one person [see PART]. The
twentieth century has seen the rise of the "chamber orchestra,"
but music for chamber orchestra is not chamber music. A chamber orchestra is just a small orchestra — there's more than one
player to a part, and there's usually a conductor.

Chamber music pieces for two players are called duos (or
sonatas — see SONATA). Pieces for three players are called trios;
for four players, quartets; for five players, quintets; for six players,
sextets; for seven players, septets; for eight players, octets; and for
nine players, nonets. Pieces for ten players are called "pieces for
ten players." There are also names for pieces written for specific
instrumental combinations. The following are among the most
common:

string trio	violin, viola, cello
string quartet	two violins, viola, cello
string quintet	usually means two violins, two violas, cello. This combination is also called a "viola quintet."
piano trio	piano, violin, cello
piano quartet	piano and string trio
piano quintet	piano and string quartet
wind quintet	flute, oboe, clarinet, bassoon, French horn
brass quintet	two trumpets, French horn, trombone, tuba

When there's a wind instrument present either with strings or in combination with piano and one stringed instrument, the piece usually takes the name of the wind instrument. A trio for French horn, violin, and piano, for example, is called a horn trio, while a quintet for clarinet and string quartet is called a clarinet quintet.

All these names, incidentally, refer both to the pieces and to the instrumental formations themselves. It's not unusual, for example, to hear a radio announcer say something like, "And now we'll hear the Tokyo String Quartet playing the Debussy String Quartet," or "And now we'll hear the Borodin Quartet playing a quartet by Borodin." String trios play string trios, string quartets play string quartets, wind quintets play wind quintets, and so forth.

⤙

Composers during the Baroque period (ca. 1600–1750) wrote plenty of chamber music, especially trio sonatas and violin sonatas, but the body of chamber music with which modern musicians and audiences are most familiar starts with Joseph Haydn (1732–1809). Known affectionately during his lifetime as "Papa" Haydn, Haydn never had any children of his own, but he was the father of the two most enduringly popular chamber music forms — the string quartet and the piano trio. He didn't actually invent either of them, but he developed them from fledgling forms, exploring and exploiting them and demonstrating expressive possibilities for them that had never been imagined. Haydn wrote twenty or more piano trios and almost seventy string quartets (among many other chamber works), and created models that inspired Mozart, Beethoven, and all who came later.

Mozart and Beethoven both composed enormous quantities of wonderful chamber music, including sonatas and duos, string trios, piano trios, string quartets, string quintets, works for winds and piano, and works for winds and strings. These two giants created far too many great works to list, but it's impossible to avoid special mention of Beethoven's string quartets. To this day, many people think of the last six of Beethoven's sixteen string quartets as the unrivaled masterpieces of the form. Of the nineteenth-century composers who carried on the chamber music tradition established by Haydn, Mozart, and Beethoven, the most significant — in terms of quality, quantity, and variety — were Franz Schubert (1797–1828), Felix Mendelssohn (1809–1847), Robert Schumann (1810–1856), Johannes Brahms (1833–1897), and Antonín Dvořák (1841–1904).

These great composers didn't only *write* chamber music, however, they also played it. They often wrote pieces to play with their friends, usually in informal gatherings in someone's home. And it's an interesting coincidence that while they all played the piano, Haydn, Mozart, Beethoven, Schubert, and Dvořák all played the viola, as well, and enjoyed playing it in their chamber music get-togethers.

With the exception of composers who have specialized in opera, almost all major composers of the nineteenth and twentieth centuries, of whatever nationality, have made important, and in some cases very extensive, contributions to the chamber music repertoire.

⌒

Chamber music rehearsals are quite different from orchestra rehearsals. In an orchestra rehearsal, it's the conductor's job to make the overall musical decisions and to ensure that the members of the orchestra carry them out. What the conductor says, in other words, goes. A chamber music group, on the other hand, is a democracy. Everybody is entitled to voice an opinion on any aspect of interpretation — how soft here, how loud there, how much to slow down, when to speed up — and nobody's opinion carries more weight than anybody else's. The process is not always smooth, and some professional groups have actually been famous for their personality conflicts. But with a group that's musically and temperamentally well matched, easy and delightful rehearsals (not to mention satisfying performances) are not at all unusual. The intimate communication and collaboration in chamber music can be wonderfully rewarding, and for many musicians, professional and amateur, there is simply no greater joy than to play great chamber music with good friends and respected colleagues.

[For discussions of specific instruments and their chamber music repertoire, see BRASS INSTRUMENTS; VIOLIN FAMILY; WOODWIND INSTRUMENTS.]

CHAMBER ORCHESTRA

[See ORCHESTRA.]

CHARACTER PIECE

Character piece is a general term that describes a variety of nineteenth-century pieces for solo piano. The nineteenth century was the era of Romanticism in music, and many Romantic composers sought to "shake off," in the words of Franz Liszt, "the yoke of old-fashioned formulas" so that they might achieve what they considered greater freedom of individual expression [see RO-MANTICISM]. They experimented with new musical forms, in other words, always hoping to find the one that best suited the particular mood, emotion, sentiment, or state of mind they wished to express. And while this Romantic search for freedom was a matter of strongly held artistic philosophy, it was also partly a matter of practicality: there was a general sense among composers that it would be difficult if not impossible to match the achievements of Haydn, Mozart, and Beethoven in such "classical" forms as the piano sonata [see CLASSICAL MUSIC~CLASSI-CAL ERA; SONATA].

Character pieces, in fact, might almost be called *non*-sonatas. They're usually much shorter than sonatas, and they're not divided into movements. And they often bear titles intended to keep notions of formality or grandiosity at a distance, to convey a bit of an "oh, this is just a little something I wrote because I was in the mood" message. In some cases the titles are picturesque or poetic, chosen to evoke a specific setting, mood, feeling, idea, or literary association. Here are some common titles:

Bagatelle — French for "trifle," a title first used by Beethoven, who himself was a Romantic pioneer as well as a Classical master. His *Bagatelles* are generally considered the first character pieces.

Ballade — Inspired by old poetic forms of the same name (stories in verse)

Caprice [see CAPRICCIO~CAPRICE]

Etude [see ETUDE]

Fantasy [see FANTASY]

Impromptu — French for "off the cuff," "spur of the moment," "improvised"

Intermezzo [see INTERMEZZO]

Nocturne — French for "night piece." The Irish composer John Field (1782–1837) was the first to use the term as a title, and he established the model for this type of piece.

Prelude [see PRELUDE]

Rhapsody — From the Greek for "recital of epic poetry," the word is associated with an outpouring of intense feeling

Scherzo [see SCHERZO]

Song without words — Title first used by Felix Mendelssohn

The nocturne is probably the most recognizable of the various character pieces, because it usually features a flowing, or "dreamy," melody in the right hand and a simple accompaniment in the left. Otherwise, there is often little in the actual musical material of the various forms to distinguish one from another. The titles may be evocative, but they're strictly subjective, and one composer's fantasy or caprice might be another's rhapsody or intermezzo.

Many nineteenth-century composers wrote character pieces, but the names most closely associated with the genre are Franz Schubert (1797–1828), Felix Mendelssohn (1809–1847), Robert Schumann (1810–1856), Johannes Brahms (1833–1897), and, especially, Frédéric Chopin (1810–1849). Chopin, unlike the others, composed almost exclusively for the piano, and to a very great extent his reputation rests on his vast output of character pieces, which include ballades, études, nocturnes, preludes, and scherzos, as well as such dance-inspired forms as the mazurka, polonaise, and waltz. Indeed, it's probably also fair to say that to a great extent the reputation of character pieces rests on the brilliance and beauty of the output of Chopin.

CHORD

[See HARMONY~CHORD.]

CLARINET

[See REED INSTRUMENTS; WOODWIND INSTRUMENTS.]

CLASSICAL MUSIC ~ CLASSICAL ERA

Classical music is not a precise term. And how could it be, embracing as it does music of countless styles, periods, and nationalities, from the Gregorian chant of the seventh century to the diverse and unpredictable products of the twentieth?

What it is, is a *practical* term: when you use it, people generally know what you mean. They know you're referring to music that fits somewhere within a framework of forms and traditions established over the centuries. And at the very least, they know what you *don't* mean. The music you'll find in the "classical" section of a record store might be Mozart, Menotti, Mussorgsky, or Monteverdi, but it won't be Mantovani . . . or folk, jazz, rock, or bluegrass.

Within the broad category of classical music, however — and here's where things can get a bit confusing — the word *classical* also has a narrow meaning. It is the label that applies specifically to the era and to the musical style of Joseph Haydn (1732–1809), Wolfgang Amadeus Mozart (1756–1791), and Ludwig van Beethoven (1770–1827). Running from approximately 1775 to 1820, the Classical era follows the Baroque era (with a short transitional period in between) and precedes the Romantic era. Most scholars view Beethoven as both the last of the great Classical composers and, with his middle and late works, the first of the great Romantics [see BAROQUE; ROMANTICISM].

Like most composers, Haydn, Mozart, and Beethoven didn't label themselves. Their music was designated as "Classical" by later writers who saw in it qualities associated with the art of ancient Greece and Rome, the art and architecture of classical antiquity. These qualities include balance, symmetry, logic, a pleasing surface, and the natural — as opposed to technically complex or overwrought — expression of feelings. In the Classical ideal — and in the Classical reality of Haydn, Mozart, and Beethoven — beauty and depth of expression are inseparable from clarity and beauty of form, and even the most passionate expression is achieved within the bounds of established conventions and proportions.

With regard to specific musical forms, the Classical era was not so much a period of invention as one of development and "perfection." The forms for which Haydn, Mozart, and Beethoven established lasting structural models and unprecedented artistic standards include the symphony, the sonata (including both the piano sonata and the sonata for piano and one other instrument), the divertimento, various chamber music forms (including the string quartet and piano trio), and the concerto, especially the piano concerto. To this day, these Classical forms remain at the heart of the concert repertoire, and at the heart of "classical music" in the broad sense. Haydn, Mozart, and Beethoven also made great advances and refinements in "sonata form," securing its place as one of the primary organizing principles in Western music. [See CHAMBER MUSIC; CONCERTO; DIVERTIMENTO~SERENADE; SONATA; SONATA FORM; SYMPHONY.]

Developments in musical composition often go hand in hand with developments in musical technology. The piano was invented in Italy in the early 1700s, but it was not until much later in the century that manufacturing technology advanced sufficiently to allow mass production and widespread distribution of the instrument. It was, indeed, precisely during the Classical era that the piano finally "caught on" throughout Europe and came into its own, replacing the harpsichord in most instrumental music and displacing the violin as the favored instrument for concertos. The great — and enormous — literature for solo piano and for piano in combination with other instruments begins with the music of Haydn, Mozart, and Beethoven. [See KEYBOARD INSTRUMENTS.]

CLAVICHORD

[See KEYBOARD INSTRUMENTS.]

CLAVIER

[See KEYBOARD INSTRUMENTS.]

CODA

Coda means "tail" in Italian, and a coda is indeed a musical tail, a passage added on to the end of a movement or piece to provide a fitting conclusion.

Sometimes the coda functions as a compact, emphatic summary, or wrap-up, of the musical material that's been presented during the course of a movement, sometimes as an extra flourish to make for a rousing, exciting finish, and sometimes as a quiet extension to allow feelings to settle — or linger. Almost always, the coda stresses in some way the return to the home key of the movement or piece, thereby reinforcing the sense of resolution and finality [see KEY~TONALITY].

In literary and dramatic forms — novels and stories, plays and movies — good authors and directors take great pains to come up with satisfying endings. In music an effective coda can make the difference between a piece that feels deeply satisfying and one that seems to end just a bit too soon. A coda may be short or long: it's the composer's job to decide what fits, what's appropriate for the character of the piece and for its proportions. Beethoven wrote positively monumental codas, for example, for the first and last movements of both his *Eroica* Symphony and his Fifth Symphony, but he needed such codas to balance the weight of the monumental material that had come before.

COL LEGNO

Col legno (pronounced "call lenyo"), Italian for "with the wood," is an instruction that composers write in the music when they want string players to sound notes by hitting the strings with the wood of their bows (the stick) instead of playing with the hair [see BOW~BOWING]. It's a special effect, used rarely — which is a good thing, because it's not exactly the best way to treat an expensive bow. Hector Berlioz (1803–1869) uses col legno to wonderful (and wild and woolly) effect in the last movement of his *Symphonie Fantastique*, where the violins and violas play col legno to evoke the sound of skeletons dancing in a graveyard.

COLORATURA

[See VOICE TYPES.]

CONCERTMASTER

The concertmaster is the violinist who occupies the first chair of the first violin section of an orchestra. Viewed from the audience, the concertmaster is the first person to the conductor's left, in the row of violins closest to the audience.

When a composer calls for a passage to be played by a solo violin in an orchestral composition (not a concerto), it is the concertmaster who plays it. The concertmaster also has the responsibility, sometimes guided by specific instructions from the conductor, of deciding which bowings the violins will use so that all the bows will move in the same direction at the same time [see BOW-BOWING]. The concertmaster makes bowing marks in his or her part before or during rehearsals (or both), and the other stands of violins, or an orchestra librarian, copy these marks. When the viola and cello sections' parts mirror the violin parts, it is the responsibility of those sections to take the concertmaster's bowings, too. Often during rehearsal, either at the conductor's request or on his own initiative, the concertmaster will demonstrate a particular kind of bow stroke or musical effect to ensure that all the violins play the same passage the same way.

Prior to the nineteenth century and the age of the modern conductor, it was sometimes the concertmaster's duty to lead the orchestra from his chair, often by waving his bow or making emphatic gestures. In modern times, the concertmaster has retained the ceremonial duty of presiding over the tuning of the orchestra onstage before a performance, and he usually has the honor of coming onstage last, after all the other musicians are seated.

When all is said and done, the greatest responsibility of a concertmaster is to play well, and to lead by playing well. The process of leading can be a bit mysterious, especially as the concertmaster is just one member of a section, and the vast majority of the time he plays exactly the same part as everybody else in that section [see PART]. But when a concertmaster plays in a manner that is emotionally committed, consistently accurate, rhythmically reliable, and always beautiful, he sets an example that exerts a strong positive influence on his colleagues and contributes in an important way to the overall quality of an orchestra's music making.

[See CONDUCTOR; ORCHESTRA.]

A concerto is a composition for one or more solo instruments and orchestra. A concerto for piano and orchestra is called a piano concerto, a concerto for violin and orchestra is called a violin concerto, and so forth.

The etymology of the word *concerto* is particularly interesting, because the Latin verb *concertare* means to "dispute," or "contend," while the Italian verb *concertare* means to "agree," or "get together." The Italian sense agrees with modern usage, as in "to work in concert," or "to make a concerted effort"; it explains why in Italy in the sixteenth and seventeenth centuries a group of performing musicians was often called a *concerto,* and also why *concerto* was used during that period as a title for various kinds of compositions that called for instrumental ensembles or combinations of voices and instruments. The Latin sense, on the other hand, points toward what would come to be the guiding principle of the pieces known as concertos: the dramatic "opposition" of a solo instrument and a full orchestra.

The modern concerto form has its roots in the Baroque period (ca. 1600–1750). By the end of the seventeenth century, Baroque composers had developed three distinct types of concertos, often utilizing just stringed instruments for both the orchestra and the solo parts. (A harpsichord would also be present to play continuo. See CONTINUO.) The first and oldest of the three types was the so-called *ripieno concerto. Ripieno* means "full," as in "full orchestra"; the ripieno concerto took its name from the fact that it didn't involve soloists. Instead it featured flashy "soloistic" passages (for the violins, usually) alternating with simpler music. The second type was the *concerto grosso,* which featured a small group of solo instruments — often two violins and cello (with harpsichord) — set against the larger forces of the orchestra. The third type was the *solo concerto,* for one solo instrument and orchestra. Of the three types, the concerto grosso and the solo concerto (especially for violin) were by far the most common, and they ranked among the most important of Baroque instrumental forms [see BAROQUE].

Some of the great names in the history of the Baroque concerto are Arcangelo Corelli (1653–1713), Giuseppe Torelli (1658–1709), Antonio Vivaldi (1675–1741), and George Frideric Handel (1685–1759). These four figured prominently in the development of the concerto grosso, but Vivaldi, in particular, was also a giant of the solo concerto. He wrote well over three hundred solo concertos, mostly for violin (including the four known as *The Four Seasons*), but also for other stringed instruments and for wind instruments. Johann Sebastian Bach (1685–1750) managed, as usual, to synthesize and expand all the developments of the period, and he brought the various concerto forms to new heights of beauty and expression. Bach's six Brandenburg Concertos, for example, include versions of the ripieno concerto and concerto grosso, but they're highly individual versions that transcend the genres and explore every possible variety of instrumental and musical contrast. One of the Brandenburg Concertos (No. 5) is a virtual harpsichord concerto in the guise of a concerto grosso, another (No. 6) features two solo violas and *no* violins, and four of the six concertos include prominent parts for wind instruments (Nos. 1, 2, 4, and 5).

After the Baroque period, the concerto grosso fell out of currency, but the solo concerto continued to flourish, with the piano concerto displacing the violin concerto as the most popular form. (Mozart wrote twenty-seven piano concertos, for example, and only five violin concertos, and Beethoven wrote five piano concertos and one violin concerto.) Since the works of Torelli, concertos had been divided into three separate movements — fast, slow, fast. This basic structure, expanded and elaborated in various ways, remained the model throughout the Classical era (the era of Haydn, Mozart, and Beethoven), and it has more or less remained the model to this day. Also remaining is the tradition, established by Torelli and others, of inserting toward the ends of movements, especially first movements, brilliant display passages called *caden-*

zas, which are played by the soloist while the orchestra is silent. Through Mozart's time, cadenzas were usually improvised by the soloist — Mozart himself set down only a few in writing — but Beethoven firmly established the practice of composing and writing out cadenzas and including them in the published versions of the music [see CADENCE-CADENZA].

The solo concerto seems to be one of those forms that has an intrinsic genius, offering drama, excitement, the persuasiveness of the individual voice, the power of massed forces — whether in opposition to or in support of the individual voice — and the chance to exploit and exhibit great individual accomplishments. Its enormous appeal increased, if anything, during the nineteenth century, and has shown no signs of diminishing in the twentieth. In fact, of all the major composers of the last 250 years, it would be hard to list more than a handful — with the exception of those who have written opera or other vocal music exclusively — who are not associated with at least one important and well-known solo concerto. The handful would include Franz Schubert, Anton Bruckner, Nikolay Rimsky-Korsakov, Gabriel Fauré, Gustav Mahler, and perhaps just a few others.

Composers almost always write concertos for specific performers. Often the intended performer is the composer himself. Otherwise it might be someone who has inspired the composer by the beauty and brilliance of his playing, or encouraged him by his interest, enthusiasm, and persistence. (The promise of a healthy commission fee can also be very encouraging.) The twentieth-century cello repertoire, for example, would be much the poorer were it not for Russian cellist Mstislav Rostropovich, for whom Sergei Prokofiev, Aram Khachaturian, Dmitri Shostakovich, Benjamin Britten, and Krzysztof Penderecki, among many others, all wrote, or have written, concertos. Performers often share in the actual compositional process, as well, offering suggestions and technical advice when their instrument is not the composer's own.

While pianists and violinists have by far the largest repertoire of concertos to choose from, there are concertos (and in many cases beautiful concertos by important composers) for virtually every instrument. The concerto repertoire for cello probably comes in third behind that of piano and violin for quantity and quality, but Mozart alone wrote four French horn concertos, two flute concertos, a concerto for violin and viola, one for flute and harp, and concertos for clarinet, oboe, and bassoon.

[See ACCOMPANIMENT; RONDO; VIRTUOSO. For discussions of specific instruments and their concerto repertoire, see BRASS INSTRUMENTS; VIOLIN FAMILY; WOODWIND INSTRUMENTS.]

CONCERTO GROSSO

[See CONCERTO.]

CONDUCTOR

A conductor directs rehearsals and performances by an orchestra, band, chorus, opera company, or other musical group. In the most general terms, a conductor's job is to shape a musical interpretation; to form ideas about the most compelling way to perform a piece and to lead a group of musicians in such a way that those ideas are realized. Conductors often serve as the "music directors" of their organizations, as well. A music director's duties include choosing programs and soloists and hiring (and firing) musicians.

In shaping a musical interpretation, a conductor has many specific responsibilities, which are similar no matter what kind of group he or she conducts. (In this discussion, an orchestra is assumed for the sake of convenience.) These responsibilities may be grouped as follows:

1. *Accuracy* — The conductor must ensure that the composer's intentions and instructions are faithfully carried out. At the very

least, this means making sure that everybody's playing all the right notes and rhythms. [See RHYTHM.]

2. *Ensemble* — The conductor must make sure everyone plays *together*, in precise rhythmic and musical coordination. The conductor is also responsible for giving "cues," signals with a hand motion, nod, or look that indicate (or confirm) the right moment for an individual player or section to make a musical entrance. [See ENSEMBLE.]

3. *Tempo and dynamics* (speed and volume) — Again, the conductor's job is to ensure the realization of the composer's intentions, but it's also to *interpret* those intentions, which means choosing general levels of tempo and volume as well as supervising all the fine shadings. [See DYNAMICS; TEMPO; TEMPO MARKINGS.]

4. *Phrasing* — Tempo and dynamics are part of phrasing, but so are such elusive factors as "direction," "emphasis," and "pacing," all of which affect the shape and coherence of musical phrases or passages.

5. *Quality of sound* — The conductor is at all times responsible for the kind of sound the orchestra produces. Whether it's full, thin, harsh, gentle, powerful, rich, light, heavy, round, lean, muscular, or "noble," the orchestra's sound should always suit the music.

6. *Balance* — The conductor must make sure that what should be heard is heard, that different but simultaneous musical "lines" are at the proper volume levels relative to their importance, that one instrument, voice, or group of instruments doesn't inadvertently drown out any others.

7. *Style* — The conductor must elicit from the orchestra an overall character of performance that is best suited to the composer, the period, and the piece.

⌐

The way a conductor ensures that all the members of an orchestra start together and stay together is to beat time. The fundamental principle is simple: the speed of the beat indicates the tempo of the music. Conductors usually beat time with a stick called a baton, held in the right hand. (Some conductors, especially choral conductors, prefer not to use a baton, but they're in a minority. Most conductors feel that the baton is very important for the visibility and clarity of the beat.) By convention, certain beat patterns are used to indicate certain metrical patterns, with the first beat of each measure always shown by a downward stroke, or "downbeat," and the last beat shown by an upward stroke [see BEAT; METER]. When the music is "in two," for example (that is, when there are two beats per measure), the stick goes down to show the first beat, then back up for the second, with the pattern repeated over and over. When the music is in three, the stick goes down for "one," to the right for "two," then back up for "three" before starting again. And when there are four beats per measure, the pattern is down, left, right, and up.

A good conductor, however, can indicate much more with the beat than just information about tempo and meter. It's not only the pattern and speed that count, but also the *qualities* of the beat. Expansive gestures, tight gestures, large or small gestures, and motions that are smooth, choppy, delicate, or violent all convey different information and can elicit different musical results. With a good conductor — and a good orchestra — the quality of sound the orchestra produces is influenced by the qualities of the beat, by the *character* of the conductor's physical gestures.

And these physical gestures are not limited to the hand with the baton. They include complementary gestures of the left hand, as well as overall "body language." In fact, especially from the point of view of musical expressiveness — dynamics, phrasing, sound quality, and so forth — conductors lead by a kind of multilevel physical seduction, a seduction of which the orchestra musicians may not even be aware. This is why even individuals who have fine musical minds and/or "great hands" — some instrumentalists turned conductor, for example — don't necessarily make good conductors if they are unrefined in their larger movements or physically awkward in a general way. Then again, people can be seductive in many different ways, and conductors of widely differing physiques, physical styles, and temperaments can be effective. In conducting, as in everything else, the absolute rule is that nothing is absolute.

A conductor does a large part of his or her work — perhaps the largest part — away from the public eye, in study and in rehearsal. It is in the many hours of studying the score that a conductor learns a piece of music in detail and formulates his interpretative ideas, and it is in rehearsal that the conductor communicates those ideas to the musicians — in both word and gesture — and sees that they are brought to fruition in the playing. (Most professional orchestras have a maximum of four rehearsals of about two and a half hours each for each concert program, with three or four different pieces per program.) Conductors have varying styles and techniques of rehearsing. Some are tense, some are relaxed; some talk quite a bit and some talk very little; some spend considerable time going over every detail and others never do much more than have the orchestra play through all the pieces a few times.

⌐

The question remains: What makes a good conductor? Musical imagination, intelligence, and judgment certainly come first, since there's no point learning how to communicate with an orchestra in the absence of musical ideas that are worth communicating. A conductor must also have confidence in his ideas and the self-assurance and personal presence to lead well, to be completely convincing, even inspiring, in the role. A good ear is essential, both for judging overall qualities and for pinpointing specific problems within large and complicated masses of sound. A well-trained "inner ear," too, or "mind's ear," is very important for studying scores and for "hearing" music just by looking at the printed page. In order for an orchestra to feel at ease and confident enough to play freely and beautifully, a conductor must also demonstrate a rock-solid sense of rhythm. Tempos must be consistent and steady, beating mistakes rare, and rhythmic complexities handled securely. A good conductor also possesses a certain physical grace, or at least coordination, which translates into a clear beat and musically meaningful gestures. A good conductor must be at ease facing large and complex forces and coordinating their efforts, and he must know how to run an efficient, well-organized rehearsal. It may seem a simplistic thing to say, but with a good conductor, both the music and the orchestra playing it should sound better *after* rehearsal than they did before. Like all good musicians, a good conductor must also have a flair for performance, the ability to remain in control and yet bring a little something extra when it counts the most.

And bad conductors? Some are unimaginative or uninteresting, even if they're technically competent. Others are just not very gifted — they have difficulty communicating musical ideas, either physically, verbally, or both. Some may even put on quite an extravagant physical show (complete with rapturous facial expressions that look great on TV), but without necessarily communicating much that's musically relevant or useful to the members of the orchestra. Other conductors are unprepared or undependable, and in fact they get in the way. They're uncertain in their gestures and cues, and they make mistakes. In rehearsal they may be disorganized or inefficient, which means they either allot their time poorly or use it poorly. They may mistake little problems for big ones and vice versa, or they may not even notice problems. And when they do notice them, they may not know how to fix them.

To the extent that they can, good orchestras try to ignore bad or mediocre conductors, both in rehearsal and in performance. As a matter of fact, it's not that uncommon for orchestras to rescue conductors from their mistakes — to play passages correctly even when the conductor beats the wrong pattern or gets lost. The truth is that most of what an orchestra needs to know is already indicated in the music by the composer, and one can do a lot worse than just to play what's written. An excellent, inspiring conductor can lift a performance to another level, but an orchestra doesn't necessarily need a conductor to "make it play" or to inspire it — the music does that. It's a matter of professional accomplishment and professional pride for the best orchestras that they simply don't allow themselves to play below a certain level.

In all fairness, it's not always easy for the audience to tell whether a conductor is good or bad. First of all, the audience doesn't get to attend the rehearsals. More importantly, though, the best music is "hard to kill," and will usually sound pretty good — or pretty terrific — no matter what, especially in the hands of a fine orchestra. Is an exciting performance the result of a great piece of music played by excellent musicians, or is it the conductor who is responsible for the excitement? It's hard to know. Familiarity with a specific orchestra or with a specific piece helps enormously. Does the orchestra sound better with this conductor than with that one, more precise, richer, more vibrant, with a wider range of sounds and qualities? Does the performance of a certain piece seem more persuasive, more beautiful, more interesting, more exciting? These are the questions to ask.

Audiences tend to see conductors in a very glamorous light. After all, these people wield authority over lots of other people, over great musical forces. A conductor stands alone, high on a podium, and calls forth oceans of sound with a wave of the baton. The image is one of great power. In the modern mythology of conductors, in fact, one of the figures occupying a prominent place is that of the glorious tyrant of days gone by, the musical giant who treated orchestras disdainfully, even cruelly. There have indeed been such figures — some of whom left behind legendary reputations and hundreds of recordings — and there are those who claim that the tyranny was worth it for the fabulous musical results; that it was all in the service of great art. But is it really necessary for conductors to be unpleasant, intimidating, or tyrannical in their behavior toward orchestras in order to achieve the highest standards?

The answer is no, and the number of wonderful conductors who are, or were, perfectly pleasant and polite proves the point. Yes, conductors need to be sure of themselves. Any leader needs to radiate confidence in order for others to follow him with confidence and enthusiasm, and the conductors that orchestras tend to respect the most are those who "know what they want and know how to get it." But tyrannical behavior, temper tantrums, insulting or belittling remarks — all are musically unnecessary, and all represent an unfortunate misuse of musical authority. Those conductors in "the old days" who were tyrants simply took personal advantage of a world in which their power was unlimited. Today there are limits: with collective bargaining agreements and the strengthening of musicians' unions over the last thirty years, orchestra players both in this country and abroad have a much larger say in their working conditions. Although conductors may still be able to say what they want, they can't always just *do* what they want. It used to be the case, for example, that a music director could summarily fire a musician at any time, and for any reason, professional or personal. No longer. When a player proves incompetent he can still be fired, but the procedures for doing so (especially in major orchestras) are specific and strict, and usually require review by a committee of orchestra members in addition to the decision of the conductor. A conductor of cruel bent can still embarrass someone and make his life in the orchestra very difficult, but he can no longer take away his livelihood in a single stroke.

It's worth emphasizing that the best conductors respect the musicians they conduct, and are respected by them in return. Orchestra musicians are certainly cynical enough when it comes to conductors of meager skills, but their cynicism is quickly replaced with enthusiasm and admiration in the presence of conductors of true stature and accomplishment.

〜

The age of the modern conductor began in the early nineteenth century. Prior to that time, most operatic and orchestral works included harpsichord, and the person who beat time was either the harpsichordist or the concertmaster (the principal violinist). The concertmaster would use his bow to give signals, and the harpsichordist might use either his hand or a rolled-up sheet of paper. As orchestral and operatic forces expanded in the nineteenth century, and as the complexity of music increased, it became a necessity to have conductors of undivided responsibilities. (It's an interesting point, though, that in the early nineteenth century it was quite common for conductors to face the audience, not the orchestra.) The first important conductors of the nineteenth century were composers who also conducted, such as Ludwig Spohr (1784–1859), Carl Maria von Weber (1786–1826), and Felix Mendelssohn (1809–1847). The composer-conductor tradition was later carried on by such figures as Gustav Mahler (1860–1911) and Richard Strauss (1864–1949). Among the first of those whose renown rested solely on their conducting accomplishments were Hans von Bülow (1830–1894), Hans Richter (1843–1916), Arthur Nikisch (1855–1922), Arturo Toscanini (1867–1957), and Pierre Monteux (1875–1964). These conductors, among others, helped establish both the image and the reality of the conductor as a powerful, revered figure in the music world.

[See CONCERTMASTER; MAESTRO; ORCHESTRA; SCORE.]

CONTINUO

"We've just heard the Collegium Baroquium of Liverpool under the direction of André-Pierre Farfelstückel, performing Heinrich Geräuschenmacher's Concerto for trumpet, strings, and continuo." Whenever a piece of Baroque music is announced on the radio, Geräuschenmacher or no Geräuschenmacher, it always seems there's something called "continuo" involved. There's a good reason for this: much of the time in Baroque music continuo *is* involved.

Continuo, however, is not the name of an instrument. It's the name of one of the component "parts" in a Baroque composition, a part usually played by a combination of instruments. One of the typical textures in music of the Baroque period (ca. 1600–1750) is a high solo line or melody supported down below by a strong, ongoing bass line, with the notes in between serving to fill out harmonies [see HARMONY–CHORD; INNER VOICES]. The term *continuo* is short for **BASSO CONTINUO**, which means "continuous bass" in Italian, and the continuo part includes the continuous, or ongoing, bass line of a composition, the lowest notes. There's more to it, though. In Baroque practice, the composer marks the notes of the bass line with numbers (called "figures") that indicate which chords or harmonies are to be built on each bass note. The continuo part includes not just the bass notes, but the bass notes plus the figures. This means that when it's played — as it's heard out loud, in other words — the continuo part includes the bass notes plus the harmonies.

And who plays continuo? Continuo parts always require a keyboard instrument, usually the harpsichord or the organ. Most often, however, the keyboard continuo instrument is joined by a second, low-voiced instrument such as the cello or viola da gamba. The second continuo instrument serves to reinforce the notes of the bass line, while the keyboard instrument covers all the harmonies.

For the keyboard player, playing continuo is an art of improvisation. The bass line is set, and the figures indicate what harmonies should be heard, but within those constraints the keyboard player is free to invent, to arrange the notes any way he likes. This may mean playing not just simple chords, but finding ways to imitate patterns in the bass line and the (composer's) primary melody, or inventing secondary melodies that complement the primary melody. Another term for continuo is **FIGURED BASS**, and playing a continuo part at the keyboard — using the figures to build a harmonically correct musical structure above the bass line — is called "realizing" a figured bass. The ability to realize a figured bass at sight was absolutely essential for keyboard players of the Baroque era, who were often judged on the skill and imagination of their improvisations. Nowadays, however, only specialists attempt it. Most modern editions of Baroque music are published with the figured bass realized by an editor.

Yet another term for *continuo* is **THOROUGHBASS**. *Thoroughbass* is actually just a translation of *basso continuo*, with "thorough" being an old spelling for "through," as in "throughout." *Continuo, basso continuo, figured bass, thoroughbass* — they're all different words for the same thing.

[See BAROQUE.]

CONTRABASS

[See VIOLIN FAMILY.]

CONTRABASSOON

[See WOODWIND INSTRUMENTS.]

CONTRALTO

[See VOICE TYPES.]

COUNTERPOINT ~ POLYPHONY

Counterpoint is the art, in musical composition, of combining two or more simultaneous lines of music. The word *counterpoint* comes from the Latin *contrapunctus*, which comes in turn from the phrase *punctus contra punctum*, meaning "note against note." The adjective derived from the word counterpoint is *contrapuntal*.

In contrapuntal writing, the simultaneous musical lines are distinct and independent: each is a theme or melody that could stand alone. But the lines are composed according to certain rules and principles so that they sound good *together*. The notes of each musical line are heard "against" the notes of the other line — *punctus contra punctum* — but that doesn't mean that they clash.

On the contrary, they "fit," so that when they sound together they create harmonies of the composer's choosing. What's fascinating and compelling about counterpoint (the word may also be used to refer to the music itself) is the way it operates on several levels at once: at the same time that each musical line retains its character and creates interest individually, the lines also act collectively. They relate and refer to one another — sometimes to the point of imitation — and combine to create a progression of harmonies essential to the beauty and sense of direction of the music. Terms such as *three-part counterpoint, four-part counterpoint,* and *five-part counterpoint* indicate how many individual melodies, or musical lines, are woven together to form the musical fabric.

The earliest contrapuntal writing is found in church music of the tenth century. From simple two-part compositions of severely limited possibilities, counterpoint developed steadily over the centuries, becoming ever more complex and sophisticated and serving as a basis for vocal and instrumental composition in both the religious and secular realms. During the Renaissance (ca. 1430–1600), counterpoint was the preeminent musical style throughout Europe, and it remained a central feature of much music of the Baroque period (ca. 1600–1750), especially in Germany. The most important Baroque contrapuntal form was the *fugue,* and the fugues of Johann Sebastian Bach (1685–1750) are generally recognized as the summit of Baroque counterpoint, astonishing for their marriage of dazzling compositional technique and profound artistic expression [see FUGUE].

As a musical style, counterpoint stands in direct contrast to the style known as "melody and accompaniment." Melody and accompaniment involves multiple musical lines sounding together and creating harmonies, but the lines are not equal and independent, as they are in contrapuntal writing. One line serves as the principal melody, and the accompanying lines, even if interesting, are of very different character, and clearly subsidiary.

After the Baroque period, the influence of counterpoint waned, and the melody and accompaniment style took on a position of undisputed prominence. Nonetheless, contrapuntal writing (and even the fugue) is an essential ingredient in the music of Haydn, Mozart, and Beethoven, and in various forms it has remained essential throughout the nineteenth and twentieth centuries. Serious training for a composer has always included training in counterpoint.

↩

Another word for counterpoint is POLYPHONY. The terms are essentially interchangeable, but *polyphony* is commonly used when referring to music composed before the seventeenth century, as in the term *Renaissance polyphony*.

[See ACCOMPANIMENT; BAROQUE; CANON; HARMONY~ CHORD; MELODY.]

COUNTERTENOR

[See VOICE TYPES.]

CRESCENDO

Crescendo means "growing," or "increasing" (from the Italian verb *crescere*, "to grow"), and in music it always refers to volume. The term is usually employed as a noun: when a musician says, "Let's make a crescendo in this passage," for instance, he means, "Let's get louder in this passage." He doesn't necessarily mean, "Let's get *loud*," however. A crescendo may lead from soft to loud, but it may also lead from extremely soft to very soft, or from very soft to moderately soft.

Of all the *mis*uses of musical terms, in fact, the use of the term *crescendo* to mean "climax" is probably the most common. For example, "As Senator Soundbite finished his speech, the roar of applause reached a shattering crescendo!" You can't "reach" a crescendo. A crescendo is a process. You can reach a climax, but you need to build up to it first — and the buildup usually consists of, or at least includes, a crescendo.

[For a discussion of terms pertaining to volume in music, see DYNAMICS.]

CYMBALS

[See PERCUSSION INSTRUMENTS.]

D

DANCE

Dance is a noun with a double meaning: it represents not just a set of repeated steps and movements, but also a musical piece or form with which those steps and movements are associated. You can dance a tango, and you can *play* a tango — whether or not anybody's dancing. Composers borrow dances for their music because of their rhythmic vitality and because they provide ready-made, concrete associations. The associations may be with specific moods, feelings, functions, or types of physical movement, or with peoples, nations, or cultures.

The possibilities for "color," for the excitement and exoticism of "foreign" dances, have always particularly intrigued composers. Mozart, Haydn, Schubert, and Brahms, for example, all made use of fast Hungarian or Gypsy dances in their music at one time or another, Mendelssohn's *Italian* Symphony has its name because it concludes with a *saltarello,* and Ravel was fascinated with Spanish forms — the *bolero,* for one. Ravel also wrote *La valse* (*The Waltz*), and the Viennese waltz has been a favorite of countless composers.

Composers have often used dances from their own countries, as well, as a means of expressing or preserving ethnic or national identity and pride. The late nineteenth century saw the rise of nationalism in music as a conscious principle or movement, starting in the 1860s with the Bohemian (Czech) composer Bedřich Smetana (1824–1884). Earlier, Frédéric Chopin (1810–1849), while not part of any specific nationalist movement, had mined his Polish roots extensively with *polonaises* and *mazurkas.* Antonín Dvořák (1841–1904), also Bohemian, followed Smetana's example, as did later composers in other countries. Smetana and Dvořák made frequent use of a fast Bohemian dance called the *furiant,* while Russian composers such as Tchaikovsky, Mussorgsky, Rimsky-Korsakov, and later Stravinsky occasionally flavored their compositions with dances like the *hopak* and *trepak.* The Spaniards Isaac Albéniz (1860–1909), Enrique Granados (1867–1916), and Manuel de Falla (1876–1946) wrote *jotas, seguidillas,* and *fandangos,* and Zoltán Kodály (1882–1967) and Béla Bartók (1881–1945) more than once appropriated a Hungarian military recruiting dance called the *verbunkos.*

When dances find their way into musical compositions — compositions meant for listening, that is, as opposed to music written specifically for dancing — it's almost always in altered or stylized form. Composers may keep the general character, flavor, or underlying rhythms, but they usually don't hesitate to modify dances to suit their artistic purposes. You couldn't dance the *allemande* to a Bach Allemande if you wanted to, for example, or the *mazurka* to a Chopin Mazurka. And nobody ever signed up for the Hungarian Army after hearing a Bartók Verbunkos.

The following dances figure in musical compositions either frequently or from time to time. Where the dances are true national dances, or are at the very least strongly identified with a single country, national identifications appear in parentheses. A number of the dances, however, originated in one country but later crossed various borders and were transformed in the process, sometimes changing just the spelling of their names, sometimes changing character totally. Transplanted versions of dances sometimes became the standard forms, in some cases taking on new national identities and in some cases losing national identity completely.

allemande	chaconne	fox-trot (U.S.)
bolero (Sp.)	courante	furiant (Bohem.)
bourrée	czárdás (Hung.)	galliard
cakewalk (U.S.)	fandango (Sp.)	galop
cancan (Fr.)	forlana (It.)	gavotte (Fr.)

gigue

habanera (Cub.-Sp.)

hopak (Belarus)

hornpipe (Eng.)

jig (Ire., Eng.)

jota (Sp.)

ländler (Aust.)

loure

malagueña (Sp.)

mazurka (Pol.)

minuet

passacaglia

passamezzo (It.)

passepied (Fr.)

pavane

polonaise (Pol.)

rigaudon (rigadoon)

saltarello (It.)

samba (Braz.)

sarabande

seguidilla (Sp.)

tango (Arg.)

tarantella (It.)

trepak (Russ.)

verbunkos (Hung.)

waltz (Aust.)

DISSONANCE

[See ATONALITY~DISSONANCE.]

DIVERTIMENTO ~ SERENADE

Divertimento, in Italian, means "entertainment," or "diversion." Composers in the latter part of the eighteenth century used the term as a title for a wide variety of instrumental pieces whose primary purpose was to be light, pleasant, and entertaining. Divertimentos (or *divertimenti,* the frequently encountered Italian plural) usually have more than four movements — sometimes as many as ten — and often include minuets, marches, and theme-and-variation movements [see MINUET; THEME AND VARIATIONS]. The number of instruments generally varies from three to ten, and the instruments may be strings, winds, or a combination of the two.

The works of great composers tend to transcend, or to redefine, categories. Haydn and Mozart both wrote dozens of divertimentos, but in their hands the "entertainment" often reached great heights — and depth. Mozart's trio for violin, viola, and cello, K. 563, for example, is called Divertimento, but by any definition it's serious music, a brilliant, beautiful, and profound piece. And like any great work of art or literature, it's effective and affecting on many levels at once.

∽

For instrumental music of the late 1700s, the terms *divertimento* and *serenade* were virtually interchangeable. The original meaning of the word *serenade,* however, or *serenata,* in Italian, was "evening song" — a song to be sung by a suitor under his beloved's window. Instrumental serenades dispensed with the requirement for love and windows, but the implication of outdoor performance in the evening, often in conjunction with meals or other festivities, remained.

DOMINANT

The dominant is the fifth note, or fifth *degree,* of a major or minor scale. The dominant of the C-major scale, for example, is G: C-D-E-F-*G*.

Dominant is also the name for the major chord, or harmony, built on that fifth degree. The major chord built on G is G major, and since the C-major scale forms the basis for the *key* of C major, it's correct to say that in the key of C major, G major is the dominant. (All keys are based on scales. See KEY~TONALITY.)

In tonal music, that is, music written in a key, the dominant harmony is of central importance because it is the harmony that leads most strongly to the *tonic,* the harmony on which the key is based.

[See HARMONY~CHORD; SCALE; TONIC.]

DOUBLE BASS

[See VIOLIN FAMILY.]

Dynamics are the degrees and shadings of volume — loudness and softness — in a musical piece or performance. The written symbols, words, and abbreviations that are included in the music to indicate those degrees and shadings are called "dynamic marks."

By tradition and convention, the terms employed for dynamics are Italian [see TEMPO MARKINGS for a discussion of the use of Italian musical terms]. This doesn't mean that they have to be pronounced with an Italian accent, though, even if it's a pretty good Italian accent. "Musicians' Italian" long ago became an international language, and it's normal for the terms to take on the flavor of local pronunciation. There's one exception: a final "e" is pronounced "ay," as in "day." The word *forte*, for example, is pronounced "fortay," and *sempre* is "sempray."

Dynamics are indicated in the music below the notes or passages to which they refer. Here are the most common terms for dynamics, their definitions, and the ways they're marked in printed music:

Dynamic	Definition	Dynamic mark
piano	soft	*p*
pianissimo (sometimes called "double piano")	very soft	*pp*
mezzo piano	medium, or moderately soft	*mp*
più piano	softer (*più* means "more"; implies the dynamic is already piano)	più *p*
meno piano	louder (*meno* means "less")	meno *p*
forte	loud	*f*
fortissimo (sometimes called "double forte")	very loud	*ff*

Dynamic	Definition	Dynamic mark
mezzo forte	medium, or moderately loud	*mf*
più forte	louder (implies the dynamic is already forte)	più *f*
meno forte	softer	meno *f*
poco forte	somewhat loud, or not too loud (*poco* means "a little"; an ambiguous marking, favored by Johannes Brahms, among others)	poco *f*
sempre piano	remain soft	sempre *p*
sempre forte	remain loud (*sempre* means "always," or "still")	sempre *f*
sforzando, sforzato	strongly accented (applies to a single note or chord; *sforzando* means "forcing," *sforzato* means "forced"; the terms are equivalent)	*sf* or *sfz*
forzando, forzato	strongly accented (same as sforzando)	*fz*
forte-piano	loud, immediately followed by soft (usually on the same note)	*fp*
crescendo	getting louder	*crescendo* or *cresc.*
decrescendo	getting softer	*decrescendo, decresc.,* or *decr.*
diminuendo	getting softer (*decrescendo* means "decreasing," *diminuendo* means "diminishing"; the terms are equivalent)	*diminuendo, dimin.,* or *dim.*

(The words *poco a poco,* "little by little," are occasionally added either before or after *crescendo, decrescendo,* or *diminuendo.*)

morendo	fading away (literally, "dying")	*morendo*

How loud is loud and how soft is soft? That's up to the performer to decide. Loud and soft are not exact measurements, and dynamic marks — like tempo markings — always require interpretation. The style of the piece, the nature of the specific musical material, the acoustics of the performing space, the size and characteristics of the instrumental and/or vocal forces and the balancing of those forces to bring out the important musical lines — all must be taken into account in choosing actual volume levels. Shaping and shading dynamics, in fact, is one of the most important aspects of a musician's responsibility in performing a piece. It's also one of the areas where individual (and group) differences in interpretation and musical ideas are most apparent.

Dynamics are relative. Forte is louder than mezzo forte, and mezzo piano is louder than pianissimo. The relationships that count, however, are within the same piece. It doesn't mean anything to compare the fortissimo in one piece with the forte in another — one piece may be for solo harpsichord and the other for a phalanx of trombones — but within the *same* piece those comparisons are crucial because they give a clear indication of the relative volume levels the composer has in mind. Because of individual differences in taste or capacity, one performer's forte may be louder than another's even when interpreting the same piece — I play TOMATO, you play TOMATO — but for that piece each performer's forte should still be less loud than his own fortissimo. Faithfulness to a composer's intentions is a matter of keeping proportions, not counting decibels.

Up until and throughout the Baroque period (ca. 1600–1750), however, a composer's intentions regarding dynamics had to be deduced mainly from the character and patterns of the music and the stylistic conventions of the time, because dynamic marks in music were infrequent. Most of J. S. Bach's works, for example, include no dynamic marks at all. And even during the Classical era (ca. 1775–1820), dynamic marks provided only a skeleton. In the music of Haydn and Mozart, for instance, *f*'s and *p*'s are common, but *ff, pp,* and *crescendo* appear infrequently, *diminuendo* even more infrequently, and *mf* and *mp* never. Haydn and Mozart and their contemporaries assumed that, for the most part, well-educated performers would know when a musical phrase required a crescendo or diminuendo, and that good musicians would use good taste in managing the subtle dynamic shadings and gradations necessary during the course of a piece.

It was Ludwig van Beethoven (1770–1827) who started the practice of providing much more detailed indications of dynamics, and most composers since Beethoven's time have followed his example. A number of these composers, including late-nineteenth-century composers like Peter Ilyich Tchaikovsky and turn-of-the-century composers like Gustav Mahler and Richard Strauss, expanded the range of dynamic marks to include such indications as *ppp* and *fff*, with even an occasional *ffff* or *ppppp*. Some might consider these amplifications a devaluation of the currency, since even in the mighty final movement of his Ninth Symphony, with a big chorus and orchestra going full guns, Beethoven never felt the need to mark anything more than *ff*. But if a composer marks a passage *fff* and nowhere else in the piece goes above *ff*, it's certainly clear where the loudest point in the piece is supposed to be.

The ending *-issimo* means "very," as in forte-*fortissimo*, piano-*pianissimo*. But what do you call *fff*, or *ppp?* Not to worry, the Italians have a solution: just add another *iss*. The term for *fff* in Italian is fortiss**iss**imo, with the accent on the second *iss*, and *ppp* is pianiss**iss**imo. Four *p*'s would be pianississississimo, and five would be pianississississississimo. In these cases, however, linguistic discretion is often the better part of pronunciatory valor: terms such as *triple forte* and *quadruple piano* convey the necessary information, and they're a lot easier to say.

[See CRESCENDO.]

E

ENGLISH HORN

[See WOODWIND INSTRUMENTS.]

ENSEMBLE

An ensemble is a group of performers. The music world is filled with instrumental ensembles, vocal ensembles, chamber music ensembles (sometimes called just chamber ensembles), early music ensembles, contemporary music ensembles, and so on.

Ensemble also refers to the quality of togetherness in performance. (The French word *ensemble* means "together.") One can say of a musical group, for example, that "their ensemble is excellent," meaning their performances are "tight" — musically accurate and well coordinated, with no rough edges.

ETUDE

An étude (from the French *étudier*, "to study") is a piece, most often an instrumental piece, composed for study or exercise purposes. Individual études often focus on one particular kind of technical difficulty or problem.

By the nineteenth century, various kinds of instrumental exercises had been around for hundreds of years, but the invention of the modern étude is generally credited to the Italian English pianist, composer, and teacher Muzio Clementi (1752–1832). Between 1817 and 1826, Clementi published three volumes of piano études called *Gradus ad Parnassum* (*Steps to Parnassus,* after a famous eighteenth-century music theory text of the same name), and what was different, or modern, about these études compared to most that had come before was that although they were still meant for practice, they were musically interesting compositions, not just mindless finger exercises. Many other nineteenth-century composers followed in Clementi's path, composers such as Karl Czerny and Ignaz Moscheles for the piano and Rodolphe Kreutzer, Jacob Dont, and Pierre Rode for the violin, whose names became (and remain) familiar to — if not exactly popular with — generations of music students. The introduction of musical, as opposed to merely mechanical, values into study materials was of great importance because in fact there is no such thing as pure technique, technique divorced from music. The only goal of technique is musical expression, and the only way for a musician to judge whether he is doing something technically "right" is to judge whether the results are beautiful or expressive.

The history of music is filled with examples of seemingly minor forms transformed by genius. After Clementi, the next important name associated with the étude is Frédéric Chopin (1810–1849). In his sets of piano études published as Op. 10 and Op. 25, Chopin created impressive and challenging pieces that were meant not just for private practice, but also for public performance. These pieces require a fabulous technique, but they were intended less for developing technique, it might be said, than for showing it off. Because of their musical beauty and brilliance, they transcended the previously imagined limits of the étude and created an entirely new category, which came to be known as the "concert étude."

There is hardly a composer of piano music after Chopin who was not influenced by him, and among the subsequent composers of concert études were such important figures as Robert Schumann (1810–1856), Johannes Brahms (1833–1897), Franz Liszt (1811–1886), Alexander Scriabin (1872–1915), Sergei Rachmaninoff (1873–1943), Claude Debussy (1862–1918), and Béla Bartók (1881–1945). On the violin side, the great nineteenth-century virtuoso Niccolò Paganini (1782–1840) also wrote a famous, and famously difficult, set of twenty-four concert études, and composers to this day continue to write concert études for various instruments. Concert études often go by other names, however. Schumann's concert études for piano, for example, are called *Symphonic Etudes*, Liszt's are known as *Transcendental Etudes*, Rachmaninoff's are *Etudes-tableaux*, and Debussy's, like Chopin's, are simply *Etudes*. Paganini, on the other hand, called his set of concert études *Caprices*.

[See CHARACTER PIECE.]

FANTASY ～ FANTASIA

Fantasy is the English translation of the Italian *fantasia*, a term that first appeared as a title for instrumental compositions in the 1500s. The fantasy has had countless specific incarnations. There have been fantasies for lute, guitar, harpsichord, viols, organ, piano, and orchestra; Renaissance fantasies, Baroque fantasies, Classical, Romantic, and modern fantasies; fantasies ranging from abstract contrapuntal exercises to extravagant variations on operatic arias. Through all these different periods, styles, and instrumental combinations, however, the general definition has remained the same: a fantasy is a composition in which the composer allows his imagination free rein, unrestrained by strict rules of form or convention. "In this," wrote the English composer Thomas Morley in 1597, "may more art be showne then in any other musicke, because the composer is tide to nothing but that he may adde, deminish, and alter at his pleasure."

[See CHARACTER PIECE.]

FIDDLE

Fiddle and *violin* are two words for the same instrument, and it's the same instrument whether it's played by a country or bluegrass fiddler or by a classical violinist. *Fiddle* is an informal term, but one that classical musicians use all the time: a classical musician might say of a colleague, "She's quite a fiddle player," or of a priceless Stradivarius violin, "That's a terrific fiddle" — high praise in both cases.

Interestingly enough, not only are a fiddle and a violin the same instrument, but the words themselves are closer than they might appear to be at first glance: they have the same etymological roots. Their closeness would have been clearer in the Middle Ages, when the words *fithele* and *fiele* (English), *vièle* and *vielle* (French), *viula* (Provençal), and *Fiedel* and *Videl* (German) all referred to the same family, or families, of instruments. The original Latin root is thought to be *vidula,* or *vitula,* meaning "to rejoice."

The words *fiddle* and *violin* weren't always interchangeable, however, nor were they even contemporaneous. Neither the modern word *violin* (*violino,* in Italian) nor the instrument to which it referred was in standard use until the 1500s, whereas by that time the various versions of the word *fiddle* and the different kinds of bowed string instruments known today as medieval fiddles had already been in existence for several centuries. For a long while, *fiddle* probably remained the generic term, with *violin* meaning a particular kind of fiddle. Only in modern times (after 1600, at the very earliest) did the paths of fiddle and violin — the words and the instruments — merge.

The word *fiddlestick,* by the way, or *fydylstyk,* in its medieval spelling, is an old word for *bow.*

[See VIOLIN FAMILY.]

FINALE

Many kinds of musical compositions are divided into distinct sections called "movements." The finale is the last movement of a composition. *Finale* is also the name for the last section of an opera or operatic act. An operatic finale itself is often divided into sections, and lasts much longer than an aria or any single number.

Throughout the eighteenth and nineteenth centuries, the finales of instrumental pieces were almost always in fast, or relatively fast, tempos, and their endings were usually loud [see TEMPO]. Composers wanted there to be no doubt about when their pieces were over, and they wanted them to end with a bang, or at least with some sort of satisfyingly emphatic (or happy, or triumphant) musical statement. The goal — artistic, philosophical, and commercial — was to leave the listener feeling uplifted and enthusiastic. It wasn't until Tchaikovsky wrote his Sixth Symphony, the so-called *Pathétique,* in 1893, that a composer closed a symphony with a slow movement (the piece ends softly, as well). In the twentieth century, composers have been much more willing to leave their listeners depressed or disconcerted: countless twentieth-century finales end slowly and softly.

While this liberation from the cliché of the Big Bang has resulted in many beautiful and moving endings, it has also spawned one of the clichés of twentieth-century music: the finale that dies away into nothingness, symbolizing uncertainty, or the meaninglessness of life, or the meaninglessness of uncertainty, or the certainty of death, or the death of certainty, or . . . something. Given the realities of two world wars, unending atrocities, and the continuing possibilities for atomic annihilation, pessimistic reflections in musical composition and philosophy have been natural, and perhaps inevitable. But a cliché is a cliché, and there's a danger when an inclination becomes an obligation. Nowhere is it written, after all, that for music to be good it must be joyless. In music as in life, it is neither dishonest nor philosophically disgraceful to find a little happiness along the way, whether at the beginning, the middle, or the end.

FLUTE

[See WOODWIND INSTRUMENTS.]

FORTE

[See DYNAMICS.]

[See KEYBOARD INSTRUMENTS.]

FRENCH HORN

[See BRASS INSTRUMENTS.]

FUGUE

Imagine three bettors: each one thinks his horse is going to triumph at the track that afternoon, and, what's more, each one decides to sing about his choice. The first thinks the winner will be Paul Revere, and he expresses his confidence with a catchy melody. He's followed in song by the second bettor, who sings the same melody while extolling the virtues of Valentine. Meanwhile, the first fellow has kept singing, but with a different, "secondary" melody. Against the continued singing of the first two, the third gentleman now joins in with the original melody, singing the praises of Epitaph. The result is "Fugue for Tinhorns," the song that opens Frank Loesser's great Broadway show *Guys and Dolls*.

To be perfectly accurate, the "Fugue for Tinhorns" isn't a real fugue according to the traditional "rules" of the form. But it illustrates the most important principles of the fugue: three or four distinct and equally important voices coming in one after the other in *imitation* of one another, each then adding a melody that complements the first, or principal, melody, and all continuing simultaneously so that all the parts fit, so that the music makes sense and sounds good. The "voices" may actually be singing voices, or they may be three or four different instruments, or they may be several distinct "musical lines" played on a single instrument.

The fugue is a highly sophisticated form of the art of counterpoint, and in particular the art of *imitative counterpoint* [see COUNTERPOINT~POLYPHONY]. It evolved during the Baroque period (ca. 1600–1750) and reached its greatest heights in the works of George Frideric Handel (1685–1759) and Johann Sebastian Bach (1685–1750). Bach was without question the supreme master of the form. He wrote countless fugues, vocal and instrumental, and his last work, *The Art of Fugue,* is a brilliant summation of virtually all the techniques of imitative counterpoint. Bach's true greatness lay in his ability to combine technical mastery of this highly ordered and structured form with an astonishing freedom of imagination and range of emotional expression. His fugues are not dry compositions intended solely for the appreciation of experts — they're beautiful pieces of music, and often profoundly moving.

Since the Baroque period, most composers have written fugues only occasionally. Nonetheless, later figures such as Mozart, Beethoven, Felix Mendelssohn, Hector Berlioz, Robert Schumann, Johannes Brahms, and, in this century, Béla Bartók, Ernest Bloch, Paul Hindemith, Igor Stravinsky, and Dmitri Shostakovich all made important, and in some cases remarkable, contributions to the form.

Here are a few technical terms used to describe the elements of a fugue:

SUBJECT: The primary melody of a fugue; it's also called a theme. The subject is what's subject to imitation. Each voice "states" the subject in turn.

COUNTERSUBJECT: A secondary melody or theme that's heard in one voice while another voice states the subject. A countersubject is designed to complement the subject — to "fit" — without overshadowing it.

EXPOSITION: The opening section of a fugue, during which the subject is stated at least once in all the voices.

EPISODE: A transitional section, during which there are no statements of the subject. A fugue may have a number of episodes, or it may do without them.

And an etymological note: *fugue* comes from the Latin *fuga,* which means "flight." The term is a metaphor for the way the voices follow one another in imitation, with each voice "fleeing" the one that comes after it.

[See BAROQUE; CANON.]

G

GLOCKENSPIEL

[See PERCUSSION INSTRUMENTS.]

GREGORIAN CHANT

Gregorian chant — also called PLAINSONG or PLAINCHANT — is a generic term for the medieval melodies used in the services of the Roman Catholic Church. Almost three thousand of these melodies have been catalogued. Most of them were probably composed sometime between the years 600 and 900, and they're all based on the medieval system of scales called "modes," or "church modes" [see MODES]. Gregorian chant is named for Pope Gregory I (also known as Gregory the Great), who, according to medieval legend, was supposed to have invented it, or at least to have introduced it to the Church. Unfortunately for Gregory, who reigned from 590 to 604, modern scholars seem to think that his role has been greatly exaggerated.

The melodies of Gregorian chant consist of a single vocal line. The melodies may be sung by one person or by a whole choir in unison, but either way, only the single line of melody is heard — there is no harmony. There is also no regular beat or meter, and the music is not divided into measures or symmetrical phrases. There's nothing to "count" in Gregorian chant, in other words. There *is* rhythm, but the rhythm flows freely, following the syllables of the Latin prayer texts. Sometimes the notes change with each syllable of text, but sometimes a number of notes are made to turn around one syllable.

Gregorian chant was invented centuries before anything re-sembling modern musical notation. Chant melodies were origi-nally notated using a collection of symbols called "neumes," which were markings placed over the words of the prayers to remind singers of the shape of the melody — where it goes up, where it goes down, where it turns around on itself. It wasn't until the 1200s that Church musicians started using actual notes on a (four-line) staff to write down the melodies in a more precise way. For a discussion of neumes and notes, see NOTATION.

[See MASS.]

GUARNERIUS

[See STRADIVARIUS.]

GUITAR

The guitar has an extremely long, complicated, and elusive history. One common theory is that the instrument originated in Asia in ancient times, and that, like the lute, it was brought to the West by the Moors when they conquered Spain in the Middle Ages. In any case, since the Middle Ages there have been many different kinds of guitars and guitarlike instruments known in Europe, some bearing names related to the word *guitar* and some not. What we now call the "classical guitar," however — the kind of guitar used to play classical music — has been with us in its present standard size and shape only since the mid-1800s.

The modern classical guitar has a flat belly, or "table," a flat back, a long neck with a fingerboard glued to it, and six strings. The upper three strings are usually made of nylon, and the lower three of nylon tightly wound with fine metal wire. At least five different kinds of wood are necessary for the construction of the body, neck, and fingerboard. Guitars also have frets, which are strips of gut, bone, ivory, wood, or metal set crosswise into the fingerboard to form a series of parallel ridges. (The spaces between the frets are also called frets.) Frets help guitarists find the right notes, but that's only a secondary benefit, and not an indispensable one — after all, guitarists can't always look at the frets when they play from printed music, yet they still know where to put their fingers.

It's for the *sound* of the instrument that frets are essential, and indeed, without them the beautiful resonance of the guitar would be impossible. Without frets, the fingertips themselves would be "stopping" the strings on the fingerboard. (Stopping a string at different points along the fingerboard changes the length of string that's vibrating, which changes the pitch, or note.) But fingertips are soft, and they absorb vibrations. In the absence of frets they would dampen the sound considerably. When the fingertips push the strings against frets, however, the *frets* actually stop the strings, not the fingertips. Because the frets are made of a hard material, the absorption of vibrations is minimal, and the strings are free to sound much longer and louder. (By tradition and convention, guitarists pluck or strum the strings with the right hand and stop the strings with the left.)

Without frets it would also be next to impossible to play chords in tune on a guitar. Frets give the player a certain leeway, since a note will be right if the finger is placed anywhere within the right fret. It's a difficult concept to grasp without holding a guitar in your hands, but this leeway is absolutely necessary for playing chords because the neck of the guitar is just too wide, the strings are too many and too far apart, and fingers can only stretch so far and twist so much.

For most of its history the guitar was used primarily as an instrument to accompany folk songs and dances, and many composers were simply not familiar enough with the instrument to know how to write for it, or to be interested in writing for it. Apart, therefore, from a number of pieces by such nineteenth-century guitar virtuosos as Fernando Sor (1778–1839) and Mario Giuliani (1781–1829), the repertoire for classical guitar is not particularly extensive. It has expanded considerably in the twentieth century, however, in large measure due to the efforts of the great Spanish guitarist Andrés Segovia (1893–1987). Segovia made his contributions by looking toward both the future and the past: on the one hand, he inspired or commissioned many modern composers to write for the guitar, and on the other, he himself took many pieces originally written in the sixteenth, seventeenth, and eighteenth centuries for the lute and the vihuela (an early type of guitar) and arranged them for the guitar [see ARRANGEMENT]. He also brought the classical guitar a popularity it had never before enjoyed, paving the way for other classical guitarists to have successful careers. Fortunately, many of these other guitarists have continued the tradition of commissioning and arranging that Segovia started. Among the twentieth-century composers who have made significant contributions to the guitar repertoire are Manuel de Falla (1876–1946), Joaquín Turina (1882–1949), Heitor Villa-Lobos (1887–1959), Darius Milhaud (1892–1924), Mario Castelnuovo-Tedesco (1895–1968), Alexandre Tansman (b. 1897), Francis Poulenc (1899–1963), Joaquín Rodrigo (b. 1901), Benjamin Britten (1913–1976), Malcolm Arnold (b. 1921), and André Previn (b. 1929), whose Concerto for guitar and orchestra dates from 1971.

[See STRINGED INSTRUMENTS; LUTE.]

H

HALF STEP

An *interval* is the distance in pitch between two notes. In traditional Western music, the half step, also called the "semitone," is the smallest possible interval: two different notes can be no closer than a half step apart [see PITCH]. Finer gradations of pitch are possible in both theory and practice, but they are found primarily in non-Western music, and occasionally for special effect in Western music. (On stringed and wind instruments, you can "bend" notes, that is, raise or lower the pitch of the notes in increments smaller than half steps. On the piano, there is no way to play an interval smaller than a half step: any two adjacent notes on the keyboard are a half step apart.)

Two half steps equal a *whole step* (also called a "whole tone"), the second-smallest interval. Notes on the piano separated by one key, black or white, are a whole step apart. Twelve consecutive half steps equal an octave. *Any* larger interval may be divided into a series of half steps.

In musical notation, placing a sharp sign, ♯, before a note raises the note by a half step. A flat sign, ♭, lowers a note by a half step. The natural sign, ♮, cancels sharps and flats, and may also therefore serve to alter a note by a half step [see ACCIDENTAL, under NOTATION].

HARMONY ~ CHORD

A chord is three or more different notes sounding together. Harmony, in the broadest sense, is the sound of chords. A *specific* harmony is the sound of a specific type of chord. To play a C-major chord, for example, is to create the harmony of C major.

Harmony is also the overall practice, or science, of creating chords and chord *progressions* according to certain rules and principles. It's in this sense that one speaks of "fifteenth-century harmony," for example, or "late-nineteenth-century harmony," or "the system of tonal harmony." Systems of harmony have changed enormously from century to century, and sometimes from decade to decade, along with notions of what's possible, or acceptable, or beautiful. To describe a harmonic system, or a harmonic language, is to describe both what kinds of chords are commonly used in that system — how notes are combined — and the principles that underlie the system's chord progressions — how the harmonies relate to one another and to the other elements of musical composition.

⌒

Harmony is called, metaphorically, the "vertical" element in music, because on a printed page of music, notes that sound simultaneously are lined up vertically. Melody is the "horizontal" element: as a melody proceeds, the notes follow each other from left to right on the page.

Any given melody may be "harmonized" in different ways. A melody consists of single notes, but each of those notes may fit into a variety of different chords. To harmonize a melody, a composer decides which chord progression will work with the melody most effectively and then "builds" the desired chords by adding notes that will be heard together with the melody notes. These chords are called a "harmonic accompaniment" to the melody. The harmony isn't usually just plugged in after the melody is written, however. More often than not, melodies come to a composer's imagination with at least some of the harmonies already attached. And sometimes it happens entirely the other way around: the idea that first comes to a composer's head is a chord progression, and he or she creates a melody to fit the chords.

In fact, one of the greatest problems in using language to describe music is that we can say or write only one thing at a time, so that when we discuss such things as melody, harmony, and rhythm they sometimes seem like separate, and separable, elements. But they're not. They exist simultaneously. They're part of one another.

There is no melody without rhythm, for example, because the notes of a melody are all measured in time, and are therefore related to one another by duration as well as by pitch [see RHYTHM]. And even when we're just humming a simple melody to ourselves, we somehow "hear" or imagine the harmonies at the same time. (You're not sure? Try listening to a familiar melody with someone playing the "wrong" chords, or even *one* wrong chord, and you'll realize how well you know, and how completely you expect, the right ones.) What we think of as a beautiful melody, in other words, is most often inseparable from its harmony. Harmony, too, has its rhythm: the beauty of a chord progression depends not just on how the harmonies change, on which specific chords form the progression, but on *when* they change — on how long the harmonies last relative to one another and to the notes of the melody.

⌐

The instruments on which it's most practical to play chords are keyboard instruments like the piano and organ, where all ten fingers are available to play at the same time, and plucked instruments like the guitar and harp. Composers often write chords for bowed stringed instruments like the violin, viola, cello, and double bass, but in actual performance such chords are usually "broken" into two consecutive parts because the physical arrangement of the strings allows the player to sustain a maximum of only two notes at once. Percussion instruments like the xylophone and the glockenspiel can play chords when the player uses two mallets in each hand, but wind instruments can generally play only one note at a time.

[See ACCOMPANIMENT; ATONALITY~DISSONANCE; KEY~ TONALITY; KEYBOARD INSTRUMENTS; SCALE.]

Here's a little secret: harpists don't use their pinkies. Since the pinkie is the weakest finger, and since on the harp it provides no reach advantage (the ring finger stretches farther), it's just along for the ride. Harpists use only their thumbs and the first three fingers of each hand. They also use their feet. The modern harp has seven separate foot pedals, which are used not to sustain or soften the sound, as on the piano, but to change the length of the strings — which means to change the actual notes the strings produce. There's a pedal for each different note of the scale: C, D, E, F, G, A, and B. The C pedal controls all the C strings on the instrument (there are seven), the D pedal controls all the D strings, and so on. Each pedal has three possible positions — the pedals fit into slots in the wood of the harp's pedestal, or base — and each change in position results in a change in pitch of a half step for all the strings controlled by that pedal. For example, depending on the position of the C pedal, all the C strings may be tuned to C-flat, or to C (natural), or to C-sharp [see HALF STEP; OCTAVE; PITCH]. It all gets quite complicated, because harpists have to set the pedals differently depending on the particular notes in each passage, which means that they're constantly setting and resetting the pedals to prepare for what's coming. The way they know how to set the pedals in advance is by following "pedal diagrams" that they draw in their parts.

Other interesting harp facts:

⋄ The harp has a roughly triangular frame, consisting of a vertical post called the "pillar," a curved top part called the "neck," and a slanting wooden resonator called the "soundboard."
⋄ There are forty-seven strings on a full-sized harp (spanning a range of more than six octaves), although there are smaller harps, including student models, that have fewer. The strings are all strung vertically, from the neck down to the slanting soundboard, and their lengths run from about 2½ inches for the shortest (and highest-pitched) to over five feet for the

longest. For the player's convenience, the strings are color-coded: all the C strings are red, and the F strings are dark blue or black. (The other strings are a neutral color.) To tune all the strings before playing, the harpist turns the pins to which the strings are attached along the neck, using a tool called a "tuning key." By turning the pins, the harpist tightens or loosens each string, thereby raising or lowering its pitch. (The pitch of a string is affected by both its length and its tautness, as well as by its thickness. See STRINGED INSTRUMENTS.) Harpists today all use electronic devices that tell them when each string is perfectly in tune, which makes the tuning process a lot easier, faster, and more accurate than it used to be.

⋄ The vast majority of professional harpists throughout the world use harps made either by Lyon & Healy, of Chicago, or Salvi, originally of Italy, but now also of London. (The two companies are now owned by the same Swiss corporation.)

⋄ It's expensive to play the harp. A harp of the highest quality can cost from $15,000 to $60,000 or so, depending on the custom details, which may include gold leaf on the pillar, platinum or gold mechanical fittings, and painted decorations. And harps don't last long: without major repair or rebuilding, the average useful life of a fine harp is between ten and twenty-five years. They wear out from stress on the wood, warping, and cracking, which are caused by temperature and humidity changes and by the enormous pulling force of the tightened strings. They also get generally beaten up from being moved around. Meanwhile, strings break, fray, or weaken and must be replaced periodically, and a full set of strings costs in the neighborhood of $350 to $400. And don't forget the price of the station wagon! There's no such thing as a professional harpist without a station wagon, or a van.

⋄ The harp is not an easy or comfortable instrument to play. It may have an angelic image, but in the words of the great French harp virtuoso and teacher Carlos Salzedo (1885–1961), "You have to work like ze devil to play like ze angel." Harpists tend to develop strong hands and arms, and they must develop — and maintain through regular practicing — thick, hard calluses on their fingertips. Without the calluses, it hurts like crazy to play. It sometimes hurts even with the calluses, and in fact one of the common occupational hazards for harpists is the formation of blisters — and blood blisters — under the calluses.

◇ Harps are heavy (the average full-sized harp weighs between seventy and eighty-five pounds), and their weight, combined with their size and shape, makes them very awkward to carry. Whenever harpists have to carry their harps — when they have to get them in or out of their station wagons, for example — they run the risk of being asked, "Don't you wish you played the piccolo?" Harpists hear this question often. Harpists hear this question *very* often.

⤺

The solo repertoire for harp in classical music is quite limited, partly because before 1810, which is about when the pedal mechanism described above was invented, the capabilities of the harp itself were fairly limited (even though the instrument had been in existence in one form or another for about five thousand years). Handel wrote a harp concerto in 1736, and Mozart wrote a concerto for flute and harp in 1778, but other than those works, there's nothing particularly noteworthy in the repertoire for solo harp before Claude Debussy's *Sacred and Profane Dances* for harp and orchestra, written in 1904. In 1919, Camille Saint-Saëns wrote *Morceau de concert* (*Concert Piece*) for harp and orchestra, and in 1956 the Argentine composer Alberto Ginastera wrote a concerto for harp and orchestra. Contemporary composers have tried to expand the solo repertoire, but there are still very few pieces for harp and orchestra that are known to the general public. In chamber music, the best-known pieces with harp are the *Fantaisie* for harp and violin (1907) by Saint-Saëns, Debussy's Sonata for flute, harp, and viola (1916), and Maurice Ravel's *Introduction et allegro* for harp, string quartet, flute, and clarinet (1905–1906).

Since the 1830s, composers of orchestral music (including the orchestral music for opera) are the ones who have really explored the harp's potential and taken advantage of its possibilities. Hector Berlioz (1803–1869) started things off with prominent and colorful orchestral harp parts in the *Symphonie Fantastique* (1830) and *Harold in Italy* (1834), and virtually every important composer of orchestral music since has made extensive use of the harp.

HARPSICHORD

[See KEYBOARD INSTRUMENTS.]

HELDENTENOR

[See VOICE TYPES.]

HORN

[See BRASS INSTRUMENTS.]

I

IMPRESSIONISM

In art, *impressionism* is the name for the style of a group of nineteenth-century French artists who included, among others, Claude Monet, Auguste Renoir, Edgar Degas, Camille Pissarro, and Edouard Manet. The word comes from the title of one of Monet's paintings — *Impression: soleil levant* (*Impression: rising sun*). In music, impressionism is the name for the style of the French composer Claude Debussy (1862–1918).

Debussy was influenced by the aesthetic ideals of the impressionist painters, whose goals had less to do with strict accuracy of representation than with capturing the atmosphere, or essence, of a scene through subtle and fluid manipulation of light and color. In a similar way, much of Debussy's music has less to do with strict compositional structures and procedures (such as the exposition, development, and recapitulation of sonata form), or the clarity of traditional melodies and harmonies, than with mood, nuance, color, and fluid and unexpected shifts of harmony. His first major impressionist work was the symphonic poem *Prélude à l'après-midi d'un faune* (*Prelude to the Afternoon of a Faun*), which was followed by the opera *Pelléas et Mélisande* and by the well-known *La Mer* (*The Sea*), among many other works.

There was never an impressionist group, or school, in music as there was in painting. Nonetheless, Debussy was too brilliant and innovative a composer not to have influenced others. Among the important composers who absorbed, and reflected, elements of the impressionist style were Charles Martin Loeffler (1861–1935), Frederick Delius (1862–1934), Paul Dukas (1865–1935), Albert Roussel (1869–1937), Maurice Ravel (1875–1937), Manuel de

Falla (1876–1946), Ottorino Respighi (1879–1936), and the American Charles Tomlinson Griffes (1884–1920).

INCIDENTAL MUSIC

Incidental music is music meant to be heard at various points during the course of a play. It may include an overture, songs, music for dance scenes or scenes performed in pantomime, instrumental interludes between scenes or acts, background music for dialogue, and music for scenes that call for specific musical cues or performances.

Since the time of the ancient Greeks, playwrights have exploited the power of music for dramatic purposes. They've recognized that music can affect the pacing of a play, help establish atmosphere, add color and excitement, and touch people subliminally in ways that words often cannot. Sometimes playwrights collaborate closely with specific composers, as Molière did with Jean-Baptiste Lully (1632–1687), John Dryden with Henry Purcell (1659–1695), and Paul Claudel with Darius Milhaud (1892–1974). But sometimes, as in certain plays of Shakespeare (*Hamlet, Othello,* and *Twelfth Night,* among others), playwrights merely indicate in the text where there should be songs or musical scenes, and leave all the musical details to the performers and producers.

Famous examples of incidental music by major composers include Beethoven's music for the play *Egmont* (Goethe), Schubert's music for *Rosamunde* (von Chézy), Georges Bizet's music for *L'Arlésienne* (Daudet), and Edvard Grieg's music for *Peer Gynt* (Ibsen). Sometimes, when the music is particularly compelling, incidental music can be removed from its dramatic surroundings to stand on its own as concert music. There's no better example than Mendelssohn's incidental music to Shakespeare's *A Midsummer Night's Dream:* it would be a masterpiece in any setting. Often, in fact, composers try to ensure that their incidental music will have a life outside the theater by extracting the best portions and arranging them into suites [see SUITE].

A modern relative of incidental music is film music. Although film music started out as an essential sonic backdrop for silent films — and as a way to cover the noise of film projectors — its dramatic functions are in many ways the same as those of incidental music.

INNER VOICES

These are not the kind that Joan of Arc heard. And they're not even necessarily voices. In a musical composition with several simultaneously heard parts, or "lines," inner voices are neither the lowest line (the bass line) nor the highest line, which is often the melody. "Inner," in other words, refers to pitch range, that is, how high or low the notes are, and means "in the middle." In a string quartet, for example, the first violin part is usually the highest and the cello part the lowest, while the second violin and the viola parts are the inner voices. In choral music for soprano, alto, tenor, and bass, the alto and tenor parts are the inner voices. Music for solo piano has inner voices, too. Only one person is playing, but the music has a number of simultaneous voices or lines shared among the fingers.

The term *inner voices* reflects the reality of the printed page: music is printed with the highest part on top and the lowest part on the bottom. These are the "outer" voices, visually, and between them lie the inner voices. But inner voices is also a metaphor: it reflects the perception that mid-range parts are "inside" the texture of a piece of music. The highest and lowest parts are more easily heard and their roles are more obvious.

Inner does not mean obscure or unimportant, however. It may not always be easy to pick out the inner voices in a composition, but their role is essential. They often serve to fill out or enrich the harmonies of a piece, to provide rhythmic propulsion, and to add interesting melodic material to other, more prominent melodies. They tend to play an important *accompanying* role, in other words, although at times they rise from the middle and play (or sing) the principal melodies, too. One of the marks of a good composer, in fact, is how interesting and expressive he or she can make the inner voice lines.

[See ACCOMPANIMENT.]

INTERMEZZO

Intermezzo is an Italian word for "interlude," from the Latin *intermedius,* "in the middle." As a musical term, *intermezzo* (Italian plural: *intermezzi*) didn't appear until the eighteenth century, when Italian musicians began to use it to describe the comic musical scenes typically performed between the acts of serious operas [see OPERA SERIA, under OPERA].

Because most eighteenth-century serious operas were in three acts, they generally included two intermezzos, with the second intermezzo usually just a continuation of the first. The result was that in one evening audiences would see the equivalent of two overlapping operas, one tragic and one comic. Eventually intermezzos became so popular and successful that they were extracted from their serious surroundings, expanded, and performed separately. In the expansion process they merged stylistically with other comic forms that had been developing independently, and they evolved into — or were subsumed into — the form known generically as *opera buffa,* or Italian comic opera [see OPERA BUFFA, under OPERA].

⤙

Nineteenth-century composers borrowed *intermezzo* as a name for certain short pieces for solo piano [see CHARACTER PIECE]. The term was meant to convey the idea of a work of charm and feeling but of no great consequence, perhaps something tossed off between — "in the middle of" — more important endeavors. It's always interesting, though, how composers of genius manage to turn little pieces of no great consequence into works of depth and beauty. The *Intermezzos* of Johannes Brahms, Op. 117 and 118, are a case in point.

K

[See OPUS NUMBER.]

KEY ~ TONALITY

The concept of key, of a piece of music being "in" a key, has been one of the fundamental organizing principles of Western music since the seventeenth century. It is a *harmonic* organizing principle. When a piece is in the key of C major, for example, or "in C major," it means that the harmony of C major serves as the music's home base, its harmonic center of gravity. Harmonies are defined by several notes sounding together, by chords [see HARMONY~CHORD]. For a piece in C major, the "home" harmony is defined by a C-major chord, which is in turn based on — or built from — the notes of a C-major scale. Every key is based in this way on a scale — major keys on major scales, minor keys on minor scales. And since there are twelve different major scales (that is, major scales starting on twelve different notes) and twelve different minor scales, there are twelve possible major keys and twelve possible minor keys.

But back to C major. A piece in C major will establish the C-major harmony at the start and return to C major by the end. In between, however, it may include a wide variety of other chords and harmonies, both major and minor. A piece that is in one particular key overall may also spend time in other keys, temporarily shifting harmonic centers in a compositional process called "modulation." And while the first and last movements of a multimove-

ment piece such as a symphony, sonata, or concerto will be in the
home key, the middle movements are usually written in a completely different key.

Another word that is often used for *key* is *tonality*, as in, "the
tonality of G minor." *Tonality* also refers to the overall system of
writing music in keys, as in, "the principles of tonality." Music
that is written in a key is called "tonal music," and in any piece,
the harmony of the home key is called the "tonic" [see TONIC].

In the world of tonality, or tonal harmony, harmonies don't
follow each other randomly. They are ordered in progressions, in
which harmonies that contain *dissonances* — jarring or unsettling
sounds — always eventually lead, or "resolve," to harmonies that
are made up of *consonances* — pleasing, comfortable sounds. In
tonal harmony, it is dissonance that creates tension and consonance that provides resolution — or repose, or solidity, or affirma-
tion of some kind.

And nothing is more solid or affirmative than the tonic, the
harmony of the home key. The crucial idea of tonality remains the
idea of gravity toward the tonic: when a piece is written in a key,
no matter how far afield the harmonies may wander, ultimately
they give a sense of gravitating back, of wanting to come home.
As we listen, much of this process of harmonic leading and gravi-
tation operates on an unconscious level: we're not necessarily
aware that we're being drawn along, either away from the tonic
key at first or back to it later. But the effects are there all the same,
and the genius of tonal music is that by virtue of these effects —
effects created by the manipulation of consonance and dissonance — harmonic progressions can create a narrative, or an entire dramatic structure complete with direction, conflict, tension,
uncertainty, and satisfying resolution.

⸛

Why do composers choose certain keys for their pieces? This
question has a variety of answers. To a certain extent, composers
choose keys the way abstract painters choose colors. Why blue for
a particular pattern, or red, or yellow? It just seems right. Sometimes music simply "comes to" a composer in a particular key, and

he or she can't imagine it in any other. A strange concept? Perhaps, but many composers have absolute pitch (or "perfect" pitch), and for them all pitches, and therefore all keys, have distinct, individual identities [see ABSOLUTE PITCH]. Indeed, some composers associate certain moods, characters, or colors — actual colors or emotional ones — with certain keys. These associations are not necessarily consistent, however, and they vary greatly from composer to composer. Even the major-minor difference is not absolute: minor keys are generally heard as "darker" than major keys, and more appropriate for expressions of sadness or seriousness, but music in major keys is by no means always "happy" or light. Aesthetic choices are often combined with technical considerations in a composer's key selection: some instruments sound better in certain keys, and fingering patterns on some instruments may be awkward or comfortable depending on the key of the composition. The key affects the range in which an instrument must play, and instruments sound different in different parts of their range, even if not necessarily better or worse. For singers, the key of a piece may determine whether they will be singing in comfort or straining at the edges of their vocal range.

Does it make a difference, then, if a piece written in D major is played in E major? Yes. Even if we don't know that we're listening to it in a different key, and even if we can't quite identify the difference, the piece will *sound* different. In some cases this isn't so bad — some pieces sound just fine "transposed," that is, shifted to another key. Most of the time, however, and especially with very familiar works, we'll have a sense that something is wrong — or at least not quite right. Would the paintings from Picasso's "blue period" look good in green?

⌒

When a piece is described as being "in C," or "in D," for instance, without mention of major or minor, it's the major key that's indicated. "Minuet in G," for example, means "Minuet in G Major." The lowercase letter is often used to indicate minor: "Symphony in f" means "Symphony in F Minor." Music written in a key includes on each printed line of music an indication called a "key signature," which specifies the key for the performer [see NOTATION].

It's worth noting that key is by no means a concept confined to classical music. We don't usually hear radio announcers saying things like, "And now Elvis Presley singing 'You Ain't Nothin' but a Hound Dog,' in C major," but the song *is* in the key of C major, and just about every pop, rock, country, bluegrass, or jazz tune in existence is written in a key.

[See ATONALITY~DISSONANCE; DOMINANT; SCALE.]

KEYBOARD INSTRUMENTS

Keyboard instruments can be used to play a number of notes at the same time, which means that they can produce melodies and harmonies simultaneously [see HARMONY~CHORD]. In fact, since playing any one note on a keyboard instrument requires just one finger, and since the player has ten fingers at his or her disposal at all times (on the organ there is also a keyboard for the feet), the possibilities for melodic and harmonic combinations and complexities on a keyboard instrument are virtually limitless. This is why keyboard instruments have long been favored by composers both as instruments of musical expression and as tools for composition, and it's also why keyboard training has played such a fundamental role in the training of so many composers.

In Western musical history, the most important keyboard instruments are the organ, the clavichord, the harpsichord, and the piano. The organ is by far the oldest keyboard instrument, with origins dating back to the Greeks of the third century B.C. [see ORGAN]. In all likelihood, no other keyboard instruments besides the organ even existed before the 1300s, and until about 1500 almost all keyboard music was written for organ. The organ is a combination keyboard and wind instrument: its sound is produced by columns of air vibrating in pipes. Depressing the keys of an organ initiates a process that leads to pipes opening and air rushing into them. The clavichord, harpsichord, and piano, on the other hand, are combination keyboard and stringed instruments: their sound is produced by vibrating strings. Depressing the keys on a stringed keyboard instrument initiates a chain of mechanical actions that causes something to strike or pluck an array of strings, setting them vibrating.

⌣

CLAVICHORD: The clavichord dates from the fifteenth century, and was in common use — primarily as an instrument for home practice and enjoyment, rather than for public performance — from the sixteenth through the eighteenth centuries. The mechanical action of a clavichord is relatively simple: to depress a key is to depress one end of a lever; the other end rises, and a metal blade called a "tangent" strikes a string. The strings run over a wooden bridge, which communicates their vibrations to a soundboard, a piece of wood that amplifies the vibrations. Clavichords are rectangular in shape — they're essentially wooden boxes on legs — with the keyboard set in one of the long sides of the rectangle, and the strings running the long way in the box, from left to right in front of the player. The clavichord, however, has one big problem: it's hard to hear. The instrument is quite sensitive to touch, and fine gradations of volume can be achieved by varying the force with which the keys are struck. But even though the relative variations in volume are significant, the total amount of sound is severely limited. It's not an instrument suited for playing in large rooms, or for playing with other instruments. Then again, what seems like a problem to some can seem like an advantage to others: the sensitivity and intimate character of the clavichord made it a favored instrument among the exponents of the *Empfindsamer Stil* (sentimental style), a style of musical composition and expression popular in northern Germany during the middle of the eighteenth century. The greatest exponent of that style, and most famous champion of the clavichord, was the composer and performer (and son of J. S. Bach) Carl Philipp Emanuel Bach (1714–1788).

⌣

HARPSICHORD: With the organ, the harpsichord was one of the two principal keyboard instruments of the Baroque period (ca. 1600–1750), although like the clavichord it dates from the fifteenth century, and possibly earlier. The harpsichord was included in almost all Baroque instrumental ensembles, large or small, usually to play the continuo part, that is, to play the bass line and fill in the harmonies [see CONTINUO]. As a continuo instrument, it was also a principal member of the instrumental contingent for the new form known as opera, and for other vocal forms such as the cantata and the oratorio. When large forces were present — instrumental and/or vocal — the harpsichord player often doubled as conductor, leading the performance by waving either his hand or a rolled-up sheet of music. The harpsichord was also featured as a solo instrument, occasionally in concertos, but more often in pieces for harpsichord alone, such as dance suites, preludes and fugues, and toccatas [see CONCERTO; FUGUE; PRELUDE; SUITE; TOCCATA].

Like the keys of a clavichord, harpsichord keys are levers, and the strings of a harpsichord also sit on a wooden bridge that transmits their vibrations to a soundboard. Instead of a blade on the far end of each lever to strike the string, however, the harpsichord has a vertical wooden piece called a "jack," and attached to the jack is a piece of quill called a "plectrum." When a key is depressed, the jack rises, and the plectrum *plucks* the string on the way up. That's the fundamental difference between the clavichord and the harpsichord: the strings of the clavichord are struck, while those of the harpsichord are plucked. Another important difference is the configuration of the instrument: harpsichord strings stretch straight out away from the player, not from left to right across the player's field of view. This gives rise to an elongated instrumental shape that is similar to the wing shape of a modern grand piano, although squared off at the corners and much narrower. Sitting down to play the clavichord looks like sitting down alongside a long wooden box; sitting down at the harpsichord looks very much like sitting down at a delicate version of a grand piano.

The harpsichord is a much louder instrument than the clavichord, and it has been admired for the clarity of its sound. It too, however, is an instrument with a problem: on a harpsichord, varying the touch on the keys has no effect on the volume or tone quality. The way to vary the sound when plucking a string — any string — is to vary the way it's plucked. To get more volume, for example, you would pull the string back farther before letting go, making it vibrate more widely, while to get a gentler or a softer sound you would pull the string back less — and touch it more gently. But you can't do these things with the keys of a harpsichord: the mechanism provides no way to vary either the distance that a plectrum pulls a string as it plucks or the touch of a plectrum on a string. Whether you bang on the keys or depress them softly, the strings get plucked in exactly the same way, with exactly the same force, and the sound of the notes is the same. The way many Baroque harpsichord makers dealt with this problem was to construct instruments with two keyboards, called "manuals," and two or three complete sets of strings, called "choirs." On instruments of this type, each choir has its own set of jacks and plectra, designed and placed to produce different sounds. (One set of quills might be harder or softer than another, for example, and the jacks might be placed nearer the ends or the midpoints of the strings.) One of the choirs is played with one manual and the other choir or choirs with the other, with mechanical means (foot pedals and/or hand pulls) used to engage the choirs separately or in combination. Depending on which choir or choirs are engaged, the sound of the instrument is different. A simple example: two choirs engaged simultaneously would produce a louder sound than one choir alone because each note would consist of the sound of two strings being plucked, rather than just one.

The different choirs and manuals can give the harpsichord several different overall sounds. Still, there's no way to vary the sound from one note to the next, no way to get gradually louder or softer or to produce subtle variations of tone quality or volume within a musical passage. This is not to say that for a harpsichordist individual musicianship is irrelevant — far from it. But without the means to manipulate tone, the player must concentrate on manipulating time. Factors such as tempo, spacing, and pacing take on critical importance, and remain a matter of individual taste and skill.

᷍

PIANO: *Piano* is the shortened form — and today much more common form — of the word *pianoforte,* which is itself an abbreviation of *gravicembalo col piano e forte,* the name given to the instrument invented by Bartolomeo Cristofori in Florence, Italy, sometime around 1700. In Italian, *piano* means soft and *forte* (pronounced "fortay") means loud. *Gravicembalo col piano e forte* means "harpsichord with (the) soft and loud." The great achievement of Cristofori's new instrument was that it could do what the harpsichord could not: it could produce changes in volume in response to changes in the player's touch on the keys.

The strings of a piano are struck with hammers. Cristofori's hammers were made of rolled parchment, but today's hammers are made of hard felt. The keys and hammers are part of an extremely complex system of rods, levers, dampers, and other mechanically related parts called the "action" of the piano. Depressing the keys on a piano starts a chain of leveraged events that results in felt-covered dampers being lifted from the strings, allowing the strings to vibrate when struck, and hammers (at the end of long, narrow wooden hammer rods) striking the strings from below and then falling away from the strings by means of an escapement mechanism. Because of the escapement, the hammers don't interfere with the vibration of the strings after they strike them. The "double escapement" mechanism of modern pianos permits rapid repetition of notes by allowing the hammers to fall away first to an intermediate position, where they can still be engaged by the motion of the keys. The hammers are not actually connected to the ends of the keys, but are kicked into motion and thrown at the strings by the system of interconnected levers. When the keys are released, the dampers drop back onto the strings, stopping their vibrations, and the hammers fall back to their original positions.

Pianos are built with one hammer per note. There's not always just one *string* per note, however. In the upper register (the notes that are highest in pitch), there are three strings per note, all tuned exactly the same and struck simultaneously by one hammer, and in the middle register there are two strings per note. It's only in the low register that there is one (thick) string per note. As on the clavichord and harpsichord, the strings rest on a bridge that transmits their vibrations to a wooden soundboard.

Modern pianos also have two or three pedals. The pedal on the right goes by any of three names: "loud pedal," "damper pedal," or "sustaining pedal." When the loud pedal is depressed, all the dampers are raised at once, and all the strings are free to vibrate. Any notes already sounding when the pedal is depressed are "sustained" (which means they keep sounding even after the keys are released), and any and all notes played *while* the pedal is down are sustained. The middle pedal, not found on all pianos, is called the "sostenuto pedal" — which can be confusing, since *sostenuto* is Italian for "sustained." The sostenuto pedal doesn't raise the dampers, however; it keeps only those dampers raised that are *already* raised. The only notes it sustains, in other words, are notes that are already sounding when the pedal is depressed. The pedal on the left is called either the "soft pedal" or the "una corda ('one string') pedal." Depressing the soft pedal shifts the entire keyboard and the hammers to the right, just far enough for each hammer to strike one less string per note than it ordinarily would. With fewer vibrating strings, the sound is softer. (The single strings in the low register are thick enough that the hammers still strike them, although slightly off-center.)

Although Cristofori invented the piano at the beginning of the eighteenth century, it took quite a while for the instrument to catch on. The main problem was that Cristofori was ahead of his time: his mechanism was very complex and sophisticated, and not easily copied or reproduced by craftsmen elsewhere. Most early pianos in other countries, in fact, were considerably more primitive — it took the better part of a century for the general level of mechanical sophistication to catch up to where Cristofori had

started. Nonetheless, by around 1775 the piano had become the
dominant instrument of keyboard composition. The later keyboard works of Haydn and virtually all the keyboard works of
Mozart (with the exception of his works for organ) were written
for the piano, not the harpsichord, and indeed, Haydn and
Mozart were the first great composers to write for the piano. (In
his operas, however, Mozart continued the Baroque tradition of
using harpsichord to accompany recitatives. See RECITATIVE.) In
short order, the piano became by far the most important and popular instrument for musical composition. Throughout the nineteenth century, composers produced music for the piano in
astonishing quantities, and today the piano repertoire is enormous, far larger than that of any other instrument. The piano also
became the most popular instrument for musical enjoyment in
the home. For most of the nineteenth century and early twentieth
century, in fact, the only way many people were able to become
familiar with symphonies, operas, and chamber music works was
to play them at home in arrangements for piano. To this day, the
piano has maintained its position as the most popular instrument,
although its role as a musical home entertainment system diminished considerably with the invention of the phonograph and the
radio, and has diminished still further in the age of stereo, televi-
sion, and home video.

The piano of Mozart's time was a lighter, less powerful instrument than the piano of today, and it had a narrower range of
notes — generally sixty-one notes as compared to eighty-eight
notes on a modern piano. In the early 1800s, various inventions
and technological advances in piano making, spurred in part by
the demands of composers and pianists, led to the manufacture of
instruments of greater power, brilliance, and range. By the 1850s,
the piano had acquired the form and the general sound characteristics that are familiar to us today. Despite modern technology
and the achievements of mass production, however, it's a curious
fact that every individual piano has a slightly different feel, or
touch, at the keyboard, and a somewhat different sound. (It's not
just that pianos from the Steinway factory are different from pi-

anos made by the Baldwin company, for example. No two Steinway pianos are exactly the same either.) This presents quite a challenge for concert pianists, who must constantly adjust to different pianos, trying to feel comfortable and to get "their" sound on unfamiliar instruments.

GRAND PIANO: *Grand* describes the shape and configuration of a piano. A grand piano is a piano whose heavy wooden case is wing-shaped — one long side (the left side, from the player's point of view) is straight and the other curved inward, with the keyboard at one end and the narrow, curved "tail" at the other. The case is usually supported by three sturdy legs, two at the corners under the keyboard and one at the tail. Inside the case is a cast-iron frame, called the "plate," to which the strings are attached under tremendous tension. The strings, soundboard, and plate are all parallel to the floor, with the strings extending straight out behind the keyboard, away from the player. The longer strings — lower in pitch — are on the player's left-hand side, and the higher, shorter strings are to the right.

Some grand pianos are grander than others. The standard concert grand piano used in concert halls is approximately nine feet long and weighs about a thousand pounds. There are also smaller grands, which use shorter strings and produce less sound. Seven-foot grands are sometimes used for concerts in rooms where a nine-foot piano would be overpowering. The smallest grands, designed for living rooms and known as "baby grands," are only about five feet long.

UPRIGHT PIANO: An upright piano is designed to take up less floor space than a grand piano. The keyboard itself — in size and in number of notes — is exactly the same as that of a grand piano, but the wooden case of the instrument is a shallow rectangular box that stands upright behind the keyboard, with the strings, soundboard, and plate all perpendicular to the floor. Well-made upright pianos can have a very nice sound, but they're limited in power, depth, and brilliance, and they're generally much more suited for practice purposes and home enjoyment than for concerts.

⌒

CEMBALO, CLAVICEMBALO, GRAVICEMBALO: Italian words for *harpsichord*.

⌒

CLAVECIN: The French word for *harpsichord*.

⌒

CLAVIER (pronounced "claveer"): The German word for *keyboard*. As used during the Baroque period, it is a generic term for any keyboard instrument, and may refer to the clavichord, harpsichord, or organ. There's no way to tell from the title, for example, the specific instrument or instruments for which J. S. Bach's *The Well-Tempered Clavier* (*Das Wohltemperierte Clavier*) may have been intended. When the same word is spelled with a "k" (*klavier*), as it is in modern German, it usually refers to the piano. *Hammerklavier* (hammer keyboard) is another, older German word for *piano*.

⌒

FORTEPIANO: In eighteenth-century English, *fortepiano* was another word for *piano*. The term is now generally used to refer to pianos of the eighteenth and nineteenth centuries.

⌒

VIRGINAL (also known by the plural, **VIRGINALS**): A type of small harpsichord, usually with just one keyboard. The virginal has a configuration similar to that of a clavichord, however. The keyboard is set in the long side of a box, and the strings run the long way in the box, from left to right in front of the player.

L

LEGATO

Legato is Italian for "tied." To play a series of notes legato means to play smoothly, without articulating or accenting the beginning of each note or making perceptible breaks between notes. Like many Italian musical terms, *legato* may be used as an adjective, adverb, or noun: notes may be legato, or played legato, or played with a lovely legato. The opposite of legato is *staccato*, which means "separated," or "detached" [see STACCATO].

For singers and wind players, singing or playing a musical phrase legato usually requires taking the phrase in one breath. On stringed instruments, legato entails playing a series of notes either in one smooth bow stroke or with very smooth changes from one stroke to the next. Pianists play legato by carefully modulating their touch; interestingly enough, how they release the keys is as important as how they strike them. (The piano's sustaining pedal can also contribute, but legato starts with the hands, not the foot.) A beautiful, effortless legato is one of the marks of every fine instrumentalist or singer.

Composers indicate legato in the music by using *slurs,* curved lines that stretch above or below two or more consecutive notes, or by simply writing *legato,* or *molto legato* (very legato).

LEITMOTIF

A *motif,* or *motive,* is a short musical figure that recurs throughout a piece. It's not a complete melody, but more of a melodic fragment, one that often has a conspicuous rhythmic aspect. The famous opening four notes of Beethoven's Fifth Symphony, for example, are a motif.

Leitmotif, from the German *Leitmotiv,* means "leading motive." A leitmotif is a motif that is meant to symbolize a specific character, thing, place, or idea. The term is most closely associated with Richard Wagner (1813–1883), who, especially in his later operas, made extensive use of leitmotifs. (Wagner himself never used the term, however. It was coined by someone else to describe Wagner's compositional technique.) In the four operas that make up Wagner's *Ring* cycle,* for example, there are a number of leitmotifs: one for the Ring, one for Fate, one for the character Siegfried, one for Valhalla (the hall of the gods), one for the "magic fire," one for a certain very important sword, and so forth. The leitmotifs don't just function as announcements or musical name tags, however. By subtly or not so subtly altering the leitmotifs as they return at different points in the operas, Wagner is able to emphasize changes in the dramatic situation or in the mental state of his characters. The use of leitmotifs is thus not merely an interesting little sidelight in Wagner's work, but a crucial mechanism for unifying the music and the drama.

The leitmotif technique was later exploited by other opera composers, most notably Richard Strauss (1864–1949). An important precursor of the leitmotif was the *idée fixe,* or "fixed idea," of Hector Berlioz (1803–1869). Berlioz first coined the term to describe the principal melody in his *Symphonie Fantastique,* a programmatic work that tells the story of a young man's desperate love and drug-induced delirium [see PROGRAM MUSIC]. The melody, representing the "Beloved One," returns again and again throughout the piece, but it's transformed in various ways to reflect the young man's different hallucinations. Bad dream, great music.

---

* In German, Wagner's cycle is called *Der Ring des Nibelungen* (*The Ring of the Nibelung*). The four operas are *Das Rheingold* (*The Rhine Gold*), *Die Walküre* (*The Valkyrie*), *Siegfried,* and *Götterdämmerung* (*Twilight of the Gods*).

The libretto is the text of an opera or oratorio. (The Italian word *libretto* means "booklet." It originally referred to a small printed book that contained the words of an opera and that was distributed or sold at performances.)

Some opera librettos are original works, but most are adaptations of plays, books, stories, or legends. Typically, when a composer decides that he wants to create an opera based on a certain subject or story, he asks a writer to draft a libretto. The librettist must take many factors into account, including the projected length of the piece, how it will be divided into scenes or acts, the number of characters, and the need for various solo arias and ensemble numbers. He must also carefully weigh the musical potential of the written words. Will their sound and rhythm make them suitable for singing? Do they suit the composer's style? After consultation and collaboration with the librettist, the composer goes about setting the words to music. The collaboration is not necessarily over when the composing begins, however, because often a composer will decide that for musical or dramatic reasons a scene or section must be added or an existing scene altered.

There have been a number of librettists who have played significant roles in the history of opera, and who have achieved great fame in the process. Pietro Metastasio (1698–1782), for example, single-handedly established many of the literary and dramatic conventions of eighteenth-century Italian tragic opera (*opera seria*). He wrote librettos for twenty-seven full-length operas, and his twenty-seven librettos were set to music more than eight hundred (!) times. Other important librettists include Ranieri de Calzabigi (1714–1795), who wrote several librettos for Christoph Willibald Gluck, and who, with Gluck, contributed to major reforms in the style of eighteenth-century opera; Lorenzo da Ponte (1749– 1838), who wrote the librettos for three of Mozart's greatest operas, *The Marriage of Figaro, Così fan tutte,* and *Don Giovanni;* Eugène Scribe (1791–1861), who wrote librettos for most of the great figures of nineteenth-century French grand opera; Hugo von Hofmannsthal (1874–1929), who collaborated with Richard Strauss on six major operas, including *Elektra* and *Der Rosen-kavalier;* Arrigo Boito (1842–1918), himself an opera composer, who wrote the librettos for Verdi's *Otello* and *Falstaff;* and W. S. Gilbert (1836–1911), who wrote the words for the music of Sir Arthur Sullivan.

Some composers write their own librettos. The greatest of the composer-librettists was certainly Richard Wagner (1813–1883), who wrote all his own texts, applying his theories of total unification of music, poetry, and drama in what he called "music dramas" rather than "operas." Hector Berlioz (1803–1869), a brilliant writer as well as composer, wrote the librettos for his operas *Beatrice and Benedict* and *The Trojans,* and in our own time the prolific Gian Carlo Menotti (b. 1911) has also served as his own librettist.

[See OPERA.]

LUTE

The lute is a plucked stringed instrument that's held and played very much like the guitar. It had its heyday in the sixteenth and seventeenth centuries, when it was extremely important all over Europe both as an instrument for serious composition, or "art music," and as an instrument for accompanying popular songs and dances. In certain circles, it was also *the* fashionable instrument for musical entertainment in the home. In recent years, specialists in early music have revived public interest in the lute, and many pieces originally written for the lute have found new life in versions for the guitar.

There are several important differences between the lute and the guitar:

⬦ The body of the guitar curves inward at the sides, giving it a kind of waist, while the lute has no waist. The outline of the lute's body is like the outline of an egg.

✧ Both the guitar and the lute have a flat belly, but the guitar also has a flat back, while the lute's back is curved outward. To come back to the egg: the shape of the lute's body is like the shape of an egg cut in half lengthwise.

✧ The guitar has six strings, while the lute usually has eleven — five double strings and one single string. (A *double string* is a pair of strings tuned to the same note and strung right next to each other so that they can be played together as if they were one string.) The strings of the lute are not tuned to the same notes as those of the guitar.

✧ Both instruments use pegs to tune the strings, but the pegbox of the guitar extends straight from the end of the neck, while the pegbox of the lute bends back from the neck at about a ninety-degree angle.

✧ The neck of the lute is shorter and wider than the neck of the guitar, and there are fewer frets. Frets on the lute, as on the guitar, were originally just strings of gut tied around the neck.

Scholars believe that the first lutes appeared in the Middle East about four thousand years ago. There have also been lutes of various kinds in Asia since ancient times. The standard lute of Western music, however, is a direct descendant of an Arabic instrument called the "'ud," brought to Spain in the Middle Ages by the Moors. *Al 'ud* (the 'ud) in Arabic became *laúd* in Spanish, which became *lute* in English.

A person who plays the lute is called a "lutenist."

[See GUITAR.]

LYRICAL ~ LYRICISM

Lyrical means "songlike." The word comes from "lyre," or *lyra*, the name of the harplike instrument that the ancient Greeks played to accompany the singing of their poetry. Any piece or passage of music that is based on a beautiful melodic line may be called lyrical. In keeping with its origins, *lyrical* also implies "expressive." To say, therefore, that a composer has a gift for lyricism is to say that he or she is able to write beautiful, expressive melodies.

A gentle reminder, however: not all melodies are "songlike," and music can be expressive without being lyrical. It can be violent and powerful, for example, or angular, compact, dramatic, choppy, mysterious, intense, colorful, playful, halting, atmospheric, funny, or funereal. The opening of Beethoven's Fifth Symphony is not the least bit lyrical, but it's certainly expressive.

On the other hand, there is something about lyricism — about the deep-rooted connection with song — that is basic to whatever it is that we need and seek in music. That same Fifth Symphony has many wonderfully lyrical passages, and indeed without them would seem merely brutal. Variety and contrast keep things interesting, but in the complete absence of lyricism music can never be completely satisfying.

[See MELODY.]

M

MADRIGAL

Madrigal is an interesting word. Some scholars theorize that it derives from the Latin *matricalis,* meaning "mother," as in "mother tongue," or "mother church." Others think it might be related to *mandrialis,* another Latin term, meaning, roughly, "My, what a lovely shepherdess you are. Mind if I help you tend your flock for a few weeks?" A slight exaggeration, but *mandrialis* does mean "pastoral," and whatever the etymological Truth, madrigals are secular Italian vocal pieces — poetry set to music — that often have to do with love or pastoral settings or both.

The first madrigals date from the fourteenth century, but when people use the term today, they're usually referring to Italian madrigals of the sixteenth century, also known as Renaissance madrigals. (The medieval madrigal and the Renaissance madrigal both consist of secular poetry set to music, but in musical style they're unrelated.) The Renaissance madrigal went through an extensive stylistic evolution from the early sixteenth century to the late, an evolution that mirrored developments in other areas of composition, such as the motet and the Mass [SEE MASS; MOTET]. Early Renaissance madrigals are generally for three or four voices, and for the most part the voices all move together, that is, they change notes at the same time, in the same rhythm. Technically, this style represents a kind of *polyphony* — music for several simultaneous parts — but because of the rhythmic homogeneity it's a polyphony of somewhat limited possibilities. The polyphony of the madrigals of the second half of the sixteenth century is much freer and more sophisticated. These later madrigals, often called "classic madrigals," are for four to six voices (although most often five), and the voices are woven together in a complex fabric of sound, with contrasting rhythms between and among them, and imitated melodies passed from voice to voice [see COUNTERPOINT~POLYPHONY]. (Classic madrigals often include rhythmically homogeneous sections, too, for contrast.) Toward the end of the century, madrigal composers experimented with yet another style, known today as *monody* [see MONODY]. The monodic style, which at the time was called simply "the new music," features a solo voice singing the melody, with instrumental accompaniment.

The Renaissance madrigal, in other words, was a kind of laboratory, with composers trying out the latest techniques and inventing new techniques, all in an effort to give musical expression to the heightened emotions of poetry. Important composers of the classic madrigal were such men as Giovanni Pierluigi da Palestrina (ca. 1525–1594), who expanded the form to include *madrigali spirituali*, madrigals of a spiritual or devotional nature, Andrea Gabrieli (1515–1586), Cipriano de Rore (1516–1565), Philippe de Monte (1521–1603), and Orlando di Lasso (1532–1594). Two of the most important madrigal composers of the "late" period were Carlo Gesualdo (1560–1613) and Claudio Monteverdi (1567–1643). Though Italy remained the most fertile soil for the madrigal, it caught on in sixteenth-century England, as well, where composers such as William Byrd (1543–1623) and Thomas Morley (1557–1602) developed their own versions using English texts.

The Italian madrigal was an extraordinarily popular form. Thousands of madrigals were printed in collections during the sixteenth century, and people often got together in social groups and meetings to sing them for their own entertainment. To this day, in fact, many devoted amateur singers still form madrigal groups in order to enjoy firsthand these wonderful gifts from four centuries ago.

[See RENAISSANCE.]

In Italy, the title *maestro,* meaning "master," is commonly used to address teachers, as well as composers, instrumentalists, singers, and conductors. In English-speaking countries, the term has taken on a somewhat lofty flavor and is used almost exclusively to address or refer to conductors.

[See CONDUCTOR.]

MAJOR ∼ MINOR

[See KEY∼TONALITY; SCALE.]

MASS

The Mass is the most important religious service of the Roman Catholic Church, and musical settings of the Mass have played a central role in the history of Western music. Before the changes instituted by the Second Vatican Council (Vatican II) in the 1960s, the Mass was always sung or spoken in Latin. The Latin word for *Mass* is *missa,* from the phrase *Ite, missa est (congregatio)* — "Go, the congregation is dismissed" — a formula traditionally intoned at the end of the service. Before Vatican II, a Mass that was sung was called High Mass, or *missa solemnis,* while a spoken mass was called Low Mass. The distinction between High Mass and Low Mass is no longer observed, but when people use the term *Mass* in the context of music history, they're referring to High Mass.

They're also usually referring to the "Ordinary" of the Mass. The Mass (High *or* Low) consists of two sets of texts, or prayers. One set is called the "Proper" of the Mass and the other is called the "Ordinary." The prayers used for the Proper aren't always the same ones — they vary depending on the day of the week or the specific religious occasion. The prayers of the Ordinary, however,

are what you might call the "regular lineup" — they never change.
Since the 1300s, musical settings of the Mass have almost always
been settings of the Ordinary of the Mass. The prayers of the Ordinary are known by their opening words:

Kyrie	*Kyrie eleison* . . . "Lord have mercy . . ."
	(This is the only prayer of the Mass in Greek rather than Latin.)
Gloria	*Gloria in excelsis Deo* . . . "Glory to God in the highest . . ."
Credo	*Credo in unum Deum* . . . "I believe in one God . . ."
Sanctus	*Sanctus, sanctus, sanctus* . . . "Holy, holy, holy . . ."
Benedictus	*Benedictus, qui venit in nomine Domini* . . . "Blessed is he who comes in the name of the Lord . . ."
Agnus Dei	*Agnus Dei* . . . "Lamb of God . . ."

In the Middle Ages, the Mass was sung to the melodies
known as Gregorian chant. Chant melodies consist of a single
vocal line. A number of people may sing a chant at the same time,
but since they all sing the same line (that is, the same notes), there
is no harmony [see GREGORIAN CHANT; HARMONY~CHORD].
In the 1300s, however, composers started setting portions of the
Ordinary in the style known as "polyphony" (also called "counterpoint"). Polyphony combines several different melodic lines simultaneously, weaving them together to create a complex musical
fabric of changing harmonies [see COUNTERPOINT~POLYPHONY].
The first composer to write a polyphonic setting of the complete
Ordinary was the Frenchman Guillaume de Machaut, who composed his *Notre Dame* Mass in about 1350.

The Renaissance period (ca. 1430–1600) was the great age of
vocal polyphony, and the great age of Mass writing. It was during
the Renaissance that the Mass took on a strong identity as a musical form, as Renaissance composers found in the Mass an inspiration — and a laboratory — for many of their most remarkable
achievements [see RENAISSANCE]. All the most important com-

posers of the Renaissance — including Guillaume Dufay, Johannes Ockeghem, Josquin des Prez, Jacob Obrecht, Giovanni Pierluigi da Palestrina, Orlando di Lasso, William Byrd, Claudio Monteverdi, and Tomás Luis de Victoria — devoted themselves extensively to writing Masses. Ockeghem wrote 14 or 15 Masses, for example, and Obrecht wrote 29, while Palestrina alone composed 104.

One of the most common musical techniques in Renaissance Masses is the use of a *cantus firmus,* or "fixed melody." The cantus firmus, usually sung in the tenor voice, functions as a kind of musical backbone: it's the starting material, the melody against which the other voice parts are added (above and below), and with which they have to fit to make the desired harmonies. In order to give a sense of unity to their compositions, Renaissance composers would use the same cantus firmus as the basis for all the sections of a single Mass. They chose their *cantus firmi* from various sources: sometimes they used Gregorian chant melodies, sometimes they composed their own melodies, and sometimes they borrowed the melodies of popular songs, including popular songs of a distinctly *non*spiritual nature. And since composers' Masses were named for the cantus firmi on which they were based, the practice of borrowing popular songs gave rise to some interestingly named Masses, including the *More and More* Mass (*Missa de plus en plus*), the *Good-bye My Loves* Mass (*Missa Adieu mes amours*), and the *If My Face Is Pale* Mass (*Missa se la face ay pale*). Many composers used the very popular tune *L'Homme armé* ("The Armed Man") as a cantus firmus, so there are quite a few *Armed Man* Masses, too.

As the Renaissance waned, the Mass gradually lost its privileged position among musical forms. Composers continued to write occasional Masses, nonetheless, in musical styles that changed with the times. Baroque composers added instrumental parts to go along with the voices, for example, and wrote arias, recitatives, and choruses for their Masses, just as they did for their operas, oratorios, and cantatas [see BAROQUE; CANTATA; ORATORIO]. Johann Sebastian Bach's Mass in B Minor is without question the greatest of Baroque Masses, and many consider it one of the crowning achievements of all Western music.

Haydn, Mozart, and Beethoven all wrote Masses (Beethoven's Mass in D Major is known as the *Missa Solemnis*), as did such nineteenth-century composers as Luigi Cherubini, Franz Schubert, Franz Liszt, Charles Gounod, César Franck, and Anton Bruckner. Major twentieth-century composers who wrote Masses include Ralph Vaughan Williams, Igor Stravinsky, Heitor Villa-Lobos, Paul Hindemith, and Francis Poulenc.

⌒

A Requiem, or Requiem Mass, is a musical setting of the Mass for the Dead. The Latin word *requiem* means "rest," and the name *Requiem* comes from the *Introit,* or opening words, of the Mass: *Requiem aeternam dona eis, Domine* ("Give them eternal rest, Lord").

A Requiem always includes three sections from the Ordinary of the Mass — the Kyrie, the Sanctus (with the Benedictus), and the Agnus Dei — but unlike a regular Mass it also includes sections from the Proper. Here is the usual sequence of sections in a Requiem:

Introit
Kyrie
Dies irae   *Dies irae* . . . "Day of wrath . . ."
Offertory:
 Domine Jesu   *Domine Jesu Christe, rex gloriae* . . .
              "Lord Jesus Christ, King of
              Glory . . ."

Sanctus and Benedictus
Agnus Dei
Communion: Lux aeterna   *Lux aeterna luceat eis* . . .
              "Let eternal light shine upon
              them . . ."
Libera me (optional)   *Libera me, Domine* . . . "Deliver me,
              Lord . . ."

Composers sometimes include other sections from the Proper, at their discretion, but the two joyful sections of the Ordinary — the Gloria and the Credo — are never included.

The earliest surviving polyphonic Requiem is by Johannes Ockeghem, and other major Renaissance Requiems include those of Palestrina, Lasso, and Victoria. Of Requiems from the modern era, the best-known are those of Mozart (left unfinished at his death and completed by his student Franz Süssmayr), Hector Berlioz, Guiseppe Verdi, and Gabriel Fauré. Johannes Brahms wrote *Ein Deutsches Requiem* (*A German Requiem*), in 1868, but technically speaking it's really an oratorio, not a Requiem, because it's not a setting of the Mass at all, but rather of various biblical passages translated into German [see ORATORIO]. In the twentieth century, the most important Requiem composers include Maurice Duruflé (whose Requiem of 1947 is his best-known work), Benjamin Britten, and Krzysztof Penderecki. Britten's tremendously powerful *War Requiem* (1961) includes English poetry along with Latin texts from the Mass, while Penderecki's *Polish Requiem,* completed in 1984, combines Latin and Polish texts. The Requiem (1985) of Andrew Lloyd Webber — a composer known primarily for his Broadway shows, including *Cats, Evita,* and *The Phantom of the Opera* — is also an extraordinary work, a beautiful and austere setting of the traditional Latin Mass.

MELODY

From lullabies to drinking songs, from the melodies of Gregorian chant to those of Bach fugues, Beethoven symphonies, and Bartók string quartets, melodies come in all shapes and musical styles. All melodies move forward through time, but they can move in an infinite variety of rhythms and tempos. And as they're moving forward, melodies also move up and down in pitch from note to note [see PITCH]. Some melodies proceed in an angular way, with big leaps in pitch between notes, while others keep a smooth profile, moving from note to note in steps rather than leaps.

Some melodies are simple tunes, easy to remember and to hum in the shower, but some are so intricate or cover such a wide

pitch range that they can only be played on instruments. Some are
long, some are short. And though many melodies are quite
square, or symmetrical, easily divided into neat sections — think
of "Twinkle Twinkle, Little Star," for example — others seem to
be spun out like yarn, without an obvious beginning or end.

For a discussion of the intimate relationship between melody
and the two other basic elements of music, harmony and rhythm,
see HARMONY~CHORD and RHYTHM. See also LYRICAL~LYRI-
CISM.

METER

We often hear about pieces of music being "in two," "in
three," or "in four," "in three-quarter time," "in four-four," or "in
six-eight." These phrases all refer to meter.

Musical time is measured in beats, and beats are grouped together into measures, with each measure consisting of a strong, or
stressed, beat followed by a weaker beat or beats [see BEAT]. To
ask "What's the meter of this piece?" is to ask "How many beats
are there per measure?" "In two" means that there are two beats to
each measure, "in three" means three beats, and so on. Pieces that
are in two — or in multiples of two, such as four — are said to be
in duple meter, while pieces that are in three are said to be in
triple meter. ("Pop Goes the Weasel," for example, is in duple
meter, while "The Star-Spangled Banner" is in triple meter.)

Meter, however, also includes the specification of what note
value is assigned to the beat. Will the beat be an eighth note, a
quarter note, a half note? The precise meter of a piece or passage
of music is indicated by the time signature [see NOTATION].
A time signature of 3/4 ("three-four," or "three-quarter time")
means that there are three beats to the measure and that each beat
equals a quarter note — 3/4 is the equivalent of 3 × 1/4. A 6/8
time signature means the beat is the eighth note, and there are six
beats to the measure (6 × 1/8).

What meter does *not* specify, or imply in any way, is tempo (speed), style, or the actual rhythms that will be used to fill up the beats allotted to each measure. The time signature of 4/4 means four quarter notes to the measure, but not all quarter notes are created equal: in a fast piece they're fast, in a slow piece they're slow, and the length of time they cover can be divided in infinite ways. There are happy pieces in 4/4 and sad pieces, simple songs and complex symphonic movements, funeral marches and furious dances.

On the other hand, certain musical forms are always in certain meters. Waltzes, for example, are always in triple meter, usually 3/4, while marches are in duple meter, either in two or in four. Sometimes it's easy to tell what the meter of a piece is, especially when the first beat of each measure is accented; very often, in fact, the regularity of the meter is an important part of the music's appeal. But metrical regularity can be constricting, too, and composers often write music in such a way as to disguise the meter.

Before the twentieth century, composers almost always wrote long sections of pieces — often entire movements — without changing meter. They might vary the rhythm in many ways, but the time signature would stay the same. In the twentieth century, however, composers began to experiment with changing meter in order to vary the rhythm, and it became common practice to change time signatures quite frequently, sometimes as often as every few measures.

[See RHYTHM; SYNCOPATION; TEMPO.]

METRONOME

A metronome is a mechanical, electric, or electronic device that produces a tick, click, beep, or other signal at regular intervals. It can be set at different speeds, as measured in ticks per minute: a setting of 60 means 60 ticks per minute, for example, with intervals of exactly one second between ticks.

The metronome is a tool for specifying tempo, how quickly or slowly a piece of music should go. A composer finds the metronome setting that corresponds to the tempo he has in mind for a piece or passage — the faster the beat, the higher the setting — and then indicates the tempo on the written page using a metronome mark. A metronome mark consists of the symbol for a note value, say a quarter note or half note (representing the beat), followed by the equals sign and a number, which represents the number of those notes, or beats, per minute: "♩ = 60," for example, means the quarter note is the beat, and there are sixty beats per minute, while "♩ = 80" means the half note is the beat and there are eighty beats per minute [see BEAT; TEMPO; TEMPO MARKINGS].

Sometimes the metronome mark is preceded by the abbreviation *M.M.* This stands for Maelzel metronome. Johann Nepomuk Maelzel (1772–1838) of Vienna invented the name *metronome* and set up a factory in Paris in 1816 to manufacture the clever new mechanical device. Helped by the endorsements of Beethoven and other famous composers, he successfully marketed his metronome all over Europe, England, and the United States. The fact that Maelzel had actually stolen the design in 1815 from a Dutch inventor named Winkel — Maelzel saw Winkel's model in Amsterdam and went home and copied it — never much got in his way, although he did lose a lawsuit over it. The Maelzel metronome is what's called a double pendulum device. A flat metal shaft swings back and forth. A lead weight is fixed to the bottom of the shaft, and another weight is positioned toward the top. The top weight slides up and down, held in different positions by little notches on the shaft; it is the position of the top weight that determines the speed of the swing and the frequency of the ticks. Interestingly, the design of the Maelzel metronome, including its pyramid-shaped wooden case, has never gone out of fashion: exact replicas of Maelzel's original model can still be found sitting on pianos all over the world. Much smaller, more accurate, and more versatile than the Maelzel metronome, however, are the many different kinds of electronic metronomes available today.

Because its beat is perfectly steady, the metronome is an excellent practice tool for musicians. Practicing with a metronome is extremely useful for developing and maintaining rhythmic precision, for learning to keep consistent tempos, for countering tendencies to slow down or speed up in specific passages, and for developing evenness and accuracy in rapid passages. Most music teachers consider the metronome indispensable, and most professional musicians, in fact, continue to practice with a metronome throughout their careers. That doesn't mean that it's always particularly pleasant to practice with a metronome (it's no fun to have a bunch of inexorable little clicks reminding you to stay on your toes), but it's good medicine for young and old, and for amateurs as well as professionals.

MEZZO-SOPRANO

[See VOICE TYPES.]

MINUET

The minuet represents one of the longest-lasting dance crazes in history. The dance most likely originated as a French country dance, but its real success began in the 1650s when it was introduced — in finer clothing and with music by Jean-Baptiste Lully (1632–1687) — at the court of King Louis XIV of France. A graceful dance in three-quarter time [see METER] and moderate tempo, it quickly achieved an enormous popularity throughout the royal courts and aristocratic salons of Europe, and remained popular for about 150 years.

During the rest of the Baroque period (until about 1750, that is) composers all over Europe frequently included minuets in their ballets and stage works, and also in their instrumental dance suites [see SUITE]. The dance suites, however, were meant for listening, not dancing. After the Baroque period, the predecessors of Haydn and Mozart and then Haydn and Mozart themselves used minuets for the third movements of their four-movement symphonies and chamber music pieces, and often included minuets in their divertimentos and serenades [see DIVERTIMENTO~SERE-NADE; SYMPHONY]. Haydn and Mozart livened up the minuet, making it quicker and less dancelike, and treating it with unlimited inventiveness. Indeed, it could be said that they took the form as far as it would go, for by the end of the eighteenth century, Beethoven had replaced it with the *scherzo* ("joke" in Italian). Beethoven's scherzos, which aren't necessarily funny, don't resemble dance forms in the slightest. They're even faster than the minuets of Haydn and Mozart, and often quite forceful [see SCHERZO].

Minuet movements of the Classical period, the period of Haydn, Mozart, and early Beethoven, are always in a symmetrical form that consists of the minuet itself, a middle section called the "trio," which is usually lighter in sound and character, and a repeat of the minuet. The trio owes its name and lighter character to the tradition, dating back to Lully, of sandwiching a "trio minuet" — a minuet for three instruments — between two "regular" (and identical) orchestral minuets. Lully favored woodwind instruments for his trio minuets, especially the combination of two oboes and a bassoon, and although Classical composers varied the instrumentation and didn't always maintain the practice of writing for just three parts, they did tend to feature woodwind instruments in the trios of their symphonies.

[See DANCE.]

MODES

Modes, also called church modes, are types of scales [see SCALE]. The system of church modes evolved in the early Middle Ages, and modes served as the basis for the melodies of Gregorian chant, the liturgical music of the Roman Catholic Church [see GREGORIAN CHANT].

There are four principal modes, known as "authentic" modes. They are the Dorian mode, the Phrygian mode, the Lydian mode, and the Mixolydian mode. A chant based on the Dorian mode is said to be "in" the Dorian mode, just as a piece by Mozart may be in the key of C major. The modes correspond to scales using the white keys of the piano, with each mode starting on a different note: the Dorian starts on D, Phrygian starts on E, Lydian starts on F, and Mixolydian starts on G.

Because the starting notes are different, the sequence of intervals (half steps and whole steps) in each scale is different, which is why the modes all sound different. It's also why they don't sound like major and minor scales. [See HALF STEP.]

The starting note of a mode is called the "final," of all things, but there's a good reason: it's the note that a melody in that mode always ends on. There are four variants on the authentic modes, all bearing the prefix "Hypo-." Each of the four — Hypodorian, Hypophrygian, Hypolydian, and Hypomixolydian — has the same final as the authentic mode for which it's named, but a different range of notes. The final of both the Dorian mode and the Hypodorian mode is the note D, for example, but the range of the Dorian is from the final D to the D an octave higher, while the range of the Hypodorian is from the A below the final D to the A above it [see OCTAVE].

⤻

The word *mode* is sometimes used in the context of major and minor keys. To say a piece is in the "minor mode" means that it is in a minor key; in the "major mode" means in a major key. No specific major or minor key is implied, however.

MONODY

Opera in the Western musical tradition was invented in Florence, Italy, toward the end of the sixteenth century by a group of musicians, poets, and intellectuals known as the Camerata, whose goal was to create a new art form based on what they imagined to be the musical style of classical Greek tragedy. The type of vocal music that the Camerata developed and exploited in their new art form is known today as monody.

Monody (from the Greek *monodia,* "singing alone") consists of a single vocal line with a sparse, flexible instrumental accompaniment. The vocal line is not purely lyrical, or melodic, however. It is a cross between speech and song, closely tailored to the rhythms of speech and the demands of poetic expression [see RECITATIVE]. The Camerata felt that this style was ideal for the individual expression necessary for dramatic action and characterization; a great improvement, for their purposes, over *polyphony,* the style that had dominated music for at least two centuries previously. (In polyphonic music, a number of equally important voices all sing at once to create a complex fabric of sound. No voice or line of text is truly isolated, which makes dramatic declamation by individuals difficult, if not impossible.)

The rise of monody represents a major turning point in the history of music. It marks not just the beginning of opera, but the first stage in the development of "melody and accompaniment" style. Melody and accompaniment style ultimately rose to prominence in all branches of Western music, and it dominates musical composition to this day.

[See BAROQUE; COUNTERPOINT~POLYPHONY; OPERA.]

The two most important composers of the Camerata were Jacopo Peri (1561–1633), generally credited with writing the very first opera, *Dafne* (now lost), in 1597, and Giulio Caccini (ca. 1550–1618), who collaborated with Peri on the earliest surviving opera, *Euridice* (1600), and who published a groundbreaking set of songs in the monodic style called *Le Nuove Musiche,* or *The New Music(s).* The most brilliant exponent of the "new" style, however, was not a member of the Camerata. It was Claudio Monteverdi (1567–1643), a composer also known for his outstanding body of work (including Masses, motets, and madrigals) in the "old," polyphonic style. Monteverdi's *Orfeo* (1607) is usually considered the greatest of the very early Italian operas.

The motet is a form that played a central role in music history for five hundred years, from the 1200s to the 1700s. During that time, most of the changes and developments in musical style and structure were mirrored in the evolution of the motet, and for this reason there's no single definition that covers every kind of motet. Generally speaking, however, a motet is a choral setting of a religious text, performed as part of church services, usually without instrumental accompaniment. For the first three hundred years or so of the motet's history, before the Protestant Reformation, the texts were always in Latin, the language of the Roman Catholic Church. Later, composers wrote motets with texts in their native languages, especially in England and Germany.

The motets of the Renaissance (ca. 1430–1600) are probably the most familiar to modern listeners and early music lovers. The first masters of the Renaissance motet were the members of the Flemish school of composers, the greatest of whom were Johannes Ockeghem (1430–1495), Josquin des Prez (ca. 1450–1521), and Jacob Obrecht (ca. 1450–1505). Composers of the Flemish school occupied prestigious musical positions in royal courts and chapels throughout Europe, and they exerted enormous influence on their contemporaries. Their texts were Latin and their music *polyphonic:* it usually consisted of four or five different voice parts, all sung simultaneously to create a complex texture and rich harmonies, with the voice parts often imitating one another by passing melodies back and forth [see COUNTERPOINT~POLYPHONY]. Important sixteenth-century composers of polyphonic motets include the Italian Giovanni Pierluigi da Palestrina (ca. 1525–1594) and the Netherlander Orlando di Lasso (1532–1594), also known as Lassus. [See RENAISSANCE.]

During the Baroque period (ca. 1600–1750), motets with instrumental accompaniment became quite common, and composers began to vary the previously uniform choral texture by entrusting melodies to vocal soloists. Important motet composers of the early Baroque in Germany include Michael Praetorius

(1571–1621), Heinrich Schütz (1585–1672), and Samuel Scheidt (1587–1654), and in Italy, Giovanni Gabrieli (1555–1612), who was Schütz's teacher. Johann Sebastian Bach (1685–1750) wrote seven motets, all in German. All seven are for chorus without soloists, but several call specifically for instrumental accompaniment. [See BAROQUE.]

By the end of the Baroque period, other forms (especially secular forms) and musical styles were coming to the fore, and the motet's day was finally done. Although later composers such as Schubert, Schumann, Mendelssohn, and Brahms occasionally wrote motets, their motets were much more of an affectionate and respectful nod to the past — and an expression of religious sentiment — than any sort of serious attempt to keep the form alive or to further its development.

[See MADRIGAL.]

MUTE

A mute is any device that softens, dampens, or muffles the normal sound of an instrument.

On stringed instruments, the strings pass over a delicately carved but sturdy piece of wood called the bridge. When the strings are made to vibrate, the bridge vibrates in turn, transmitting the vibrations of the strings to the body of the instrument. Mutes for stringed instruments come in many varieties, but in one way or another they all clamp onto the top of the bridge, reducing its ability to vibrate. With their vibrations cut down, stringed instruments produce a gentler, "darker" sound than usual. String players sometimes use extra-heavy mutes called "practice mutes," which reduce the volume of sound to an extreme degree. Practice mutes can be especially helpful for maintaining good relations with neighbors in apartment buildings.

Brass players mute their instruments by inserting a pear-shaped or cone-shaped device of wood, wood fiber, cardboard, or metal into the bell, the flared end of the instrument. (Tuba mutes are particularly impressive; they look like big closed-end mega-phones, complete with handle.) Mutes for brass instruments all work in the same way: they dampen the vibrations of the metal and trap some of the sound inside the instrument. But mutes of different shapes and materials produce different kinds of sounds. On the trumpet, for example, a pear-shaped metal mute will produce a slightly nasal, thin, sometimes very penetrating sound, very different from the mellower sound of the so-called "wa-wa mute" (often used in jazz and jazz-inspired compositions), which consists of nothing more than the business end of a toilet plunger held in one hand and used to cover and uncover the bell. The French horn can be muted either with a conventional mute or by a technique known as "hand-stopping," which requires the player to block the opening of the bell using his or her right hand.

Muting a bassoon entails stuffing a handkerchief (or sock) in the top end of the instrument. The other instruments of the woodwind section — flute, oboe, and clarinet — are almost never muted. Handkerchiefs also come in handy for timpanists (kettle-drum players), who mute their instruments by laying a handker-chief on the head of each drum.

The Italian word for "mute" is *sordino,* and *con sordino,* "with mute," is the written indication most commonly used by composers when they want a passage muted. *Senza sordino,* "without mute," is the indication to take the mute off. French and German composers, however, sometimes use their own languages: the French word for "mute" is *sourdine,* and in German it's *Dämpfer.*

The use of mutes — and of the different varieties of mutes — vastly expands the range of instrumental color available to composers. Mutes are called for in all kinds of pieces, whether solo compositions, chamber music, or orchestral works, and their musical value and effectiveness are limited only by the imagination and creativity of the composer.

[See STRINGED INSTRUMENTS; WIND INSTRUMENTS; ORCHESTRATION.]

N

"Do you read music?" Not an unusual question at all, is it? And yet think of the implications. We take it completely for granted that music can be notated on paper; that it can be written down, not just played; read, not just heard. We assume, in other words, that visual symbols can represent sounds. Moreover, we assume that such symbols will correlate not approximately but precisely with particular sounds, and that their meaning will be interpreted in exactly the same way by all those who read music, no matter where they're from, what language they speak, or what instrument they play. And it follows that someone can "compose" music on paper, and that even if the composer is long dead, or just not around for rehearsals, the composition can be preserved and performed with perfect accuracy on the basis of the written text.

It was not always this way. The system of notation that is now standard throughout the world of Western music has existed only since the early 1600s. Before that, going back to the first attempts four or five thousand years ago in Egypt, all systems of notation were either approximate or variable.

For a system of notation to be precise, it must be able to represent both the pitch and the rhythm (that is, the relative duration) of musical sounds [see PITCH; RHYTHM]. Up until about the thirteenth century, no such system had ever existed. Music was passed on exclusively by oral tradition, from one person to the next or from one generation to the next, and the function of notation was simply to remind people of musical patterns that they already knew.

In vocal music, the notational reminders often consisted of

141

various symbols or accents placed over the words to be sung. The Greeks used such accents (although they also had systems based on letters of the alphabet for instrumental music), as did the Hebrews, whose ancient system is still used in synagogues today for chanting the Torah (Five Books of Moses) and other holy texts. The Greek and Hebrew accent systems were the ancestors of an elaborate set of markings and symbols called "neumes," which were used by monks of the Roman Catholic Church during the Middle Ages to notate Gregorian chant [see GREGORIAN CHANT]. Neumes, which can still be found in some liturgical texts, have all sorts of interesting Latin names, such as *punctum, podatus, clivis, climacus, torculus,* and *porrectus,* and these names (and neumes) describe the melodic "shapes" of the components that go together to make up a chant. (A *climacus,* for example, indicates a group of three descending notes, while a *porrectus flexus* indicates a four-note group in which the second and fourth notes are lower than the first and third.) As involved and highly descriptive as this system is, it is still approximate, an auxiliary to oral tradition and memorization: neumes can indicate neither precise pitch nor duration.

Developments in musical notation are inseparable from developments in music itself. Over the centuries that followed the era of Gregorian chant, musical compositions became more complicated and sophisticated, with forms that involved multiple melodic lines sung simultaneously [see COUNTERPOINT~ POLYPHONY]. In order to keep track of all the lines while composing, and in order to teach, learn, and preserve complicated works, it became very important to find precise notational devices. These devices in turn made possible further advances in composition.

In the 1200s, the first notational symbols that could be called "notes" made their appearance, and from about 1225 to 1325 many advances were made in the notation of pitch and rhythm. This period saw the development of "mensural notation," which used notes of different shapes and durational values, and symbols to indicate rhythmic rules and relationships. (The word *mensural* means "pertaining to measurement.") Notes were placed on a staff

(see STAFF, p. 145), but there were no bar lines or measures (see
MEASURE, p. 148), and depending on which rules were in effect,
notes of a particular type might be equal in durational value to
either two or three notes of the next smaller value. Mensural notation was never standardized — even the number of lines in the
staff varied — and as it evolved from century to century it remained a complicated system, comprehensible only to specialists.
In various forms, however, it lasted until about the end of the sixteenth century, when, again, musical evolution demanded a corresponding leap in notational possibilities. Modern notation is the
direct descendant of mensural notation.

Perhaps the greatest advantage derived from the logical refinements, improvements, and standardization of modern notation is flexibility. The same system can be used to notate works of
widely divergent styles, periods, or levels of complexity, from
fourteenth-century vocal pieces to delicate seventeenth-century
keyboard pieces to huge modern symphonies. Another important
benefit is accessibility. Musical notation is no longer just the domain of those who have served a long and hard apprenticeship.
With a little effort and a certain basic training, anybody can learn
to read the language of Bach, Mozart, and Beethoven, of Debussy, Stravinsky, and Bartók.

Here are some important terms of modern musical notation:

NOTE: the basic symbol for representing a musical sound.
Notes in the modern system are oval. A note can be white, that is,
just an outline; or black, which is to say filled in. White or black,
the oval is also called the "note head." Most notes also have a
"stem," a vertical line attached to the note head. If the note is
black, there may be one or more wavy lines called "flags" at the
end of the stem. The stems of two or more notes with flags are
often connected with solid heavy lines called "beams," which replace the flags; notes with one flag apiece are connected with one
beam, two flags with two beams, and so forth.

The color of a note, presence or absence of a stem, and number of flags (or beams) are used to indicate a note's "value," that is,

its duration relative to other notes. The most common "note values," or kinds of notes, are whole notes, half notes, quarter notes, eighth notes, sixteenth notes, thirty-second notes, and sixty-fourth notes. (The English use the term *crotchet* for a quarter note, *quaver* for an eighth note, *semiquaver* for a sixteenth note, and *demisemiquaver* and *hemidemisemiquaver* for thirty-second and sixty-fourth notes.)

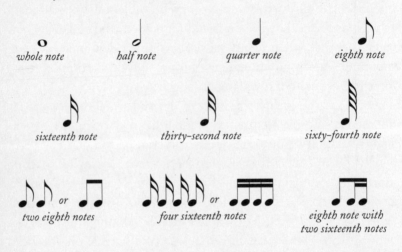

Each note value is equal in duration to two of the next smaller value: a whole note equals two half notes, a half note equals two quarter notes, and so on. It's very important to remember that these note values represent relative, not absolute, durations. The actual duration of any note depends on the tempo of the music, how fast the music "goes." A half note in a slow piece lasts longer than a half note in a fast piece, for example, and if the difference in tempo is great enough there's no reason the half note in one couldn't last longer than the whole note in the other.

DOT: A dot placed next to a note increases the value of the note by half. A dotted quarter note, for example, lasts one and a half times as long as a plain quarter note. It is the equivalent of a quarter note plus an eighth note.

REST: A rest is a period of silence of precise duration, but the word is also used to mean the notational sign for such a period.

Eighth rest, sixteenth rest, half rest — each note value mentioned above has a corresponding rest, each indicated with a different sign. A "quarter rest," for example, refers either to a silence lasting as long as a quarter note, or to the quarter rest sign. A rest can be "dotted" to increase its value by half, just as a note can.

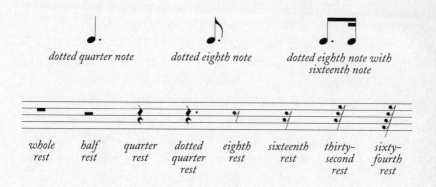

dotted quarter note   dotted eighth note   dotted eighth note with
                                                         sixteenth note

whole   half   quarter   dotted   eighth   sixteenth   thirty-   sixty-
rest   rest   rest   quarter   rest   rest   second   fourth
                          rest   rest   rest

STAFF: The staff is the set of five parallel horizontal lines on which notes are placed. To use a metaphor, the staff is the canvas on which music is painted. The placement of a note on the staff determines its pitch, that is, its name, and how high or low it is relative to other notes [see PITCH]. (The names used for pitches in the American and English system are the letters A through G. After G, the series starts back again at A and repeats.) The higher a note is placed on the staff, the higher the pitch. Notes may be written on the lines (with the lines bisecting the note heads, in other words), or in the spaces between the lines. Each line and each space of the staff represents a specific pitch, which is why the location of a note on the staff determines its pitch. For example: if one line represents the note B, then the space above it represents C, and the next line above represents D. Notes may also be written above or below the staff using added lines called "ledger lines."

Music is read from left to right on the staff. Music for single voices and for most instruments is written on one staff at a time, but piano music is notated on two parallel staves — one for the right hand, one for the left — and orchestral and choral music may consist of many parallel staves at once [see SCORE]. (In piano music, each set of two parallel staves is called a "system.") Notes that occur simultaneously — chords on the piano, for example — are aligned vertically (or "stacked") on the same staff, or aligned vertically with notes on another staff or set of staves.

CLEF: The lines of the staff represent pitches, but the clef is the symbol that determines what those pitches will be for each staff. *Clef* is French for "key," and indeed the clef — located at the far left end of the staff — is the key to the meaning of the staff. (The word does *not*, however, mean key in the sense of "in a minor key," or "in the key of C major.") With one clef, or *in* one clef, to use the common expression, the lines of the staff might stand for a certain set of pitches, say, E-G-B-D-F (the famous "Every Good Boy Deserves Favor," or "Every Good Boy Does Fine"), while in another clef the lines might mean F-A-C-E-G ("Forget About Cleaning Ernie's Garage" — less famous). If the clef changes, the same placement of a note on the staff results in a different pitch. There are three kinds of clefs: the G-clef, F-clef, and C-clef, so called because they indicate where those pitches lie on the staff. They all have different shapes. The G-clef is also called the *treble clef,* and the F-clef is known as the *bass clef.* The C-clef has several incarnations: depending on where the clef symbol itself is placed on the staff, it's called the *alto clef, tenor clef,* or *soprano clef.* The various clefs cover different pitch ranges — treble is for high ranges, alto is in the middle, tenor a little lower, and bass the lowest (the soprano clef is rarely used today). The clef, or combination of clefs, that different instruments and voice types use, or "read," depends therefore on how high or low they play or sing. Among the stringed instruments, for example, the violin uses only treble clef; the viola reads alto clef primarily and the treble clef for notes in its upper range; the cello reads bass clef primarily and tenor clef for higher ranges, skipping to treble clef for its highest notes; and the double bass reads bass clef. The piano reads two clefs at once: the upper staff, for the right hand, is usually in treble clef, and the lower staff, for the left hand, is usually in bass clef.

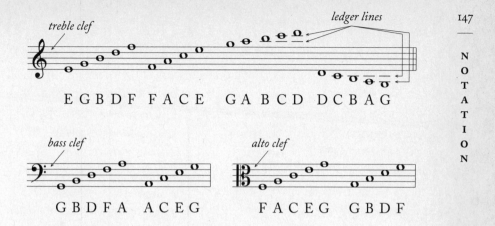

treble clef   *ledger lines*

E G B D F   F A C E   G A B C D   D C B A G

bass clef   *alto clef*

G B D F A   A C E G   F A C E G   G B D F

ACCIDENTAL: An accidental is a sign placed in front of a note to raise or lower its pitch by a *half step* (also called a "semi-tone"), which is the smallest unit of pitch in traditional Western music. The sign that raises the pitch is called a "sharp," and the one that lowers it is called a "flat." Notes that sound the same may be spelled differently using sharps or flats, depending on the context. The note C-sharp is a half step higher than C, for example, but so is the note D-flat. And they're both a half step *lower* than D. In fact, C-sharp and D-flat are equivalent: they are the same note spelled differently.*

The accidental that is used to cancel a sharp or a flat sign is called a "natural." As signs or written out as words, accidentals are also attached to the names of notes when simply naming pitches, as in "Please sing the notes C-sharp, A-flat, and B-natural." The word *natural* is often attached just to indicate for certain that a note is neither a sharp nor a flat.

♯   ♭   ♮   ♯○   ♭○   ♮○

sharp   *flat*   *natural*   *C-sharp*   *A-flat*   *B-natural*

*See footnote about equivalent pitches on p. 186.

KEY SIGNATURE: Music that is written in a key requires a key signature. Keys are based on scales, and all scales (with the exception of C major and A minor) have at least one note that is always a sharp or flat. A key signature simply consists of one or more accidentals (or *no* accidentals, in the case of C major and A minor). The key signature is always found at the left end of the staff, just to the right of the clef, with the accidentals placed on the appropriate lines or spaces of the staff to show which notes will always be sharps or flats unless otherwise specified. In the key of D major, for example, there are two sharps in the key signature, representing the notes F-sharp and C-sharp from the D-major scale. Since in any one scale there may be either sharps or flats, but not both, sharps and flats are never combined in a key signature. In printed music, the key signature appears on every staff on the page. [See KEY~TONALITY; SCALE.]

MEASURE, BAR LINE, BAR: A measure is a metrical unit, a unit of time. More precisely, it is the unit of time that is the exact duration of a certain number of beats, or that "contains" a certain number of beats [see BEAT]. If a piece or passage is said to be "in three," for example, that means that there are three beats to every measure, and that the combination of notes and silence in every measure must last for the exact amount of time covered by those three beats. A measure is also a *visual* grouping of beats on the printed page. Bar lines are vertical lines drawn through the staff and used to mark off measures. The space between two bar lines covers one measure. Through common usage, the word *bar* has become interchangeable with *measure*. Measures and bar lines are an extremely convenient means of organizing music, both visually and conceptually. For the last four hundred years or so, in fact, almost all music has been conceived and written in measures.

TIME SIGNATURE: The time signature is found on the staff just to the right of the key signature. It indicates the meter of a piece, which is to say how many beats there are in each measure and what note value each beat represents [see METER]. The time signature usually consists of two numbers, one above the other.

The upper number indicates how many beats there are per measure, and the lower number indicates the note value of the beat. For example, 2 over 4 (called "two-four time") means that there are two beats per measure and that the beat is a quarter note. Each measure lasts as long as two quarter notes. In 6/8, or six-eight time, there are six beats per measure, and the beat is the eighth note. Four-four time (4/4) is often indicated by the symbol c in place of the numbers, while c with a vertical line drawn through it (¢) indicates 2/2. Although 4/4 is also known as "common time," the c doesn't stand for "common." As a matter of fact, it doesn't even represent the letter "c." It's a relic of mensural notation, and it was originally just a partially opened circle. The time signature is not repeated for every staff. It's printed at the beginning of a piece, on the first staff, and then only again if it has to be changed to show a change in meter.

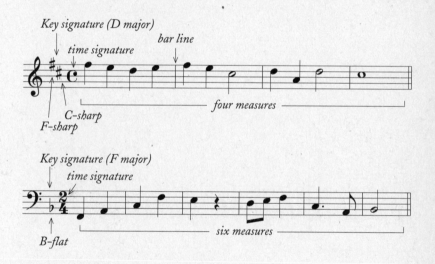

As composers have experimented over the last forty-five years or so with new musical forms and techniques, they have also experimented with different notational devices. Some composers, for example, have sought greater exactness, and have devised charts and graphs with precise timings indicated in seconds. Others have tried by various means to give performers more discretion or to emphasize the elements of chance. They've used pictures, for example, with or without a staff, or signs that indicate ranges of choices rather than specific notes. While some of these innovations have from time to time proved interesting and musically fruitful, none of them has seriously threatened the preeminence of standard notation.

[See DYNAMICS; TEMPO MARKINGS.]

O

OBBLIGATO

Obbligato is an Italian word meaning "essential," or "obligatory." During the Baroque era (ca. 1600–1750), especially, but even as late as Beethoven's time (the late eighteenth and early nineteenth centuries), composers used the term *obbligato* to describe instruments or instrumental parts that were essential to a composition. Sometimes the essential instruments were the solo instruments in a concerto, as in Antonio Vivaldi's Concerto for four violins and orchestra, Op. 3, No. 1, which was published with the title *Concerto con 4 violini obbligati* (Concerto with 4 obbligato violins). Often the term was applied to important instrumental parts in vocal compositions. In a Baroque aria for soprano, strings, continuo, and "trumpet obbligato," for example, you would expect to find a trumpet part as prominent as the soprano part. Beethoven himself included a lengthy obbligato part for solo violin in the *Benedictus* section of his *Missa Solemnis,* a work for vocal soloists, chorus, and orchestra. (In a less solemn vein, Beethoven also wrote a piece for viola and cello — for himself and a cellist friend, most likely — which he called *Duett mit zwei obligaten Augengläsern,* which means "Duet with two obbligato eyeglasses.") As is frequently the case with Italian musical terms, *obbligato* can be an adjective or a noun: an obbligato instrumental part is sometimes simply called an obbligato.

The opposite of obbligato is *ad libitum,* or "optional." In the nineteenth century, however, through a mysterious musical/linguistic transformation, obbligato merged with its opposite, so that in many cases the term *obbligato* was used for instrumental parts that were in fact optional. Early in *this* century, for example, the violinist Fritz Kreisler added violin parts to many songs for voice and piano, for the purposes of joint recitals and recordings with the great Irish tenor John McCormack. Kreisler's optional (and very beautiful) violin parts are called violin obbligatos.

OBOE

[See REED INSTRUMENTS; WOODWIND INSTRUMENTS.]

OCTAVE

An "interval" is the distance in pitch between two notes. An octave is the interval between a note and the next higher or lower note of the same name. Take the notes of a C-major scale: C-D-E-F-G-A-B-C. The interval between the two C's is an octave. Another way to describe an octave is to say that it is the interval between the first and eighth notes, or tones, of a major or minor scale. It spans eight scale tones, in other words, hence the root of the word, *oct-*, from the Greek word for "eight." (An octave can also be divided into twelve equal intervals called "half steps," or "semitones." See HALF STEP.)

Scales continue, though: they don't necessarily stop at the eighth note. As notes continue upward in pitch, they go into a "higher octave"; notes that progress downward enter a "lower octave." Octave, therefore, can also serve as a term for *range,* as long as it's understood that each range in question covers eight scale tones.

The really interesting question is, Why do different notes, or pitches, have the same names? Why does the series A-B-C-D-E-F-G keep repeating itself in different octaves? The answer is that notes that are exactly an octave apart — or two octaves apart, or three, and so on — somehow have the same identity. The note that is two octaves higher than a G, for instance, is a G. Strictly speaking, the two G's differ in pitch, but there's something about them that sounds the same. Part of the relationship has to do with physics: the pitch of a note is determined by the frequency, measured in cycles per second, of its sound waves, and the frequency ratio for notes that are an octave apart is exactly two to one. Frequency doubles with the octave, in other words. But this is a description, not an explanation. The note that vibrates at 440 cycles per second sounds like an A. The notes that vibrate at 220, 880, and 1,760 cycles per second also sound like A's, only higher or lower A's. Precisely *why* the notes sound the same remains a mystery.

[See PITCH; SCALE.]

To "play an octave" on an instrument is to play two notes that are an octave apart simultaneously. String players are often called upon to play octaves — which have a very distinctive sound on stringed instruments — and pianists play octaves all the time, sometimes in flashy (and difficult) passages in which each hand has to play rapid successions of octaves. A musical passage is said to be "in octaves" when it consists of a sequence of octaves rather than single notes. Another common expression is "doubled at the octave," as in, "the violas played the melody, doubled at the octave by the oboe," which means that the oboe played the melody along with the violas, but played the same notes an octave higher.

OP.

[See OPUS NUMBER.]

OPERA

Opera is musical theater. It may be tragic or comic or a mixture of both; it may be simple or elaborate, short or long, and it may be in any language. An enormous number of different works and different *kinds* of works fit in the general category of opera, but there are certain features that all operas share, including the staged presentation of a story; words set to music and characters who sing their roles — mostly or entirely — rather than speak them; and an orchestra or other instrumental ensemble to complement and accompany the singers.

Opera is commonly referred to as a marriage of many arts, including music, poetry, drama, acting, stagecraft, painting and set design, costume design, lighting design, and choreography. In the best operas and the best productions, the marriage — though admittedly of the polygamous variety — is a happy, harmonious one, with all the artistic elements supporting and enhancing one another, fitting together to compelling effect. That being said, there is no question that the most important element in opera is music. People often just *listen* to operas — either in concert (that is, unstaged) performances or on recordings — and though the experience is incomplete, it can still be very satisfying. Nobody, on the other hand, ever presents an opera without the music.

Over the centuries, opera has often been criticized, and justly, for any number of reasons: silly or unrealistic plots, bad acting, extravagant production expenses, an air of social exclusivity, exorbitant ticket prices, and characters who should be at least a little out of breath on account of their dying of consumption or having just been stabbed in the heart but who nonetheless manage to sing lengthy arias at the top of their lungs. But despite these problems, opera has never lost its popularity because music, unlimited in its emotional implications and associations, can elevate and transform — or transcend — even the most banal words or ridiculous situations, and because the human voice has the power to touch our hearts in ways nothing else quite can. Audiences love drama and spectacle, and these factors have always contributed greatly to opera's appeal. But the essence of opera is wonderful singers singing beautiful music.

There is no such thing as a brief history of opera. (Donald Jay Grout's *A Short History of Opera*, a classic work in the field, is eight hundred pages long.) But for discussions of various subjects touching on opera and its history, see the following: ARIA;

BAROQUE; BEL CANTO; CASTRATI; INTERMEZZO; LEITMOTIF; LIBRETTO; MONODY (for the beginnings of opera); OPERETTA; PRELUDE; PRIMA DONNA~DIVA; RECITATIVE; TESSITURA; and VOICE TYPES.

One historical note: Opera was invented by a group of Italian composers and poets called the Camerata who came together in Florence in the late 1500s and whose goal was to recreate what they imagined to be the musical style of ancient Greek tragedy. The earliest surviving opera, *Euridice,* by Giulio Caccini and Jacopo Peri, was written in 1600. The Italian word *opera* means "work," from the Latin *opus,* and the term was originally an abbreviated version of *opera in musica,* "work of music."

Here are a few opera terms, with very brief descriptions:

ARIA: A lyrical piece for solo voice with instrumental accompaniment. Arias, which are usually more elaborate and vocally demanding than pieces called "songs," are the musical numbers in which operatic characters express their thoughts and feelings, and they've been the most important ingredient in opera since the mid-1600s. The music of most operas consists of arias alternating with recitatives and ensemble pieces (such as duets, trios, or choruses).

RECITATIVE: From the Italian word for "reciting," recitative is a type of vocal music that is tailored to the rhythms of speech, and that is in fact almost like "speaking in music." Recitative can be expressive, but its primary function is not so much to convey emotion as to convey information, and to advance the plot. The term may also be used to refer to a passage or section, as in, "The Countess's aria in the third act is preceded by a lengthy recitative."

LIBRETTO: The text that is set to music to make an opera. The Italian word *libretto* means "little book," or "booklet." The author of a libretto is called a librettist, and the librettist's job is often to adapt an existing play or story for operatic purposes. Some composers write their own librettos; famous composer-librettists include Hector Berlioz (1803–1869), Richard Wagner (1813–1883), and Gian Carlo Menotti (b. 1911).

OPERA SERIA: Italian for "serious opera," or tragic opera, specifically a standardized type of Italian opera that held a dominant position throughout Europe in the eighteenth century and was influential into the nineteenth. It is now largely forgotten, partly because its librettos, dramatic conventions, and music all seem dated, but also because much of the music was never published. The most important figure of opera seria was not a composer, but rather the poet and librettist Pietro Metastasio (1698–1782), who set the standards for the genre's formal structure and aesthetic ideals.

OPERA BUFFA: Italian for "comic opera," the term refers to Italian comic opera of the eighteenth century. In the early 1700s, Italian composers wrote two types of comic operas: full-length operas and shorter intermezzos, which were comic scenes performed between the acts of serious operas. Later, as intermezzos were performed independently and expanded into full-length productions, the distinctions between the two types faded. The subjects of opera buffa are humorous or light, with elements of parody, and the same can be said of the music, which is often popular in style. The characters are ordinary people, rather than noble or mythological figures, as in opera seria. One of the innovations of opera buffa was the regular use of bass voices, which were rarely heard in opera seria. Also, whereas opera seria was built around solo singing and the occasional duet, opera buffa introduced "ensemble finales," extended scenes at the ends of acts with three or more characters all singing at once [see FINALE].

The greatest of all opera buffa composers was not an Italian, but an Austrian: Wolfgang Amadeus Mozart (1756–1791). In his three Italian masterpieces, *Le Nozze di Figaro* (*The Marriage of Figaro*, 1786), *Don Giovanni* (1787), and *Così fan tutte* (*Thus Do They All*, 1790), Mozart incorporated many of the elements of traditional opera buffa, but he went beyond mere farce or parody to achieve — through music of matchless beauty, wit, and depth — an astonishing richness of human characterization.

During the eighteenth century, England, France, and Germany all produced comic opera in their own languages. In England, comic opera took the form of the BALLAD OPERA, which parodied serious opera and featured "low" character types and new words fitted to popular songs or folk songs. *The Beggar's Opera* (1728) by John Gay is the most famous example. In France the comic form was the OPÉRA-COMIQUE, and in Germany the SINGSPIEL (singing play). Ballad opera, opéra-comique, and singspiel — but *not* opera buffa — all include spoken dialogue along with singing. Mozart's *Die Entführung aus dem Serail* (*The Abduction from the Seraglio*, 1782) is generally considered the greatest of all singspiels. His German opera *Die Zauberflöte* (*The Magic Flute*, 1791) is harder to classify: it includes broad humor and spoken dialogue, but it combines comic elements with loftier philosophical goals and content, and is therefore not usually considered "just" a singspiel.

GRAND OPERA: Originally a term used in early-nineteenth-century France to distinguish serious opera, which was entirely sung, from opéra-comique, which included spoken dialogue. Giacomo Meyerbeer (1791–1864) was the most important of the grand opera composers. Because Parisian productions of grand opera tended toward the extravagant, with huge choruses, legions of extras (including animals), and spectacular stage effects, the term eventually took on the general meaning of opera "in the grand manner": big, lavish productions presented in big, lavish opera houses before wealthy and distinguished audiences.

BEL CANTO: Italian for "beautiful singing." Today the term *bel canto* is most often associated with certain early-nineteenth-century Italian operas and with the florid, virtuoso singing style they require. Gioacchino Rossini (1792–1868), Vincenzo Bellini (1801–1835), and Gaetano Donizetti (1797–1848) are three of the most famous composers of bel canto opera. The term was first used, however, to describe the astonishing vocal technique of the castrati, the great singers of Italian opera in the 1600s and 1700s, and is still properly used as a generic term. The essence of bel canto is a seeming effortlessness, a vocal technique that permits great range, power, and virtuosity along with a fundamental beauty and purity of sound.

VERISMO: Italian for "verism," a kind of realism. *Verismo* is the name of a late-nineteenth-century artistic movement that promoted the importance of portraying the events of everyday life, and of portraying them in an absolutely truthful and realistic way even when that meant focusing on the violent, ugly, or vulgar. The term usually refers, however, to the highly melodramatic and colorful operatic style that's based on the principles of that movement. The two most famous examples of verismo are *Cavalleria Rusticana* (1890) by Pietro Mascagni (1863–1945) and *Pagliacci* (1892) by Ruggiero Leoncavallo (1858–1919). Giacomo Puccini (1858–1924), who composed the operas *La Bohème, Tosca, Madama Butterfly,* and *Turandot,* among others, was strongly influenced by the movement, but his work is too lyrical, sensual, and sentimental to be considered pure verismo.

꘏

Among the greatest of history's great composers, there are two who restricted their creative efforts almost entirely to opera: Richard Wagner and Giuseppe Verdi (1813–1901). There are also two who *never* wrote an opera — Johann Sebastian Bach and Johannes Brahms — and two who tried but weren't very successful — Franz Schubert and Robert Schumann. Some great opera composers were also highly successful in other forms: Mozart is by far the best and most illustrious example, but others include Hector Berlioz, Peter Ilyich Tchaikovsky (1840–1893), Richard Strauss (1864–1949), Alban Berg (1885–1935), and Benjamin Britten (1913–1976). Ludwig van Beethoven (1770–1827) wrote just one opera, *Fidelio.*

OPERETTA

Operetta is light opera. Its goal is to amuse: to be witty, charming, funny, not serious either in style or substance. Operetta makes liberal use of spoken dialogue and eye-catching dance numbers, and its musical material is generally of an appealing, tuneful, uncomplicated nature. Attempts at profound emotional expression or multidimensional characterization are beside the point: we're not particularly expected to believe in operetta characters, or to identify with them. Along with lots of sentimental romance, operetta may involve varying amounts of parody, social satire, or farce, but mainly it should be fun.

The greatest composers of operetta were Jacques Offenbach (1819–1880), in Paris, Johann Strauss, Jr. (1825–1899), in Vienna, and Sir Arthur Sullivan (1842–1900), in London. Offenbach, the composer of *Orphée aux enfers* (*Orpheus in the Underworld,* 1858) and *La Belle Hélène* (1864), was the father of the form (which had its roots in the earlier French opéra-comique), and his operettas strongly influenced the works of Strauss. Strauss, "the Waltz King," incorporated waltzes and marches into his operettas, and it's because of such Strauss pieces as *Die Fledermaus* (*The Bat,* 1874) and *Der Zigeunerbaron* (*The Gypsy Baron,* 1885) that the Viennese operetta became an internationally popular form. Between 1871 and 1896, Sullivan wrote the music and W. S. Gilbert the words for thirteen of the most famous operettas in English, including *H.M.S. Pinafore* (1878), *The Pirates of Penzance* (1879), and *The Mikado* (1885). In the United States, Victor Herbert (1859–1924), the composer of *Naughty Marietta* (1910), was the most important operetta composer.

The modern descendant of operetta is the musical comedy, or musical, a form that rose to prominence in this country in the 1920s and 1930s.

[See OPERA.]

OPUS NUMBER

Opus is the Latin word for "work," as in "a work for violin and orchestra." Opus numbers are numbers assigned to a composer's works to indicate their chronological order, although they often reflect the order of publication rather than the exact order of composition. They are always written with the abbreviation *Op.,* or *op.,* plus a number, and are often included as part of a work's title, as in, "Sonata for viola and piano, Op. 147." Sometimes a group of related pieces is published as a set with one opus num-

ber, in which case each piece in the set is given an additional iden-
tifying number. Beethoven's Op. 59, No. 3, for example, is the
third of three string quartets published as Op. 59. His Op. 1 consists of three trios for piano, violin, and cello, and Op. 18 includes
Nos. 1 through 6, all string quartets, of which No. 3 was actually
composed first.

Sometimes composers assign opus numbers to their own
works, and sometimes their publishers do it for them. In certain
celebrated cases, the task has been accomplished by cataloguers
working long after the composer's death. The works of Mozart,
for example, all bear Köchel numbers — K. 219, K. 364, K. 563,
K. 622, and so on — named for Ludwig Köchel (1800–1877), a
wealthy Austrian lawyer, botanist, and mineralogist who spent his
retirement years compiling the first chronological catalogue of
Mozart's music. Köchel's catalogue has been revised several times
by other scholars, but it still serves as the standard. The works of
Franz Schubert all have D. numbers, or "Deutsch listings," from
the chronological catalogue compiled by the Viennese scholar
Otto Erich Deutsch (1883–1967), and Johann Sebastian Bach's
works have BWV numbers, also called "Schmieder listings." *BWV*
is the abbreviation for *Bach-Werke-Verzeichnis* (catalogue of Bach's
works), which is itself an abbreviated version of the title of
the catalogue edited by the Leipzig musicologist Wolfgang
Schmieder and published in 1950. (Schmieder organized the
works by *category*, however; the numbers do not indicate chronological order.) Complete and accurate catalogues of composers'
works are especially important for the study of stylistic development and contemporary influences, and the rigorous scholarly
process of compiling such catalogues often leads to the discovery
of previously unknown works and the uncovering of fakes or mis-
taken attributions.

Mozart started keeping a personal catalogue of his pieces in
1784, almost eight years before he died, but Beethoven was the
first major composer to assign opus numbers to his own works in
a serious, systematic way. Many important composers in the 1800s
followed suit. In the twentieth century, a number of major com-

posers, including Jean Sibelius, Arnold Schoenberg, Alban Berg, Sergei Prokofiev, Paul Hindemith, Dmitri Shostakovich, Samuel Barber, and Benjamin Britten, have used opus numbers, while many others have been content to keep track of their works simply by title and date of composition.

ORATORIO

An oratorio is a large-scale composition for vocal soloists, chorus, and orchestra. Oratorio texts are usually religious narratives, often drawn from the Bible, but oratorios are works intended for concert performance, not religious observance. They're also concert works in the sense that they're not staged: they're performed without scenery, costumes, or acting.

The oratorio is a musical form with the unusual distinction of being named for a building. In the 1550s in Rome, a priest named Filippo Neri (later to become *Saint* Filippo Neri) initiated a series of religious gatherings that included readings, discussions, sermons, and, to attract more participants, performances of sacred stories with music. His musical meetings became so popular that he had to build a special prayer hall, called an *oratorio* (from the Latin *oratio*, "prayer"), to accommodate his followers, who subsequently became known as *oratoriani*. Neri and the oratoriani were recognized by the Pope as a separate religious order, the Congregation of the Oratorio, and their influence spread throughout Italy and the rest of Europe. The sacred stories with music continued to evolve, growing more elaborate and sophisticated and developing into a new musical form, which eventually became known by the name of its first home.

Along with opera and the cantata, the oratorio is one of three important vocal forms to develop in Italy during the Baroque period (ca. 1600–1750) [see CANTATA; OPERA]. The relationship between Italian Baroque opera and oratorio was particularly close. The subjects and often the language were different — many oratorios were in Latin, as opposed to Italian — and oratorios weren't staged, but the musical styles and compositional techniques were the same, and both forms were made up of the same ingredients: recitatives, arias, duets, and choruses, all with instrumental accompaniment [see ARIA; RECITATIVE]. (Italian cantatas of the period also included recitatives and arias, but rarely duets or choruses.) If there was one important musical difference — and it's a difference that has remained between the two forms to this day — it was that the role of the chorus was generally more prominent and elaborate in oratorio than in opera. Most of Italy's important composers of oratorio, including Giacomo Carissimi (1605–1674), Alessandro Stradella (1642–1682), Alessandro Scarlatti (1660–1725), and Antonio Caldara (1670–1736), were equally well known for their operas.

Heinrich Schütz (1585–1672) was the first important composer of German oratorio, and Johann Sebastian Bach (1685–1750) followed in Schütz's footsteps a century later with his *Christmas Oratorio,* and with his *St. Matthew Passion* and *St. John Passion,* which are essentially oratorios by another name. (The Passion is the story of Jesus' suffering and crucifixion. *Passion* is also the name for a musical setting of that story.)

The greatest figure in the history of oratorio, however, was George Frideric Handel (1685–1759), who combined dramatic and religious elements in his music with matchless skill, and who set unsurpassed standards for choral writing. Handel was born in Germany and received a good German musical education, but he also lived in Italy for several years and became a master of the style and techniques of the Italian Baroque. At the age of twenty-seven, he settled in London, and, during his first two decades there, devoted himself primarily to writing and producing Italian operas. Eventually, though, his Italian works lost their commercial viability, especially after the huge success, in 1728, of John Gay's *The Beggar's Opera.* Gay's smash hit was in English and was filled with popular tunes and familiar London characters, and it made fun of the seemingly artificial conventions of Italian opera. Handel's response was to turn to English himself, and in particular to the colorful and dramatic stories of the Old Testament,

King James Version. These were stories that Handel's middle-class Protestant public knew well — and to which his own flair for rendering drama in music were perfectly suited. Weaving together Italian and German traditions, and having assimilated as well the influence of the French and the English, Handel created a new form — the English oratorio. His first English oratorio was *Esther,* followed by *Deborah, Saul, Israel in Egypt, Messiah, Judas Maccabaeus,* and *Jephtha,* among many others. *Messiah* is a true phenomenon in the history of music. A tremendous success from its first performance in 1742, it has never gone out of fashion, and its astounding popularity is such that if Handel had written nothing else before or after, his undying fame would still be assured. Interestingly, *Messiah* is very atypical for Handel — and for oratorios in general — in that it does not tell a story.

Handel's style very much influenced two later composers, Joseph Haydn (1732–1809) and Felix Mendelssohn (1809–1847). Haydn wrote several major oratorios, including *The Seven Last Words of Our Savior on the Cross, The Creation,* and *The Seasons* (a secular oratorio), and Mendelssohn contributed *St. Paul* and *Elijah. L'Enfance du Christ (The Childhood of Christ)* by Hector Berlioz (1803–1869) and *A German Requiem* by Johannes Brahms (1833–1897) are often considered the most important oratorios of the second half of the nineteenth century. (The Brahms Requiem is considered an oratorio because it's a setting of biblical texts of the composer's choosing, not a setting of the texts of the traditional Roman Catholic Requiem Mass. See MASS.) Important twentieth-century oratorios include *The Dream of Gerontius,* by Sir Edward Elgar (1857–1934), *Le Roi David (King David),* by Arthur Honegger (1892–1955), *Oedipus Rex,* by Igor Stravinsky (1882–1971), *Belshazzar's Feast,* by Sir William Walton (1902–1983), and *Passion According to St. Luke,* by Krzysztof Penderecki (b. 1933).

A word about the spelling and pronunciation of Handel's name: the original spelling was Georg Friederich Händel, with the family name pronounced "Hendle" in German. After he settled in England, Handel spelled his name George Frideric Handel. Inasmuch as he became a naturalized Englishman — and lived in England far longer than he had ever lived in Germany — it's entirely appropriate to refer to him by the English version of his name and to pronounce his last name "Handle."

ORCHESTRA

A full-sized modern orchestra consists of more than one hundred musicians usually playing anywhere from eighteen to twenty-five different kinds of instruments. The instruments are divided into four overall "sections": the strings, woodwinds, brass, and percussion. Within these sections there are groups of instruments that are also called "sections": the viola section is part of the string section, for example, and the trumpet section is part of the brass section. Here is how the sections break down, with the standard number of players per section:

I.	Strings	64–68
	1. Violins	32–34
	a. First violins	16–18
	b. Second violins	16
	2. Violas	12
	3. Cellos	12
	4. Double basses	8–10
II.	Woodwinds (sometimes just called Winds)	16
	1. Flutes	4
	(One section member specializes in piccolo.)	
	2. Oboes	4
	(One section member specializes in English horn.)	
	3. Clarinets	4
	(One section member also plays bass clarinet, and one plays a higher-voiced instrument called an E-flat clarinet.)	

4. Bassoons   4
(One section member specializes in
contrabassoon.)

III. Brass   14–15
  1. French horns   5–6
  2. Trumpets   4
  3. Trombones   4
   (One section member specializes in
   bass trombone.)
  4. Tuba   1

IV. Percussion   4
  1. Timpani   1
  2. Other percussion instruments   3
   (These include such instruments as snare drum,
   bass drum, triangle, cymbals, glockenspiel,
   chimes, xylophone, celesta, and tam-tam.)
  Also:
  Harp   1–2
  Piano (used occasionally)   1

Other instruments, such as the saxophone and the guitar, are
added on the rare occasions they're needed. And among the regular members of an orchestra, not everybody plays all the time: for
any one piece, the kinds and (especially in the case of the woodwinds and brass) numbers of instruments on stage depend on
what the composer has specifically called for in the music. [See
STRINGED INSTRUMENTS; WOODWIND INSTRUMENTS; BRASS
INSTRUMENTS; PERCUSSION INSTRUMENTS.]

Because most orchestra members play sitting down, a person's
position in an orchestra is called a "chair." (Percussion players
stand, and double bass players support themselves with special tall
stools or chairs.) The player who occupies the "first chair" in a section is called the "principal" of that section. The first-chair oboist
is called the "principal oboe" (or "principal oboist"), for example,

and the first-chair cellist is called the "principal cello" (or "principal cellist"). The first-chair player of the first violin section, however, is called the "concertmaster," and has special responsibilities [see CONCERTMASTER]. In general, the responsibilities of the principal players include playing the orchestral solos that are written for their instrument, setting the style and tone for their section, and leading their section by setting high standards of beauty, accuracy, and rhythmic reliability. In each string section, all the players, including the principal, generally play the same part. They play the same notes, in other words [see PART]. Composers usually write *different* parts for each woodwind, brass, and percussion instrument, with the parts for the principal players being the most prominent. A piece with four French horns, for example, will generally have separate parts called "first horn" (played by the principal French horn), "second horn," "third horn," and "fourth horn." Second horn, third horn, and fourth horn are also the names of the positions, or chairs, of the people who play those parts [see SECOND VIOLIN].

Because they play separate parts, the woodwind, brass, and percussion players all need separate music stands, too, while the string players sit two-to-a-stand. In the string sections, it's the job of the person on the "inside" chair of the stand — the chair farther from the audience — to turn the pages of the music. In the old days in professional orchestras, and as recently as fifteen to twenty years ago in this country, the seating arrangement in each string section was fixed, and constituted a rigid hierarchy. The front of the section was better than the back, and an outside chair was "higher" than an inside chair. In theory, the hierarchy was based on skill or accomplishment, but in practice it was often a matter of seniority. Nowadays, in the interest of equity and morale, many professional orchestras use rotating seating plans for the string sections, with only the first two or three positions in each section fixed.

Musicians get their jobs in most professional orchestras through a competitive audition process. Major American orchestras announce their openings by placing advertisements in *The*

International Musician, the official monthly news organ of the American Federation of Musicians, the musicians' national union. Each orchestra announces openings by specific position, such as principal trumpet, second horn, assistant principal viola, or "section cello" (member of the cello section, but not principal or assistant principal). Musicians send résumés, and sometimes tapes, as part of an initial screening process, and if accepted they then audition in person. Anywhere from a dozen to two hundred people may show up for an audition, depending on the orchestra and the opening. There are usually at least two stages in the audition process: preliminaries and finals. Preliminary auditions take place before a committee of orchestra members, often with a screen separating the committee and the candidate to preserve the candidate's anonymity and reduce the opportunities for favoritism. Only the most highly qualified candidates pass on to the finals. For the finals, the music director (conductor) joins the audition committee. He or she may consult with the committee, but in most orchestras the music director has complete and final authority to choose the winner of the audition — or to decide that none of the candidates is acceptable. Once a musician joins an orchestra, there is usually a one-year probationary period, at the end of which he can be retained or dismissed at the music director's discretion. If the musician is asked to remain in the orchestra, his position is then considered tenured. Music directors may still dismiss players after they're tenured, but in orchestras with strong union contracts there are strict dismissal procedures, which usually include official warnings, opportunities to demonstrate improvement, and appeals to a committee of orchestra members.

Is there a difference between an orchestra that calls itself a "philharmonic" orchestra and one that calls itself a "symphony" orchestra? No. They're exactly the same kind of orchestra; they have the same makeup and they play the same kinds of music. (Both words have Greek roots, too: *philharmonic* is from the Greek word for "music-loving," and *symphony* is from the word for "sounding together.") The only difference is that *symphony orchestra* can also be used as a generic term, while *philharmonic orchestra* only occurs as part of a proper name. It's correct to say that the Los Angeles Philharmonic Orchestra is a symphony orchestra, for example, but you wouldn't say that the National Symphony Orchestra is a "philharmonic orchestra." Basically, orchestras pick their names because they like the way they sound, and some orchestras, like the Cleveland Orchestra and the Philadelphia Orchestra, have avoided the "Symphony" versus "Philharmonic" issue completely.

↬

The first instrumental groups that could be called orchestras were assembled for Italian opera in the early 1600s, but throughout the Baroque period (ca. 1600–1750) the makeup of orchestras, whether for opera or for purely instrumental music, varied widely. In any particular city, or for any particular occasion, the size and constitution of the orchestra usually depended on the forces — and the money — available. Baroque composers often didn't even specify which instruments, or how many, would be required to perform their pieces.

By the mid-eighteenth century, orchestral instrumentation had become standardized to a great extent, partly as a result of the example set by the famous orchestra of Mannheim, Germany. The Mannheim Orchestra, reputed to be the best in all of Europe, normally consisted of strings — first and second violins, violas, cellos, and double basses — and two each of flutes, oboes, bassoons, French horns, and trumpets, along with two timpani. This formation, which was enlarged later in the century by the addition of clarinets, became the foundation for the modern orchestra. The total number of players, especially string players, in eighteenth-century orchestras was usually much smaller than what's typical today, but as in earlier times, this was not always a matter of choice. There's evidence, in fact, that eighteenth-century composers were very happy with big orchestras when they could get them. In April 1781, for example, Mozart wrote a letter to his father telling of a recent performance of one of his symphonies. The orchestra, especially for those days, had been huge — forty violins, ten violas, eight cellos, ten double basses,

and twice the normal number of winds (including six bassoons) —
and Mozart described the performance as "*magnifique.*"

The nineteenth century, the era of Romanticism, saw an
enormous expansion in the forces of the orchestra, and it was
Ludwig van Beethoven (1770–1827) who set the process of expansion in motion [see ROMANTICISM]. Before Beethoven, composers had used the trombone, for example, mainly in opera,
usually reserving it for special or "supernatural" effects. Beethoven
included trombones in his Fifth, Sixth, and Ninth symphonies. In
the Ninth Symphony, he also augmented the standard orchestra
with triangle, cymbals, bass drum, piccolo, and an early form of
the contrabassoon, and he called for four French horns instead
of the usual two. He also used the contrabassoon in the Fifth
Symphony, and the piccolo in the Fifth and Sixth. Other instruments that joined the orchestra in the nineteenth century, after
Beethoven's time, include the harp, the tuba, the English horn,
the bass clarinet, the modern contrabassoon, the bass trombone,
and the E-flat clarinet. Among the Romantic composers for
whom better definitely meant bigger — especially when it came
to the woodwind, brass, and percussion sections — were Hector
Berlioz (1803–1869), Richard Wagner (1813–1883), Anton Bruckner (1824–1896), Gustav Mahler (1860–1911), and Richard Strauss
(1864–1949). Berlioz and Wagner, especially, were truly revolutionary figures in the history of orchestration [see ORCHESTRA-
TION].

⤴

CHAMBER ORCHESTRA: A chamber orchestra is a small
orchestra, usually consisting of twenty to forty players. Like larger
orchestras, chamber orchestras are usually led by a conductor.
The term itself is a twentieth-century invention, and the first
pieces specifically written for chamber orchestra were by such
composers as Béla Bartók (1881–1945), Igor Stravinsky (1882–1971),
and Paul Hindemith (1895–1963). Many composers, including
Bartók, Stravinsky, and Hindemith, have written both for large
orchestra and for chamber orchestra.

[See CONDUCTOR.]

At any moment, an orchestra has a particular sound that is determined by the instruments and combinations of instruments that are playing and by the kinds of musical material they are playing. Orchestration is the art of designing that sound; it's the *composer's* art of distributing the musical material of a composition among the various instruments and instrumental sections of the orchestra to produce desired effects.

Like all arts, the art of orchestration is built on a foundation of craft. Through a combination of training and experience, a composer must know how to write for all the instruments of the orchestra. He or she must know the technical capabilities of the instruments — their range of notes, how fast they can play, how loud or soft, how long they can sustain notes — as well as how they sound in each part of their range, how they sound with mutes, how they sound playing different kinds of material, and how they sound in any number of different combinations [see MUTE].

The reason orchestration is indeed an art, however, is that it involves creativity and imagination. With an infinite range of possibilities from which to choose, a composer must be able to imagine sounds in his head, imagining at the same time the instrumental combinations that will create those sounds. Often music is born in a composer's imagination complete with orchestration — the orchestration is as much a part of the original idea as the melody, harmony, or rhythm. Sometimes an idea starts out in a more abstract form and the composer must choose an orchestral "color." Will a certain theme sound more beautiful, for example — or more dramatic, or powerful, or tender — played by the oboes or by the trumpets? Or by one oboe or one trumpet, or an oboe and a trumpet together? Never mind oboes and trumpets, why not give the theme to a single clarinet plus the cello section? And meanwhile what will the violas and flutes be doing? Some composers write at the piano and "orchestrate" the music later, but even in those cases, orchestral colors are usually part of the original conception to some degree.

Hector Berlioz (1803–1869), Richard Wagner (1813–1883), Richard Strauss (1864–1949), Nikolay Rimsky-Korsakov (1844–1908), and Maurice Ravel (1875–1937) are among the composers who are commonly referred to as "masters" of orchestration. What these men had in common, along with a complete mastery of the craft, was the ability to create wonderfully varied and inventive orchestral colors and sounds, ranging from the gentlest to the most powerful and often complete with brilliant or startling instrumental effects. Berlioz, Wagner, and Strauss, in particular, were also innovative in the matter of size: they wrote music that demanded not just highly skilled orchestras but *huge* orchestras. Good orchestration, however, does not have to be flamboyant, dazzling, or overpowering, as long as it's imaginative and effective. Mozart, Beethoven, and Brahms were also wonderful orchestrators, not because their orchestration is in some way overwhelming — although it doesn't lack for power, when necessary — but because it is highly personal and persuasive, perfectly tailored to the expressive purposes of their music. Like anything that is done with great artistry, it always seems just right, as if it couldn't possibly have been done differently.

The word *orchestration* is also used to refer to an arrangement for orchestra of a piece originally written in a different form [see ARRANGEMENT].

ORGAN

It was none other than Mozart who first declared the organ the "king of instruments." He was most likely swayed, as so many others have been, by the immensity and nobility of the organ's sound, and by the tremendous variety of sounds the instrument can produce. Mozart was also certainly aware of the organ's long history, and of its leading role in the development of such important musical forms as the fantasy, the prelude, the toccata, and the fugue [see FANTASY; PRELUDE; TOCCATA; FUGUE].

The organ is a hybrid, a combination wind instrument and keyboard instrument. It's a wind instrument because it produces

sound by means of air vibrating in pipes. And it produces different notes (that is, notes of different pitch) by setting the air vibrating in pipes of different lengths: the longer the pipe, the
longer the vibrating air column and the lower the pitch. The
shorter the pipe, the higher the pitch [see WIND INSTRUMENTS;
PITCH]. The pipes of an organ sit on a "wind chest." There are
various types of organs, but they all have some mechanism to
force air at steady pressure into the wind chest and from the chest
into the bottoms of the pipes. To play the instrument, the organist
uses keyboards and pedals. The pedals are like an extra set of keys,
but played with the feet. (Their function is not in any way related
to that of piano pedals.) In fact the keys and pedals are really just
one end of a system of valves that open and close the pipes at the
bottom, allowing forced air in or shutting it out.

But what about the "tremendous variety of sounds" an organ
can produce? On a piano, the way the player depresses the keys
(the "touch") determines the quality of the sound. But on an
organ, this is not the case: the function of the keys is strictly to
control which pipes will be opened. With certain minor exceptions (and no exceptions in the case of organ keyboards that operate electrically), the touch has nothing to do with how the notes
will sound.

The "how" is determined by the pipes themselves. Variations
in the materials, shape, and functional design of organ pipes can
produce effects ranging from subtle gradations of tone color to
drastic differences in volume and character of sound. The reason
the organ offers such a remarkable panoply of sounds is that many
different types of pipes can be used — separately or simultaneously — to play the same notes.

Most organ pipes are metal, some are wood. They range from
the size of a pencil to monsters that are thirty-two feet (or even
sixty-four feet) long and a foot and a half to two feet in diameter.
The pipes are organized in sets of similar type and sound quality
called "ranks," with most ranks encompassing the entire range of
notes on the keyboard, one pipe per note. (Some ranks cover only
the notes played by the pedals.) Most organ keyboards span sixty-

one notes, and a large organ may have as many as fifty, seventy-five, or one hundred or more separate ranks. The result? *Lots* of pipes.

To give a simplified example: if an organ has eighty ranks of pipes and a keyboard span of sixty-one notes, and if each rank covers the entire keyboard span, that organ will have almost five thousand pipes. Four thousand eight hundred eighty, to be exact, or 80 × 61, not counting the pedal ranks. Some very large organs have as many as ten thousand pipes, or even twelve thousand.

In fact, everything about the organ has to be simplified to discuss at anything less than book length, because the instrument is so complicated. Also, although there are certain conventions in organ building and certain general types (based on the nature of the keyboard/valve systems), there is no such thing as a standard organ. The organ builder — in consultation with the client and after considering such factors as the size, acoustics, and design of the church or concert hall for which the instrument is intended — determines the size, shape, pipe arrangement and exterior decoration, interior works and mechanisms, kinds of pipes, number of pipes, and possibilities of combining pipes for each individual organ.

Here are a few important organ terms:

STOP: A stop is a set of pipes. It may consist of one rank of pipes, or it may include multiple ranks. If an organist selects a stop that combines ten ranks of pipes, for example, then depressing any key on the keyboard will open ten pipes (all tuned to the same note) simultaneously. Because the ranks all have different sounds, the stops an organist chooses will determine the organ's sound at any given moment. Stops have names that reflect either what kinds of pipes they're composed of or how they sound. Some of these names are simple, like Flute, or Trumpet, but others are a bit more esoteric: Nazard, for example, or Furniture IV, or Contra Salicional, or Tierce, or Double Open Diapason.

To complicate matters, *stop* is also the name for the knob or other device (mechanical or electric) that controls the flow of air to the set of pipes in a particular stop. A stop controls a stop, in other words, bringing it "on-line" or taking it "off-line" by opening or closing the air passages to its pipes. Stops are arrayed on the organ console, or control board: mechanical stops are usually knobs, and electric stops are usually tabs or buttons. Mechanical stops, which are attached to rods and levers, are pulled out to open stops, and pushed in to close them. The expression "to pull out all the stops" comes from organ terminology, and is believed to have been first associated with Johann Sebastian Bach. Bach was famous in his time not just as a great organist, but also as a great organ tester, and whenever he tried a new organ his practice was to start off by playing with all the stops pulled out, that is, with every rank of pipes on-line at once. (Just to be clear: if an organ had fifty ranks, then for each note Bach played on the keyboard fifty pipes would sound simultaneously. If he played ten notes at once, five hundred pipes would sound.) In this way, he said, he could see what kind of "lungs" an instrument had.

REGISTER: *Register* is another word for the complete set of pipes — one rank or multiple ranks — that makes up one stop. That is, *register* is another word for stop.

REGISTRATION: The registration is the specific set of stops and stop combinations used to play a piece, or passage, of music. Registration is also the art of choosing stops, of knowing which kinds of sounds will work most effectively with a particular piece or passage and which combinations of pipes will produce those sounds. Before the nineteenth century, composers rarely indicated which registrations to use in their compositions. Registration was considered part of the art of the performer, not of the composer, and for the most part was left up to the organist. This attitude changed considerably during the course of the nineteenth century, however, and modern composers tend to be quite fastidious about specifying registrations.

MANUAL: *Manual* is another word for keyboard, but specifically one played with the hands. (The array of pedals is called the "pedal keyboard," and usually covers thirty-two notes.) Most organs have at least two manuals, but there are often as many as four, and sometimes up to seven. Each manual controls a different "division" of the organ, meaning a different group of stops. Manuals can also be "coupled," however, so that one manual's control is extended over other divisions.

BELLOWS: Organs have existed in one form or another for over two thousand years. The earliest organs, those of the ancient Greeks and Romans, used hydraulic pressure — created by water rising and falling in a closed system of tubes and reservoirs — to force air into pipes. Later organs all depended on bellows for their pressurized air supply. Some bellows were operated by hand, some by foot, but either way, the organist himself didn't operate them. Someone else did, or, in the case of large organs with multiple bellows, a whole team of people did. By the turn of the twentieth century, bellows systems had given way to electric blowers, and organists were finally free to play their instruments without assistance.

TRACKER ORGAN: An organ whose keyboard/valve system is mechanical, as opposed to electric. A tracker is a rod, usually of wood, that connects a key or pedal with the valve that opens and closes a pipe. From about the fourteenth century until the age of electricity, all organs were tracker organs. Tracker organs fell out of fashion for a number of decades in the wake of the industrial revolution, but they have made a strong return, and are preferred by many modern organists and organ builders. Perhaps the greatest reason for their renewed popularity is that with "tracker action" there's a direct (mechanical) connection between how fast the keys are depressed and how fast air is allowed into the pipes, which allows the organist somewhat more control of the sound.

ELECTROPNEUMATIC ORGAN: An organ whose keyboard/valve system is operated by a combination of electricity and air pressure. The keyboard functions as a kind of electric switchboard. Depressing a key closes an electric circuit, which activates a magnet, which deflates an air-filled leather pouch, which pulls down a "pallet," or valve, which opens a pipe. When the key is released, the circuit opens, the pouch reinflates, the pallet goes up, and the pipe is closed.

ELECTRIC ORGAN: In some organs, the keyboard/valve

system is strictly electric. The key closes a circuit, which activates a magnet, which pulls a valve directly to open a pipe.

ELECTRONIC ORGAN: A keyboard instrument that sounds like an organ but produces sounds electronically, without pipes. [See KEYBOARD INSTRUMENTS.]

OSTINATO

Ostinato is Italian for "obstinate," and in its most common usage it's short for *basso ostinato,* or "obstinate bass." "Stubbornly repeated bass" would be more to the point, since a basso ostinato is a musical phrase in the bass line (the lowest line) that is repeated over and over, continuously, during the course of a piece or passage. The ostinato itself is not necessarily of any special melodic interest: its primary purpose is to serve as a foundation for all sorts of melodic, harmonic, and rhythmic variations and elaborations taking place in the musical lines above it. The heyday of the basso ostinato as a compositional device was the Baroque era (ca. 1600–1750), and two Baroque forms that often featured ostinatos were the chaconne and the passacaglia [see CHACONNE~PASSACAGLIA].

Basso ostinato is sometimes called "ground bass" in English, and a piece that features a ground bass may be called a "ground." Basso *continuo,* by the way, is a bass of a different stripe, not to be confused with ostinato [see CONTINUO].

OVERTURE

An overture is an orchestral introduction to an opera, oratorio, ballet, play, or other large work. The word itself comes from the French word *ouverture,* which means "opening." It's not an accident that the term is of French origin: the earliest standard form of overture was the "French overture," invented in the mid-1600s by Jean-Baptiste Lully (1632–1687), court composer to Louis XIV of France. Lully — who was actually Italian, but who lived his entire ambitious, power-hungry, greedy, unscrupulous, promiscuous, and brilliantly productive adult life in France — borrowed from the work of earlier Venetian composers to create a type of overture that had two sections. The first section was slow, of a stately or pompous nature, and the second section was fast, featuring the musical style known as "imitative counterpoint," in which several equally important instrumental lines all sound the same melody one after the other, then play off one another, overlapping and interlocking [see COUNTERPOINT~POLYPHONY; FUGUE].

Lully used this form for his ballets, operas, and other dramatic works, and it was soon copied by many other composers. One of these was George Frideric Handel, who favored the French overture even for operas in Italian and oratorios in English. The overture to Handel's oratorio *Messiah*, for example, is a typical French overture.

Toward the very end of the seventeenth century, the Italians got back into the act. Alessandro Scarlatti (1660–1725), in particular, developed a form that became standard for the Italian overture. This form, known as the *sinfonia*, consisted of three separate sections, or movements, in the arrangement fast-slow-fast. By the middle of the eighteenth century, it had completely eclipsed the French overture as the most popular type of opera overture. The sinfonia itself developed in two different directions, however. On the one hand, opera composers had started expanding the first movement and dropping the second two, so that by the end of the eighteenth century the opera overture had become a one-movement form. On the other hand, in their purely instrumental works, various composers had been expanding the whole three-movement structure, and even adding a movement. The offspring of this expansion was none other than the symphony [see SYMPHONY].

It was the composer Christoph Willibald Gluck (1714–1787) who first proposed that the overture should be closely linked, both musically and emotionally, with the opera that follows, and his ideas later found expression in the overtures of Wolfgang

Amadeus Mozart (1756–1791), Ludwig van Beethoven (1770–1827), Carl Maria von Weber (1786–1826), and in the works of virtually all the important opera composers of the nineteenth century. From an entertaining but insignificant curtain raiser, the overture developed into a piece in which composers tried to set the emotional stage for the dramatic action, often borrowing musical material from the body of the opera in order to establish the proper mood or atmosphere. (Mozart's overture to his opera *Don Giovanni* is an excellent example. From the first notes, we know that powerful forces will be unleashed, that something — or somebody, as it turns out — will be cooking before the evening's over.) The overture also developed, especially in the operas of Richard Wagner (1813–1883), into a piece that usually led directly into the action of the opening scene without a pause. Wagner himself abandoned the word *overture* and instead used the title *prelude* (*Vorspiel,* in German) for the orchestral introductions to all his later operas [see PRELUDE].

An interesting and important development of the nineteenth century was the form called the "concert overture." Precursor of the form that Franz Liszt would call the "symphonic poem" [see SYMPHONIC POEM], the concert overture doesn't introduce anything: it's an independent, one-movement piece usually inspired by — and named after — some sort of literary, artistic, or historical idea or scene from nature. Famous concert overtures include the *Hebrides* Overture of Mendelssohn (also called *Fingal's Cave*), the *Corsair* Overture of Berlioz, the *Academic Festival* Overture of Brahms, Rimsky-Korsakov's *Russian Easter* Overture, and Tchaikovsky's *1812* Overture.

Concert overtures are by no means the only overtures that stand on their own, however. Many opera overtures have led long, healthy, independent lives in the concert hall, and in many cases these overtures have far outlived the operas to which they were originally attached. Rossini's *William Tell* provides a perfect example: the opera itself is hardly ever performed now, but the overture is immortal.

[See OPERA; ORATORIO.]

P

PART

A part is the music written for a particular instrument or voice in a piece that includes other instruments or voices. A part is like an individual musical line, woven together with other lines to form the fabric of a composition. One speaks of playing the violin part of a string trio, for instance, or the second violin part of a string quartet, or of singing the soprano part or second tenor part of a choral work. In an orchestra, all the members of each section of stringed instruments usually play the same part: all the violists play the viola part, the cellists play the cello part, and so forth.

Part is also the word commonly used for the written or printed piece of music from which the individual performs. In order for an orchestra's first violins to play the first violin part in a symphony, all the first violin parts must be on the music stands.

[See SECOND VIOLIN.]

PASSACAGLIA

[See CHACONNE~PASSACAGLIA.]

PERCUSSION INSTRUMENTS

Percussion instruments are instruments that are sounded by being struck, shaken, or scraped. The percussion instruments most often played in symphony orchestras are the TIMPANI, SNARE DRUM, BASS DRUM, CYMBALS, TRIANGLE, TAM-TAM (GONG), GLOCKENSPIEL, XYLOPHONE, CELESTA, TAM-

179

BOURINE, and CHIMES (also called TUBULAR BELLS). Percussion instruments fall into two categories. The first category, which includes the timpani, glockenspiel, xylophone, celesta, and chimes, consists of instruments that produce sounds of definite pitch (they produce specific *notes,* in other words). In the second category, which includes the snare drum, bass drum, cymbals, triangle, tam-tam, and tambourine, are instruments that produce sounds of indefinite pitch.

The TIMPANI, also called kettledrums, are the original percussion instruments of the orchestra. Their history can be traced back to ancient times in the Middle East, but they first appeared in Europe in the 1400s, imported from Turkey for use in cavalry bands. They were first played in orchestras in the 1600s, and they've been regularly employed in the orchestra since about 1700. Up until the early nineteenth century, timpani were generally used in pairs, and they were invariably teamed with trumpets to provide festive or martial effects. Each drum usually played just one note: if a piece were in the key of D major, for example, one drum would be tuned to the note D, the *tonic* of the key, and the other would be tuned to A, the *dominant* [see TONIC; DOMINANT]. With Beethoven, however, the timpani came into their own. He liberated them from the trumpets, expanded the range of notes they played, and even wrote distinctive solo passages for them. In the Beethoven Violin Concerto, for example, a timpani solo at the very opening of the piece announces one of the principal musical figures, or motifs, of the first movement. Romantic composers such as Hector Berlioz (1803–1869) and Richard Wagner (1813–1883) expanded the role of the timpani still further and increased the number of timpani in the orchestra as well [see ROMANTICISM]. The Berlioz *Requiem,* which calls for sixteen timpani and ten timpanists, may be an extreme example, but nineteenth- and twentieth-century orchestral compositions regularly require three, four, or even five timpani. Usually the timpani are played by one person.

The "kettle" of a kettledrum is called the "bowl" and is made of copper or brass. The "head" of the drum, the surface that the player strikes, is a piece of Mylar plastic stretched over the rim of the bowl. (Timpani heads were originally made of calfskin. Many players still prefer the sound of calfskin — they feel that calfskin gives a warmer, deeper sound than plastic — but for a variety of practical reasons, including the cost of calfskin and its sensitivity to changes in temperature and humidity, calfskin heads are now rarely used.) Tuning the drum to specific pitches is a matter of adjusting the tension of the head: to raise the pitch, the tension must be increased (the head tightened, in other words), and to lower the pitch, the tension must be lessened. This is accomplished with a pedal mechanism on most modern timpani, although hand screws around the rim are still used for fine adjustments. Timpanists can vary the sound of a drum by using drumsticks with harder or softer heads, and by striking the drum at different distances from the rim. While the heads of the softest sticks are made of sponge and those of the hardest are solid wood, the heads of "normal" timpani sticks are made of hard felt covered with soft felt.

When a percussionist says, "I'm playing bells in this piece," he means he's playing the GLOCKENSPIEL. *Glocke* is the German word for bell, and *Glockenspiel*, translated literally, means "bell-play." The modern orchestral glockenspiel, in use since the mid-1800s, consists of thirty tuned steel bars mounted in a portable case that's set flat on a four-legged stand. The bars are rectangular, and they're laid out in two rows, the arrangement corresponding to the arrangement of the black and white keys of a piano keyboard. The size of each bar determines its pitch — the longer the bar, the lower the note. The heads of the mallets that the player uses to strike the bars are small, round, and hard, and may be made of plastic, rubber, wood, or metal. As with timpani sticks, different materials produce different sounds. In general, the sound of the glockenspiel is bright and penetrating. It can be *extremely* penetrating for orchestra members who happen to be seated right in front of it, especially if the glockenspiel player is using metal mallets.

The XYLOPHONE is built very much like the glockenspiel, but xylophone bars are made of wood, not steel. Orchestral xylophones also have an array of metal tubes set beneath the bars to act as resonators. Camille Saint-Saëns used the xylophone in his *Danse Macabre* (1874) to depict the sound of rattling skeletons, and twelve years later he poked fun at himself by including a xylophone solo in the "Fossils" section of his *Carnival of the Animals.*

Definitive statements about the origins of instruments are rare, since most instruments evolve from earlier forms, with details of the evolutionary stages often lost to history. No uncertainty surrounds the origins of the CELESTA, however. It was invented in Paris in 1886 by a French instrument manufacturer named Auguste Mustel. The celesta (or *céleste* in French, meaning "heavenly one") looks like a very small upright piano, and it has a keyboard like a piano's. It's more closely related to the glockenspiel than to the piano, however, since its keys are connected to hammers that strike steel bars. (Piano hammers strike strings. See KEYBOARD INSTRUMENTS.) On the other hand, the celesta's sound is much softer and more ethereal than that of the glockenspiel. Tchaikovsky, who had heard the new instrument in Paris and found its sound captivating, was the first composer to write for the celesta: the "Dance of the Sugar Plum Fairy" from his ballet *The Nutcracker* (1892) features a prominent celesta part.

CHIMES, also called TUBULAR BELLS, are long, hollow steel tubes usually between an inch and two inches in diameter. A standard set consists of eighteen chimes ranging in length from about three feet to just over five feet. The length of the tube determines the pitch — the longer the tube, the lower the pitch. The chimes hang from a frame, and the player strikes them at the top with heavy, rawhide-covered wooden mallets. (Each chime is fitted with a steel cap that protects the rim of the tube.) Chimes are usually used in orchestral compositions to imitate the sound of church bells.

It was a fad that brought the BASS DRUM, CYMBALS, and TRIANGLE to Europe from Turkey. The fad was for a kind of Turkish military music known as Janissary (or Janizary) music. The Janissaries, personal guard of the Turkish Sultans from the fourteenth century until 1826, when the corps was abolished, were renowned for their bands, which relied on the bass drum, cymbals, triangle, and an instrument called the Turkish crescent for their distinctive sound. (The Turkish crescent is a handheld stick with lots of bells and jingles hanging from crescent-shaped cross-bars.) During the eighteenth century, military bands all over Europe copied the style — and imported the instruments — of the Janissary bands, and by the end of the century European composers had begun to include bass drum, cymbals, and triangle in their orchestral compositions to provide exotic flavor. Mozart used the three instruments in his opera *The Abduction from the Seraglio* (1782) to establish a "Turkish" atmosphere, and Beethoven used them in the finale of his Ninth Symphony (1824) to evoke the sound of a military band on the march.

The **SNARE DRUM** is another instrument with a military background, and military drummers still play it, the instrument strapped to their side as they march. Another name for the snare drum, in fact, is the "side drum." Snare drums have two heads, with the top head, called the "batter head," being the one the player strikes. The "snares" of a snare drum are strings of plastic or twisted wire that run across the center of the bottom head ("snare head") and vibrate furiously against it when the drum is struck. The snares can be disengaged if a softer or duller sound is required.

Snare-drum stroke combinations have colorful names: there's the "flam," for example, and the "drag." The flam produces the sound "ba-*dum*," and the drag produces either "ba-da-*bum*" or "ba-da-ba-*bum*." The longer of the drags is also called a "ruff." A "roll" is an extremely rapid alternation of strokes, and although there's no way for the listener to tell (it happens much too fast to hear or see), a snare drum roll is a not a simple alternation of single strokes, but rather an alternation of *double* strokes — left-left, right-right, left-left, and so on — or even of triple or quadruple strokes. Snare drum sticks are made of hard wood, usually hickory; each stick is a single piece of wood, tapered at the playing end to an oval tip less than half an inch wide.

The familiar **TAMBOURINE** seems to have ancient origins in both the Near East and Far East, but the orchestral gong, called the **TAM-TAM**, is of purely Asian ancestry. (The word *gong* is from Java. *Tam-tam* is Chinese.) A bronze disk anywhere from about two feet to four feet across, the tam-tam can produce soft, mysterious sounds, as well as shatteringly loud sounds. The heavy, soft-headed stick used to strike the tam-tam is called a "beater."

⌣

The principal timpanist of an orchestra, though a thoroughly trained percussionist, usually plays only timpani. The other members of the percussion section, however, must be prepared to play all the percussion instruments, including timpani if necessary, and including such foreign or exotic instruments as the bongos, maracas, and gourds. (The celesta is a separate case: it's considered a percussion instrument, but it's usually played by a pianist, not a percussionist.) In any one piece, a percussionist may be called upon to play several different instruments, which sometimes requires switching very quickly from one instrument to another. There are even times when a percussionist has to play two instruments at once, playing the bass drum with one hand, for example, and a cymbal suspended on a stand with the other. In a piece with multiple instruments and quick changes, percussionists have to make sure that their choreography is right: they have to know in advance which instrument they'll be playing when, they have to plan and practice their moves, and they have to arrange their instruments — and their music stands — in just the right positions.

The percussion section is also responsible for producing orchestral special effects, which may mean playing the wood blocks, rattle, sleigh bells, cowbells, car horn, slide whistle, wind machine, chains, anvil, or any number of other interesting devices.

[See ORCHESTRA.]

PERFECT PITCH

[See ABSOLUTE PITCH.]

[See KEYBOARD INSTRUMENTS; DYNAMICS.]

PICCOLO

[See WOODWIND INSTRUMENTS.]

PITCH

Pitch is the measure of the highness or lowness of a sound or musical tone. Most people have an instinctive understanding of the term and a familiarity with the concept of highness and lowness: a scream is high, or high-pitched, and a growl is low; the meow of a kitten is a higher sound than the roar of a lion; a crow's caw is lower than a canary's tweet.

Pitch, however, is not just a term used for relative measures, for distinctions like "higher" and "lower." It is also an absolute measurement, the indicator of a sound's precise level of highness or lowness along a continuous scale. When something vibrates at a certain frequency, measured in vibrations per second, it generates sound waves, or sound, of that frequency. Precise pitch is determined by frequency: the higher the frequency of the sound — the more vibrations per second — the higher the pitch. A sound that consists of regular vibrations at a specific frequency has a specific pitch, and that pitch is given a name.*

---

* To be more precise: Most sounds or tones are actually composed of tones of a number of different frequencies. The tone of lowest frequency produced by the vibrating medium is usually the strongest. It is called the "fundamental," and it determines the pitch that is perceived. The tones of higher frequency that are also part of the tone — but that can't be detected separately by the ear — are called harmonics, or overtones. Sounds of irregular frequency or of combinations of irregular frequencies are heard as noise.

The names of pitches, or notes, in the American and English system, are the first seven letters of the alphabet — A-B-C-D-E-F-G. (A *note* is a musical sound of specific pitch. A note whose pitch is C, for example, is called a C.) After G, the series starts back again at A and repeats in the next higher octave [see OCTAVE]. The signs for sharp (♯) or flat (♭) are added to indicate notes that are a half step higher or lower [see HALF STEP; SHARP~FLAT]. The "spelling" of notes can sometimes get tricky, however, because for every sharped or flatted note there's another note that's equivalent in pitch but spelled differently. The choice of spelling depends on which of its immediate neighbors a note is being compared to: the note that's a half step higher than a C, for example, is the same note that's a half step lower than a D, thus C♯= D♭.* Here's a quick "spelling chart" for equivalent notes:

A♯ = B♭	D♯ = E♭	G♯ = A♭
B♯ = C	E♯ = F	C♭ = B
C♯ = D♭	F♯ = G♭	F♭ = E

The upshot is that, with spelling taken into account, the total number of different possible notes in an octave is twelve. Here are two possible ways to spell the twelve notes:

A - A♯ - B - C - C♯ - D - D♯ - E - F - F♯ - G - G♯ - (A)
A - B♭ - B - C - D♭ - D - E♭ - E - F - G♭ - G - A♭ - (A)

---

* This description of equivalent pitches is accurate, in the strictest sense, only for the piano and other keyboard instruments, on which small inflections ("bending") of pitch are impossible. On other instruments and in the voice, "equivalent" pitches may actually differ to a very tiny degree, a degree that's barely perceptible. In certain circumstances, for example, a C-sharp might be ever so slightly higher than a D-flat, or a B-flat just a smidgen lower than an A-sharp. The subject is highly technical, having to do with acoustical physics and with the harmonic function of notes — with how notes relate to one another in a chord and how they relate to the notes of other chords in a series.

On the piano, the sharps and flats in these two examples correspond to the black keys, and the notes without sharps or flats correspond to the white keys. [See NOTATION; SCALE.]

The pitch names in the system used by the Italians, French,
and Spanish are:

Do (pronounced "doh")*   C
Re (pronounced "ray")   D
Mi (pronounced "mee")   E
Fa   F
Sol   G
La   A
Si (pronounced "see")   B

Each pitch has its own specific frequency, and the frequency
of any pitch is precisely doubled when it is an octave higher. The
A above middle C on the piano, for example (middle C being the
C that's right in the middle of the keyboard), is generally tuned to
a frequency of 440 vibrations (also called cycles) per second. The
A an octave higher has a frequency of 880 cycles per second, and
the A an octave higher than that, 1,760 cycles per second. The octave relationship is a mysterious one: nobody can explain exactly
why, but when the frequency doubles, the pitch identity somehow
stays the same. That's why the series of seven alphabetical pitch
names is simply repeated for each octave. An A sounds like an A,
a B like a B, and so forth, even when one is in a high range and
the other is in a low range.

Frequencies may be absolute, but pitch is not eternal: pitches
have not always been set at the same frequencies as they are now.
As a matter of fact, standardization of pitch is a relatively recent
phenomenon, dating only to the mid-nineteenth century. Before
that, the "same" pitches varied greatly: the note A, in Paris, might
have been tuned to a very different (frequency) level from the A
in Venice, which was itself different from the A in Florence,

* The French also use the syllable *ut* for *do*.

which in turn was not the same as the A in Rome. Organs in different cities, or even in the same city, were tuned to different pitch levels, which differed from the levels for string and woodwind instruments, which were not the same as the pitch for brass instruments. For the most part (there are exceptions), pitch has risen over the years. The note C during the Baroque period (ca. 1600–1750), for example, might have been as low as the note that today would be called B, or even B-flat — unless it was a C on a brass instrument, in which case it might have sounded considerably higher, perhaps as high as today's D.

A conference in Paris in 1859 established that in France the A above middle C would be set at 435 cycles per second. "A = 435" would be the reference point for tuning pianos, and for tuning the instruments of the orchestra. This pitch was officially adopted as an international standard at a conference in Vienna in 1885. The standard was changed to "A = 440" at an international conference in London in 1939, and it has remained there, although in practice pitch keeps creeping up: many orchestras around the world routinely tune their instruments to an A that is higher than 440 cycles per second.

[See ABSOLUTE PITCH.]

PIZZICATO

Pizzicato is the Italian word for "plucked." To play pizzicato on a stringed instrument (such as the violin, viola, cello, or double bass) means to make the notes sound by plucking the strings with the fingers rather than by using the bow. The word may be used as an adjective, as in "Those notes should be pizzicato"; as an adverb, as in "Those notes should be played pizzicato"; or as a noun, as in the name for the technique itself. The term is not associated with instruments that are *always* plucked, such as the harp and the guitar.

To play pizzicato, the player generally uses the index finger (and sometimes the middle finger or thumb) of the right hand, the hand that holds the bow. For extended pizzicato passages it's sometimes convenient to put down the bow, but usually the player keeps it in his hand while plucking. Pizzicato passages may be fast or slow, loud or soft. In addition, the player can produce different kinds of sounds by varying the specific manner in which he plucks the strings. Plucking with the fingernail, for example, will give a sound that is much harder, or "nastier," than plucking with the fleshy part of the fingertip, and plucking at different points along the string will cause the string to resonate in different ways. A stiff finger versus a flexible finger will also change the sound, and even the direction or manner of follow-through will have an effect.

In the nineteenth century, as part of his ongoing commitment to violinistic R and D — razzle and dazzle — the Italian virtuoso violinist and composer Niccolò Paganini (1782–1840) developed the technique of left-hand pizzicato. This technique requires simultaneous fingering and plucking of notes with the left hand, and usually involves throwing in bowed notes in rapid alternation with those that are plucked. The twentieth-century composer Béla Bartók (1881–1945) was the first composer to call for a "snap" pizzicato, so named because the string is plucked so violently that it snaps back against the fingerboard. A snap pizzicato is sometimes called a "Bartók" pizzicato.

Composers since the Baroque period (ca. 1600–1750) have used pizzicato to provide color and contrast in their works. And they've used it often, whether for gentle accompaniments to arias or instrumental melodies (sometimes in imitation of a guitar or harp), resonant countermelodies or rhythmic punctuations, percussive effects, or flashy displays. In his Fourth Symphony, Peter Ilyich Tchaikovsky (1840–1893) included one movement where the strings play *only* pizzicato for the entire movement, and the effect is extraordinary.

A word on notation: *Pizzicato* is one Italian musical term that is never translated. When a composer wants a note or notes plucked, the universal indication is the abbreviation *pizz.* And how does the performer know when to resume playing with the bow? Again, the Italian indication is universal: *arco,* meaning "bow."

[See COUNTERPOINT~POLYPHONY.]

PRACTICING ~ REHEARSING

"We've got a rehearsal this afternoon, so I'd better do some practicing this morning." The distinction between practicing and rehearsing is that practicing is something you do by yourself, and rehearsing is something you do with others. Take the members of a string quartet, for example: each member practices his or her part individually, but when the four of them get together, they rehearse. [See PART.]

PRELUDE

In ordinary, nonmusical language, a prelude is a preliminary, an introduction, related or connected in some manner to whatever it precedes. That's what a prelude is in music, too . . . sometimes.

In music of the Baroque era (ca. 1600–1750), suites of dances for keyboard instruments, solo stringed instruments, or orchestra often begin with a movement called a prelude [see SUITE]. The prelude of a dance suite is not itself a dance, but is instead a movement in a style of the composer's choosing. Often this style is very "free" — the composer follows his fancy rather than any strict compositional form or procedure. In Baroque keyboard music, pieces called preludes are often attached to fugues, as in the famous preludes and fugues of *The Well-Tempered Clavier*, by Johann Sebastian Bach. *The Well-Tempered Clavier* is divided into two volumes, Book I and Book II, and each volume consists of twenty-four preludes and fugues — one pair for every possible major and minor key. Like the preludes to the dance suites, these "attached" keyboard preludes are composed in a free, almost improvisatory style, and their pairing with the fugues, which are highly structured contrapuntal pieces, exemplifies the important Baroque principle of contrast between freedom and order [see BAROQUE; COUNTERPOINT~POLYPHONY; FUGUE].

Another type of Baroque prelude is the "chorale prelude." A chorale is a Lutheran hymn, and a chorale prelude is a piece for organ based on a chorale tune. Chorale preludes were originally (in the 1600s) short, simple pieces that served as introductions to the chorales sung by the congregation. Later, however, the preludes grew longer and more complex, and they evolved into independent pieces. Bach, who in addition to being a great composer was the foremost organ virtuoso of his time, wrote well over 150 chorale preludes.

In the nineteenth century, *prelude* was one of the many names composers gave to the kinds of short, evocative pieces for solo piano known generically as "character pieces" [see CHARACTER PIECE; ROMANTICISM]. These pieces served no introductory purpose; their goals were purely expressive. The greatest composer of piano preludes was Frédéric Chopin (1810–1849), whose twenty-four preludes, one for every major and minor key, set an extraordinary standard for beauty and variety. Twentieth-century composers continued to find the form appealing. Claude Debussy (1862–1918), for example, also wrote twenty-four preludes (between 1909 and 1913), although he gave them such picturesque titles as "The Girl with the Flaxen Hair," and "Homage to S. Pickwick Esq. P.P.M.P.C." In the early 1930s, the Russian composer Dmitri Shostakovich (1906–1975) joined the twenty-four-prelude club. (Later, in homage to Bach, Shostakovich also wrote a complete set of twenty-four preludes and fugues.) Other important composers of piano preludes include Alexander Scriabin (1872–1915), whose total of eighty-three preludes includes one complete set of twenty-four, Sergei Rachmaninoff (1873–1943), and George Gershwin (1898–1937), whose *Three Preludes* (1926) have always been audience favorites.

Prelude is sometimes used instead of *overture* as the title for the orchestral introduction to an opera or operatic act. (In German, the word for this kind of prelude is *Vorspiel;* in Italian, *preludio.*) Is there a difference between a prelude and an overture? It depends partly on who's using the terms. Nineteenth-century Italian opera composers such as Gaetano Donizetti (1797–1848), Vincenzo Bellini (1801–1835), and Giuseppe Verdi (1813–1901) used the title *prelude* for short introductions, and *overture* for long ones. The preludes to Richard Wagner's operas *Tristan und Isolde* (1847) and *Die Meistersinger von Nürnberg* (1867), on the other hand, are longer than most overtures. Preludes invariably lead right into the opening scenes of operas without coming to a full stop, but many overtures — including several by Mozart — do that, too. Perhaps the most consistent difference is that overtures almost always have a fast, brilliant ending, while preludes usually don't. [See OVERTURE.]

PRIMA DONNA ~ DIVA

Prima donna, Italian for "first lady," refers to the leading lady in an opera, the singer of the principal female role. The terms *seconda donna,* "second lady," and *altra prima donna,* "other first lady," denote singers of lesser female roles. For the men, it's *primo uomo* and *secondo uomo.*

The term *prima donna* has been in use since the 1600s, the earliest days of opera. Originally a simple descriptive term, by the 1700s it was already associated with the artistic and commercial cult of the glamorous leading lady, and with singers who were monumentally demanding egomaniacs (to put it politely). Some prima donnas have demanded to be called *prima donna assoluta,* "absolute leading lady," and some have even had claques, groups of people in the audience paid to cheer them and throw flowers and to boo and hiss other singers. To a certain extent, the clout of prima donnas (and of famous leading men) has influenced the course of music history: big stars have often insisted that the style, and number, of arias in an opera be tailored to their strengths and desires, and many composers have had no choice but to comply.

The stereotype of the impossible prima donna still flourishes in the world of opera, not without reason, although the vast majority of singers (including famous ones) are conscientious musicians and unpretentious people. *Prima donna* is such an evocative term, however, that long ago it made its way into general use as a label for anyone, singer or civilian, male or female, who exhibits the requisite personality traits.

Diva means "goddess" — it's the feminine form of "divine one," in Italian. The term was popularized by nineteenth-century opera impresarios eager to create glorious reputations for their prima donnas. Like *prima donna,* the title *diva* may be used in flattering or less than flattering ways.

PRODIGY

A prodigy is a person whose talents or achievements — in music or in any other area — are so extraordinary as to seem miraculous. The term is most often applied to children.

No one has ever been able to explain why some children demonstrate musical gifts far beyond those of other, even very talented children. Musical families, a musical environment, early and excellent training, hours of practice — all certainly contribute, but a child of six or seven or even ten years of age has simply not lived long enough for prodigious achievement to be the result of hard work and positive influences. And more difficult to explain than fast and accurate fingers is the level of seemingly mature musical expressiveness that many child prodigies achieve.

Interestingly enough, child prodigy performers have not been so very rare in the history of music. Every generation seems to have its famous prodigy, if not several. (The most famous was undoubtedly Wolfgang Amadeus Mozart, who was taken on tour by his father starting just before his sixth birthday, and whose playing at the keyboard and on the violin astonished professional musicians and royal audiences throughout Europe.) And yet the public's interest never ceases: there is an endless fascination with stunning musical feats performed by people who are years away from being able to carry on an adult conversation.

Far more rare than the child prodigy performer is the child prodigy composer. People tend to think of Mozart in this regard, as well, and it's true that he started writing music at the age of four or five. But of the many great pieces on which Mozart's fame as a composer rests, few were written before his twentieth birthday. Felix Mendelssohn (1809–1847), on the other hand, composed works when he was fifteen, sixteen, and seventeen that far surpass the adolescent Mozart's, and that are still considered masterpieces. The Octet for Strings, for example, is a brilliant and profound composition, one of the great works of chamber music, and Mendelssohn was just sixteen when he wrote it. The manuscript of the Octet even has the sweet, very careful, and slightly stiff look of a young person's hand. Another great compositional prodigy was Franz Schubert (1797–1828), who wrote many of his most celebrated songs (in addition to various symphonies, string quartets, and choral works) when he was seventeen and eighteen years old. In this century, the Vienna-born Erich Wolfgang Korngold (1897–1957), later famous as a composer of film scores, was writing music of astonishing complexity and expression by the time he was thirteen.

The rarity of child prodigy composers should probably not be surprising, since the process of creation is even more mysterious than that of interpretation and performance, or of physical accomplishment, precocious or otherwise. From what sources, after all, does a child creator draw inspiration? How can a fifteen- or sixteen-year-old start with a blank sheet of paper and write music that in countless ways stirs the souls of men and women far beyond him in years and life experience?

Program music is instrumental music that attempts to tell a story, render a scene or picture in a realistic way, or convey impressions of a character, place, or event. The "program" of a piece is the story or subject; it may be set out in a preface or accompanying text (prose or poetry), or it may simply be indicated by the piece's title.

For centuries, composers have used music to imitate the sounds of life and nature, real or mythological. Nightingales and grasshoppers; dragons and thunderbolts; angry gods and valiant heroes; crickets, cuckoos, and cannons — since the time of the ancient Greeks, all have found their counterparts in instrumental shrieks, cries, tweets, toots, hiccups, roars, or booms of various kinds. Strictly speaking, however, the presence of this kind of imitation does not, by itself, make a piece "programmatic." The underlying theory of program music, as described by the man who coined the term, the Hungarian composer Franz Liszt (1811–1886), is that the composer must allow the program to determine the actual form of the piece. The introduction and unfolding of the various musical elements, in other words, must reflect the unfolding of the story or the progression of images.

Although Liszt invented the term and applied the theory in a number of his works, particularly in the orchestral pieces he called "symphonic poems," he didn't invent program music. In one form or another, in fact, it had already existed since the 1600s, if not before. The many early examples include such well-known pieces as Antonio Vivaldi's *Four Seasons* (1720s), four violin concertos that are all preceded by a "program" in verse.

The nineteenth century, however — the period of Romanticism in music — is the period during which program music achieved the height of its popularity and prestige, as many composers sought an intimate connection between music and the other arts, including literature and painting [see ROMANTICISM]. Program music wasn't more popular than other kinds of music:

none of the Romantic composers wrote program music exclusively, some went no further than the occasional picturesque title, and some, like Johannes Brahms (1833–1897), wrote virtually no program music. But it was in the air, and among those whose compositions reflected its influence to a greater or lesser degree were Ludwig van Beethoven (1770–1827), Hector Berlioz (1803–1869), Robert Schumann (1810–1856), Bedřich Smetana (1824–1884), Camille Saint-Saëns (1835–1921), Modest Mussorgsky (1839–1881), Peter Ilyich Tchaikovsky (1840–1893), Antonín Dvořák (1841–1904), Nikolay Rimsky-Korsakov (1844–1908), Isaac Albéniz (1860–1909), Claude Debussy (1862–1918), Richard Strauss (1864–1949), Paul Dukas (1865–1935), Alexander Scriabin (1872–1915), Sergei Rachmaninoff (1873–1943), and Manuel de Falla (1876–1946).

Beethoven's Sixth Symphony, the *Pastoral* (1808), is often considered the first great modern programmatic work. Each of its movements bears a descriptive title ("Awakening of happy feelings on arriving in the country"; "Scene by the brook"; "Merry gathering of the country-folk"; "Thunderstorm"; "Shepherd's song — glad and grateful feelings after the storm"), and it also includes fairly realistic depictions of birdcalls. The composer himself, however, was careful to describe the piece as "more expression of feeling than painting." Berlioz, by contrast, provided a detailed program for his *Symphonie Fantastique* (1829), involving an extremely sensitive young musician (guess who), obsessed by love, who poisons himself, hallucinates the murder of his beloved and his own march to the scaffold, and then dreams he is a witness to the "witches' sabbath." The five movements of the symphony depict the various scenes in a manner that sometimes seems quite graphic; in the final movement, for example, Berlioz conjures up the sound of skeletons dancing in a graveyard.

One of the more heated critical and philosophical debates of the nineteenth century was the one between the proponents of program music and those who favored so-called "absolute music," music whose appeal is made in "strictly musical" terms. Nowadays, though, the distinction itself seems a bit artificial, in that music by its very nature must remain abstract: sounds can't convey concrete meaning the way words can. Music can only evoke feelings and stimulate associations, and the same piece of music will inevitably evoke different feelings and associations for each listener.

A work of program music, therefore, no matter how sonically descriptive or how closely tailored to a story line, is always subject to a vast range of interpretations. And by the same token, the very same program is bound to be interpreted differently by different composers. In his symphonic poem (or "tone poem") *Also Sprach Zarathustra* (1896), for example, Richard Strauss, inspired by Friedrich Nietzsche's book of that name, attempts to wrestle in music with a series of philosophical ideas. But are Nietzsche's ideas — or the wit and irony with which he expresses them — actually recognizable in the music? Absent the title, would one have even the faintest idea of what the music was "about"? The music critic James Huneker, writing in 1899, said that if Nietzsche had heard the piece, he probably would have laughed himself crazy. "[It] is Strauss mirroring his own moods after feeding full on Nietzsche," wrote Huneker, "and we must be content to swallow his title, 'Also Sprach Zarathustra,' when in reality it is 'Thus Spake Richard Strauss!'"

It was not Huneker's intention, however, to disparage the work. In fact, he called the music itself "astounding in its scope, handling, and execution." The point is that the value of a work of program music — like that of any composition — lies, ultimately, in its inherent musical qualities and its capacity to move us, not in how accurately it tells a story or paints a picture. The important distinction in music, in other words, is not between "programmatic" and "absolute." It's between compelling and not compelling, good and . . . not so good. If programs have proved inspiring and fruitful for many composers and have provided added levels of interest for audiences, so much the better. But far more powerful than any program is what Joseph Conrad called the "magic suggestiveness" of music. Works like the *Pastoral* Symphony and the *Symphonie Fantastique*, for example, would remain masterpieces even if the words attached to them were to vanish, never to reappear.

[See SYMPHONIC POEM.]

R

RECITATIVE

In many operas, oratorios, and cantatas, there are passages or sections in which the singers seem almost to be speaking, rather than singing. These passages are called recitative (pronounced "ressita*teev*") or recitatives. The purpose of recitative is to convey information that's necessary to advance the story or action, and to do so with perfect clarity. The rhythms in recitative are intended to follow the natural rhythms and flow of speech, and the range of notes is often quite restricted.

As opera developed in Italy in the 1600s and 1700s, recitative (*recitativo*, in Italian, from the verb *recitare*, "to recite") took several different forms:

RECITATIVO ARIOSO: "songlike recitative." The earliest operas consisted almost entirely of this type of recitative, which is a kind of semilyrical, expressive declamation, with very simple and flexible instrumental accompaniment. (Another name for this style of vocal music is *monody*. See MONODY.) Recitativo arioso evolved in two different directions: it is the precursor of both the *recitativo secco*, which is even more like speech, and the aria, which is pure singing [see ARIA].

RECITATIVO SECCO: "dry recitative." Very common in eighteenth-century Italian opera, as well as in the operas of Wolfgang Amadeus Mozart (1756–1791) and Gioacchino Rossini (1792–1868), recitativo secco takes its name from the fact that it's much less melodic and expressive than recitativo arioso. Its usual function is to get a lot said in a very little time between arias, so in addition to being dry it tends to be quite fast, and often features series of rapid-fire repeated notes. The instrumental accompaniment for recitativo secco is also rather dry, usually consisting of nothing more than a harpsichord playing occasional chords, or a harpsichord and cello.

RECITATIVO ACCOMPAGNATO: "accompanied recitative." This is recitative accompanied by the full orchestra playing continuous music, not just chords, and is therefore stricter rhythmically, since the singer has to keep in time with the orchestra. It's much more lyrical and expressive than recitativo secco. In eighteenth-century operas, including those of Mozart, accompanied recitatives often serve as introductions to arias that occur at especially dramatic moments. Most operatic recitative after the early 1800s is accompanied recitative.

In his cantatas and other works with vocal soloists and orchestra, Johann Sebastian Bach (1685–1750) used his own versions of both dry and accompanied recitative, and George Frideric Handel (1685–1759) did the same in his operas and oratorios.

[See OPERA; CANTATA; ORATORIO.]

REED INSTRUMENTS

The reed instruments of the orchestra are found among the woodwinds. They include the members of the clarinet family — clarinet, bass clarinet, and E-flat clarinet, which are *single-reed* instruments — and the members of the oboe and bassoon families — oboe, English horn, bassoon, and contrabassoon — which are *double-reed* instruments. (The saxophone is also a reed instrument — a single-reed.)

A woodwind instrument is really just a long tube. In order for the instrument to produce a sound, something has to make the column of air inside the tube vibrate. On a reed instrument, that something is the reed: the player's breath causes the reed to vibrate, and the vibrating reed causes the column of air to vibrate. On a single-reed instrument, the reed vibrates against a mouthpiece; on a double-reed instrument, the two halves of a slit reed vibrate against each other.

While a reed, strictly defined, is any thin strip of material that can be made to vibrate to produce sound, the reeds for woodwind instruments are always made of *cane* (a generic term for various hard, bamboolike grasses). Not just any cane will do, however. The type of cane used by almost all professional reed players goes by the Latin name *Arundo donax,* and almost all the best *Arundo donax* grows in fields near the small town of Le Lavandou, not far from the city of Toulon, in the south of France.

A double reed is made by folding a narrow strip of cane in half to make the ends meet, tying the ends together with thread, and then slitting the reed in two along the fold. Oboe reeds are only about a quarter-inch wide at the slit end, which is the "double" end the player puts between his or her lips. Bassoon reeds are about a half-inch wide. On double-reed instruments, the reed itself is all that touches the player's lips.

Single reeds, for the clarinet, are single slips of cane about a half-inch wide. Clarinetists use a mouthpiece of hardened rubber or crystal, with a flat slot on one surface to hold the reed. The reed rests on the player's lower lip, and the player's upper lip and upper teeth rest on the upper surface of the mouthpiece.

Professional reed players spend many hours a week making their reeds. Double-reed players usually make them from scratch, while clarinetists usually start with precut blanks, which they buy in quantity and finish individually. Both single reeds and double reeds must be tapered to an almost paper thinness at the playing end, but the exact degree of taper and the precise contour of the edge are very much matters of personal preference. The player uses an extremely sharp knife called a reed knife to scrape the end of the reed into just the configuration he wants. (Many a touring reed player has had to explain — or surrender — his reed knife at airport security checkpoints.)

Why do players spend so much time on their reeds? Two reasons. The first is that the reed bears an enormous influence on the quality of the sound. Depending on the quality and configuration of the reed, an instrument's sound may be darker, brighter, smoother, rougher, harder, or softer, and it may be more or less clear, or "focused." To a great degree, the reed also affects the ease of sound production (the instrument's "response"), and it can even affect accuracy of pitch [see PITCH]. The second reason is that reeds don't last very long. They're sensitive to the slightest changes in temperature, humidity, and altitude, and they easily dry out, swell up, or crack: a reed may sound and feel wonderful one day and prove completely useless the next. Even under perfectly stable atmospheric conditions, reeds simply wear out from normal use. An orchestral clarinetist's reed, for example, might last as long as a month, if the player is very lucky, but it might also last a week, or less. Bassoon reeds last about a week and a half in an orchestra, on average, and oboe reeds usually last only a couple of days. Players often rotate their reeds to preserve them, saving the best ones for concerts and using others for home practice and rehearsals.

[See WOODWIND INSTRUMENTS.]

REGISTER

Register is another word for range. Upper register, middle register, lower register — the terms have to do with pitch, that is, with how high or low notes are, and where they lie on an instrument or in the voice [see PITCH]. A register is more like a general area of notes, though, than a set of strict boundaries. "The violin is playing in its upper register," for example, doesn't tell you the specific notes the violin is playing, it tells you that the notes are high. And registers are relative: a piccolo's upper register is a lot higher than a tuba's. The term can also be used without reference to an instrument or voice, as in, "The melody was repeated, but in a higher register."

Register is also a specific technical term for the complete set of pipes controlled by one stop on an organ [see ORGAN].

For the purposes of music history, the Renaissance is the period from roughly 1430 to 1600. Stretching for centuries before the Renaissance is the medieval era, and following it from about 1600 to 1750 is the Baroque era. As with so many historical designations, the term *Renaissance* was not used by people at the time, but was coined much later.

The Renaissance was the great age of vocal polyphony, music consisting of a number of equally important voice parts all woven together to create a complex tapestry of overlapping melodies and beautiful harmonies. In religious music, the primary compositional forms were the Mass and the motet, while in secular music they were the French *chanson*, or song (for three or four voices), and the Italian madrigal [see COUNTERPOINT~POLYPHONY; MADRIGAL; MASS; MOTET]. Instrumental music was not, for the most part, as formalized during the Renaissance as it would later become. Instruments were used in varying combinations to accompany singers (in both religious and secular music), to provide music for private entertainment and dancing, and to provide festive or ceremonial music for towns and royal courts. Principal instruments of the period included the lute, organ, and harpsichord, viols, recorders, shawms (double-reed precursors of the oboe), crumhorns (also double-reed instruments), trombones, and trumpets [see BRASS INSTRUMENTS; KEYBOARD INSTRUMENTS; LUTE; ORGAN; VIOL; WOODWIND INSTRUMENTS].

Among the most important composers of the Renaissance were Guillaume Dufay (ca. 1400–1474), of the so-called Burgundian school, centered at the court of the dukes of Burgundy in Dijon, France, and Johannes Ockeghem (1430–1495), Jacob Obrecht (ca. 1450–1505), Josquin des Prez (ca. 1450–1521), and, later, Orlando di Lasso (1532–1594) of the Flemish school. The composers of the early Flemish school were the true pioneers and progenitors of the musical Renaissance. They came not from Italy, where so many earlier (and later) musical developments got their start, but from northern France and the Netherlands, including what is now Belgium. They traveled widely, however, occupying many of the most important musical positions at royal courts and chapels all over Europe, and their impact was enormous. Through their musical accomplishments and the influence of their positions, they determined the compositional style that dominated all of European music from the second half of the fifteenth century through the sixteenth century. Important English composers of the Renaissance were John Dunstable (ca. 1380–1453), William Byrd (1543–1623), and John Dowland (1562–1626), while the greatest Italian master — and usually considered the greatest of all composers of sixteenth-century music — was Giovanni Pierluigi da Palestrina (ca. 1525–1594). Tomás Luis de Victoria (1548–1611), a Spaniard who lived many years in Italy, was another giant of the (late) Renaissance, as was the Italian Claudio Monteverdi (1567–1643). Monteverdi was also a musical trailblazer who led the way from the Renaissance into the Baroque era.

REPERTOIRE ~ REPERTORY

The word *repertoire* means the entire collection of works in a particular category. You might say, for example, "*The Marriage of Figaro* is one of the greatest operas in the repertoire," or "Compared to the string quartet repertoire, the repertoire for string trio is quite limited." *Repertoire* may also refer to the specific list of works that a musician or organization knows or performs regularly: "The brilliant young violinist's repertoire includes twenty concertos, dozens of sonatas with piano, and countless other solo and chamber works." In English, as in the original French, the "r" at the end of *repertoire* is pronounced.

The term *standard repertoire* refers to pieces that are performed often, or pieces with which musicians and audiences are likely to be familiar. The Beethoven Violin Concerto is standard repertoire; the symphonies of Ignaz Holzbauer are not. (It's also correct to say that the Beethoven Concerto is *in* the standard repertoire.) Times and tastes change, though, and so does the standard repertoire. In eighteenth-century Germany, Holzbauer was a very important and well-respected composer. It's always interesting to consider why certain pieces have remained in the standard repertoire while others haven't, and to try to predict which currently popular pieces are likely to retain their standing in the future.

Repertory is another word for *repertoire*.

REQUIEM

[See MASS.]

RHYTHM

Music is "spirit, but spirit subject to the measurement of time," wrote the German poet Heinrich Heine. "I got rhythm," wrote George and Ira Gershwin a century later. They were talking about the same thing.

Rhythm is the way music is organized and measured in time. It is the structuring of music according to sounds and silences of varying duration, and the forming of measured sounds and silences into patterns. The patterns fit in a framework of beats, subdivisions of beats, and groups of beats [see BEAT]. We think of music as something that moves. Rhythm is what makes it move; it is the carriage on which music rides through time. And the patterns and combinations of rhythm determine *how* music moves through time, whether it flows or marches or dances, whether it skips or shuffles.

Rhythm is also a generic term used to refer to any measured pattern in either sound or movement. The various combinations of long and short sounds — dots and dashes — that make up the alphabet in Morse code, for example, are all "rhythms," or "rhythmic figures," even though they're not music. Think, too, of the rhythms of speech, the rhythm of the waves, or the rhythm of a horse's gallop.

In musical notation, the different durational values of sounds and silences are indicated by the various kinds of notes and rests — whole notes and whole rests, half notes and half rests, quarter notes and quarter rests, eighth notes and eighth rests, and so on [see NOTATION]. These notes, or note values, can be combined and connected to create an infinite variety of rhythms and rhythmic patterns. Differences in *tempo,* in the speed of music, change the absolute duration of notes but not the relative duration. Changing the tempo, in other words, does not change the rhythm, it just speeds it up or slows it down.

Meter is not the same thing as rhythm, although it falls into rhythm's domain. *Meter* refers specifically to the organization of recurring groups of *beats* into *measures.* A beat and a measure are both units of time, and each can be divided in an infinite number of ways, into any pattern of longer, shorter, or equal note values and silences, into any *rhythm.* Rhythm and meter are not always easy to separate, however, because they exert a mutual influence: certain rhythms can imply certain meters, and certain meters can give rise to characteristic rhythms. [See METER.]

"The body is a rhythm machine," in the words of Mickey Hart, drummer of the rock group the Grateful Dead. We breathe in a rhythm, and our hearts beat in a rhythm. Every physical movement, conscious or unconscious, creates a rhythm, implies a rhythm, or is governed by a rhythm. It comes as no surprise, then, that rhythm is an essential element of all music. There can be rhythm without melody — think of a drumbeat — but no melody without rhythm, without some notes lasting longer than others. Harmony, too, always has a rhythmic component: *when* harmonies change can be as important as the changes themselves. For every moment in a musical composition, the composer must decide which rhythm or rhythmic pattern, in the context of the tempo and in combination with the melody and harmony, will be the most effective, the most persuasive, the most beautiful. The motion of a piece of music, after all, has a lot to do with how moving it will be.

[See DANCE.]

ROMANTICISM

The Romantic period in music history runs roughly from 1820 to 1910. It follows the Classical era, the era of Haydn, Mozart, and (early to middle) Beethoven, and precedes the many and varied developments of the twentieth century.

Musical labeling is a notoriously sticky business, and any label that's supposed to apply to almost a century of music and to dozens of different composers — composers as diverse as Schubert and Sibelius, Berlioz and Puccini, Wagner and Tchaikovsky — is bound to be exceedingly broad, if not completely arbitrary. In some ways, in fact, *Romantic* has simply become a chronological term, a convenient synonym for *nineteenth-century*. There are certain important elements and ideals, nonetheless, that form the foundation of Romanticism in music, and that provide common ground for composers whose styles don't seem, on the surface, particularly similar. They include the following:

✧ The ideal of music as an art intimately linked with and nourished by the other arts, especially poetry and drama, but also painting and philosophy. Hector Berlioz (1803–1869) and Robert Schumann (1810–1856), two great composers who were also excellent (and prolific) writers, were among the early Romantic composers who most clearly articulated — and exemplified — this ideal. That Romanticism came to be closely associated with program music — music inspired by a story, a set of images, or a poetic text — is not an accident [see PROGRAM MUSIC].

✧ Innovation in musical language, especially in the language of harmony. Although there are many more similarities than differences between Classical and Romantic harmony, Romantic composers greatly expanded the harmonic vocabulary of music, using chords, and, especially, sequences of chords unheard of in the Classical era [see HARMONY~CHORD]. There are differences in melodic style, as well. Romantic melodies tend to have a different shape from Classical melodies, with greater leaps in pitch between notes, a wider overall pitch range, and less rhythmic regularity and predictability [see MELODY].

✧ Innovation and experimentation in the realm of instrumental sounds and combinations, and in particular, expansion of the forces of the symphony orchestra. This expansion led eventually to the huge orchestras required for the music of Richard Wagner (1813–1883), Anton Bruckner (1824–1896), Richard Strauss (1864–1949), and Gustav Mahler (1860–1911). In addition to great improvements in the quality and capabilities of wind and brass instruments, the nineteenth century saw the adoption of the trombone, piccolo, triangle, cymbals, bass drum, harp, tuba, bass trombone, English horn, bass clarinet, E-flat clarinet, and contrabassoon as regular members of the orchestra [see ORCHESTRA]. Another major nineteenth-century advance was the development of concert grand pianos powerful enough to be heard against the sonic mass of big orchestras [see KEYBOARD INSTRUMENTS].

✧ A preoccupation with the expression of personal feelings. The idea of expressing personal feelings in music was certainly nothing new. But Classical composers generally expressed themselves eloquently within the bounds of established forms and procedures, while in their search for complete freedom of subjective expression Romantic composers accepted fewer constraints. Questions of form remained extremely important to the Romantics, but their emphasis was on the freedom to expand or revise traditional forms, or to invent new ones to suit their specific expressive purposes.

Among the musical forms developed in the nineteenth century as direct offspring of Romantic ideals and principles are the character piece for piano, the symphonic poem, and the song cycle [see CHARACTER PIECE; SYMPHONIC POEM; SONG CYCLE]. The art song itself, or *Lied,* had earlier roots, but it flowered during the Romantic period, thanks initially to the incomparable efforts of Franz Schubert (1797–1828). With its perfect marriage of music and poetry, it's often considered a typical Romantic form [see ART SONG]. (Schubert's mastery of the art song is also one of the main reasons he's often considered a Romantic composer.)

Ludwig van Beethoven (1770–1827), the last of the great Classical composers, was also the trailblazer of the Romantic movement. He wrote the first song cycle (*An die ferne Geliebte,* "To the Distant Beloved"), the first character pieces (*Bagatelles*), one of the first great programmatic works (the *Pastoral* Symphony), and, perhaps most importantly, he dramatically expanded both the structure and the expressive possibilities of such forms as the symphony, piano sonata, and string quartet.

In addition to those already mentioned, even an abbreviated list of important Romantic composers would include the following names: Niccolò Paganini (1782–1840), Carl Maria von Weber (1786–1826), Felix Mendelssohn (1809–1847), Frédéric Chopin (1810–1849), Franz Liszt (1811–1886), Giuseppe Verdi (1813–1901), Charles Gounod (1818–1893), Clara Schumann (1819–1896), César Franck (1822–1890), Bedřich Smetana (1824–1884), Johannes Brahms (1833–1897), Camille Saint-Saëns (1835–1921), Georges Bizet (1838–1875), Max Bruch (1838–1920), Modest Mussorgsky (1839–1881), Antonín Dvořák (1841–1904), Edvard Grieg (1843–1907), Nikolay Rimsky-Korsakov (1844–1908), Gabriel Fauré (1845–1924), Edward Elgar (1857–1934), Hugo Wolf (1860–1903), Isaac Albéniz (1860–1909), and Sergei Rachmaninoff (1873–1943).

⌒

The romance at the heart of Romanticism is not the boy-meets-girl, candlelight-dinner variety. In the Middle Ages, the *romance* was a literary form, a type of story or poem that described heroic or legendary people and dramatic, even supernatural, events. This is the "romance" from which the word *Romantic* derives, and to which it owes its connotations of unbounded imagination and passion.

RONDO

The rondo is a musical form that was frequently used by Haydn, Mozart, Beethoven, and their contemporaries in the Classical era (ca. 1775–1820) for the final movements of concertos, sonatas, chamber music pieces, and symphonies.

A rondo always starts with a lively or cheerful tune. This tune is called the "rondo," or "rondo theme," and it serves as a refrain, returning again and again throughout the movement. In between the recurrences of the rondo theme are sections called "episodes," which provide changes of pace, mood, or character. Sometimes the episodes include flashy passages, designed to show off the virtuosity of the performer or performers, and usually at least one episode will be of a darker or more serious nature, although not too serious, as there's more melodrama in rondos than real drama. At the end of the movement, the cheerful rondo theme always returns: in Classical times it was still considered important to send the audience home with a smile.

[See FINALE.]

RUBATO

Rubato (from the Italian *rubare,* "to steal") is the shorter and more common version of the term *tempo rubato,* whose literal meaning is "stolen time." In music, the way to "steal time" is to slow down or speed up — to stretch notes out for longer than their indicated value, or to squeeze them together and push ahead. Thus, when a composer marks a passage *rubato* or *tempo rubato,* he is directing the performer to take liberties with the tempo, to be flexible [see TEMPO]. And because stretching or squeezing notes changes their duration relative to other notes, rubato is not just a matter of tempo flexibility, but also of rhythmic flexibility [see RHYTHM]. Rubato is originally an adjective, but it's also used as an adverb, as in "I think this passage should be played rubato," or as a noun, as in "I think this passage calls for more rubato." The opposite of playing (or singing) with rubato is playing strictly "in tempo," or "in time."

Performers use rubato all the time, not just when composers call for it. It's one of the performer's essential tools, in fact, because it provides a way to highlight selected notes or passages and thereby intensify musical expression. Rubato is also indispensable for conveying a sense that a piece of music "breathes." Music is most expressive and most affecting, after all, when it seems to follow natural patterns of tension and relaxation; when the forces behind it seem human, not mechanical. Rubato can be extreme, or extremely subtle, to the point that it's hardly noticeable. But even when a composer does specifically call for rubato, the "how" and "how much" are always the performer's responsibility — a matter of taste, thoughtful consideration, and the inspiration of the moment.

S

SAXOPHONE

[See REED INSTRUMENTS; WOODWIND INSTRUMENTS.]

SCALE

A scale is any series of ascending or descending musical notes. Since notes can follow one another up and down in all sorts of patterns, there are many kinds of scales, but the kind most of us have in mind when we use the term is known technically as the *diatonic* scale. In its two most familiar forms, the *major* scale and the *minor* scale, the diatonic scale has been a fundamental element of Western music since about 1600.

The word *scale* comes from the Latin word for *ladder* (*scala*), and the notes of a scale — also called "scale degrees" — may be thought of as rungs on a ladder. All the rungs are not necessarily the same distance apart, though. Scale degrees are separated by distances in pitch called "intervals," which are the spaces between the rungs. The smallest interval in traditional Western music is a *half step*, also known as a *semitone*. The next larger interval, but still a very small one, is a *whole step* — or *whole tone*, or just *tone* — which is equal to two half steps. A diatonic scale is a ladder with eight rungs and seven spaces, where five of the spaces are always whole steps and two are half steps. Major and minor scales both contain five whole steps and two half steps, but the order of the whole steps and half steps is different: the interval between the second and third degrees in a major scale, for example, is always a whole step, and in a minor scale it's a half step. [See HALF STEP.]

The eight degrees of a diatonic scale cover the span, or interval, known as an octave. From a note to the next higher or lower note of the same name — from A to A, or B-flat to B-flat, for example — is the distance of an octave. In the American and English system of notation, the names used for notes, or *pitches*, are the first seven letters of the alphabet — A-B-C-D-E-F-G. The signs for sharp (♯) or flat (♭) can be added to indicate pitches that are a half step higher or lower. (The note C♯ is a half step higher than C, for example, and B♭ is a half step lower than B.) After the letter G, the series starts back again at A and repeats, in the next higher octave. [See PITCH; OCTAVE.]

A diatonic scale may start on any note. A C-major scale goes from C to C, for instance, and consists of the eight notes, C-D-E-F-G-A-B-C. A D-minor scale consists of the notes D-E-F-G-A-B♭-C-D. Consecutive octave spans of the same scale may be strung together, though, to form two- or three-octave scales or larger, with the pattern of notes and intervals simply repeated in each octave. In such cases the scale is like a set of stairs and landings, with the same pattern of stairs between each landing:

C-D-E-F-G-A-B-*C*-D-E-F-G-A-B-*C*-D-E-F-G-A-B-*C*

and so on

The first note of a scale is called the *tonic*, or key note. It is the note that gives the scale its name. C is the tonic of the C-major and C-minor scales, B-flat is the tonic of the B-flat-major and -minor scales, and so forth [see TONIC]. There are twelve major scales (that is, major scales starting on twelve different notes) and twelve minor scales.

The primary reason that diatonic scales are so important in Western music is that they form the basis for all *keys*, major and minor, and therefore for the whole system known as tonal harmony [see KEY~TONALITY]. In the key of C major, for example, the harmonic "home base" is the harmony, or chord, called C major, which consists of notes drawn from the C-major scale. It's also extremely common for composers to construct melodies or parts of melodies from scales and scale fragments. The relationship between melody and harmony is an intimate one [see HARMONY~CHORD].

↜

After the diatonic scale, the most frequently encountered scale is the *chromatic* scale, which also spans an octave but proceeds entirely by half steps. Because the notes of the chromatic scale are all separated by half steps, they fill in the spaces, so to speak, between those notes of the diatonic scale that are separated by whole steps. A chromatic scale, in other words, necessarily includes more than just the eight notes of the diatonic scale. It includes all the possible notes in an octave, a total of twelve different notes before the starting note is repeated.

To play a chromatic scale on the piano is to play all the keys in an octave, black and white, without skipping any.

↜

Singers warm up their vocal cords by singing scales, and instrumentalists warm up their fingers by playing them. But musicians don't just use scales for warming up — they practice them all the time. Students are assigned scales as exercises almost right from the start, and if the result among the young is not always a love of scales, still the benefits can be great. Practicing scales is important for training the ear and learning to play or sing precisely in tune, for learning to produce an even and beautiful tone, for developing evenness and exactness of rhythm, for developing speed and technical facility, and for maintaining those skills, all of which are essential to good musicianship. Also, because so many compositions include melodic material based on scales and scale patterns, facility with scales often finds very direct applications.

SCHERZO

During the time of Joseph Haydn (1732–1809) and Wolfgang Amadeus Mozart (1756–1791), the third movement of a four-movement work such as a symphony or string quartet was invariably a stylized dance movement called a minuet [see MINUET]. By the end of the eighteenth century, Ludwig van Beethoven (1770–1827), in one of his many important musical innovations, had replaced the minuet with a movement called a "scherzo." The word *scherzo*, which means "joke" in Italian, had appeared in music as early as the 1600s, and Haydn had even applied the term to the minuet movements of several of his string quartets published in 1781. But it was Beethoven who gave the scherzo its modern character and established a permanent place for it.

Like the minuet, the scherzo is usually in three-quarter time [see METER], and also like the minuet it has a contrasting middle section called a "trio" sandwiched between two identical outer sections. The scherzo is generally faster and more energetic than the minuet, however, and far removed from anything resembling a dance, or at least any dance that could be performed in powdered wigs and multiple petticoats. The element of outright humor that you might expect in a musical "joke" is by no means always present in Beethoven's scherzos, but a certain gleam-in-the-eye playfulness — characterized by speed, sparkle, abrupt accents, surprises, and changes of musical direction — usually is.

Composers after Beethoven — such as Franz Schubert (1797–1828), Hector Berlioz (1803–1869), Felix Mendelssohn (1809–1847), Robert Schumann (1810–1856), and later Anton Bruckner (1824–1896), Jean Sibelius (1865–1957), Sergei Prokofiev (1891–1953), and Dmitri Shostakovich (1906–1975) — continued the practice of writing scherzos in their symphonies and other multi-movement works. All of these composers were directly influenced by Beethoven, but each brought his own distinctive touch to the form.

⌒

Frédéric Chopin used the title *scherzo* for four of his character pieces for solo piano, and Johannes Brahms also wrote a scherzo for solo piano [see CHARACTER PIECE]. These are wonderful works, very dramatic and beautiful, but they're not in the least bit playful. The only feature they share with Beethoven-type scherzos is that they have a symmetrical form, with a contrasting middle section analogous to a trio.

SCORE

A score is the written or printed music that shows all the instrumental and/or vocal parts that make up a composition. It includes notes, tempo markings, dynamics, special instructions, and, in the case of a vocal work, text [see DYNAMICS; TEMPO MARKINGS]. "All the parts" may be as few as two, or as many as are heard simultaneously in an opera or symphony [see PART].

How is a score laid out? Very logically, but it can look quite complicated. Music is notated on staves (the plural of *staff*), with each staff being a set of five parallel horizontal lines [see NOTATION]. For musical compositions with more than one part, each part is written on one staff. (Harp parts and parts for keyboard instruments require two staves, one for each hand.) In a score, the staves for the different parts are "stacked" one above the other; each page, therefore, contains a set of parallel staves, and there are as many staves on a page as there are different parts at any one time. For pieces with large and diverse forces, such as big orchestral works, works for chorus and orchestra, or operas, each page of score can get very crowded, with sometimes as many as twenty or thirty parallel staves to a page. (To be clear: there is not a staff for each *player*, but for each *part*. Thus, there is just one staff for the first violin part, even though there may be as many as eighteen or twenty violinists playing it, and only one staff for the soprano part, no matter how many sopranos are in the chorus.) The music is read left to right, and the score continues for as many pages as necessary.

To make sure that all the parts "line up" with one another in time and are visually coordinated on the page, each page of score is also divided by vertical lines, *bar lines,* that run the length of the page straight down through all the staves and divide the music into *measures*. This marking of bar lines through the staves is in fact where the use of the word *score* in music comes from: to score means to notch, or to make a cut or mark. (To "score," in sports, or to "keep score," comes from the same meaning.)

There are certain other conventions about how scores are arranged, one of which is that higher-pitched instruments or voices are usually placed higher on the page than lower-pitched parts. In orchestral scores, the groupings are by instrumental "family": woodwinds on top of the page, and below them, in descending order, brass, percussion, harp and keyboards, soloists (instrumental or vocal), voices, and strings. Within each family, the arrangement is still from top to bottom by pitch, so that in the strings, for example, the violins are at the top and the double basses at the bottom.

Conductors conduct "from the score," and they spend many hours studying scores in order to learn works in detail and formulate their interpretative ideas [see CONDUCTOR]. The individual performers in a multipart piece, on the other hand, whether instrumentalists or singers, rarely use scores to perform. The "full score" for a piece is usually either too big and unwieldy, or inconvenient to read because of the small print size necessary to fit all the parts on the page. More often, performers perform from music that contains just their individual part, using the score only for study or reference purposes. Opera singers, especially, often use what is called a "piano score," or "piano-vocal score," which contains the vocal part plus a version of the orchestral score reduced to two staves, playable on the piano. (An exception: in chamber music pieces with piano, the pianist always plays from a full score, but the piano part itself is printed in regular size in the score, while the other parts, which are printed above the piano part, are much reduced.)

The word *score* can also refer to the music itself, as in, "Erich Korngold wrote the score for the film *Captain Blood*," or "Did you hear that piece? What a beautiful score!"

SECOND VIOLIN

The term *second violin* may refer to a part, section, or position.

The second violin part in a musical composition such as a string quartet or symphony is an individual musical line that forms part of the fabric of the composition [see PART]. To the question, "What part are you playing in that piece?" a violinist might answer, "I'm playing the second violin part." In a string quartet, one person plays the second violin part, while in an orchestra, all the members of the second violin section (as many as sixteen people) play it. The second violin part of a piece is usually less prominent than the first violin part; often it provides an accompaniment while the first violin part carries the melody. In printed scores of pieces with two violin parts, the parts are written on separate lines and are designated Violin I and Violin II, with the first violin part above the second violin part on the page [see INNER VOICES; SCORE].

A person playing a second violin part might also say, "I'm playing second violin," or, in common abbreviated form, "I'm playing second." In this sense, "second violin" describes not just a part, but also a position in a group, just as "second base" describes a position on a baseball team. When referring to the entire second violin section of an orchestra, musicians often say "the second violins," or "the seconds." In a string quartet, the person who plays the second violin part is usually called the "second violinist."

The term *second violin* does not, however, refer to an instrument that's somehow different from a "first violin." A violin is a violin. And although the term *second fiddle* [see FIDDLE] has become a synonym for any subordinate or less important role, it's a mistake to think that someone playing second violin in a chamber music group or orchestra is necessarily a less accomplished violinist than someone who plays first. While the second violin part of any particular piece may be less prominent or complex than the first violin part of the same piece, second violin parts are often extremely demanding — and always indispensable.

⤶

The viola, cello, and double bass sections of a symphony or- chestra are not divided into firsts and seconds, but in the wood- wind and brass sections there *are* firsts and seconds . . . and sometimes thirds and fourths, with one person to a part. In terms of musical characteristics, first and second parts in the winds and brass are related in much the same way as first and second violin parts.

[See ORCHESTRA.]

SERIAL MUSIC

[See TWELVE-TONE MUSIC.]

SHARP ~ FLAT

A note that's a little higher in pitch than it's supposed to be — not high enough to be the next note in the scale, but "out of tune" on the high side — is described as "sharp." A note that's a little lower than it's supposed to be is called "flat." *Sharp* and *flat* may also be used as general terms, as in, "I think her instrument is tuned a bit sharp, compared to the piano," or "He's been singing flat most of the evening."

Sharp and *flat* are also the names of *accidentals,* musical sym- bols that raise or lower the pitch of a note by a half step. The sym- bol for sharp is ♯, and for flat, ♭. [For further discussion of accidentals, see ACCIDENTAL, under NOTATION. See also HALF STEP; PITCH.]

SINGSPIEL

[See OPERA.]

[See PERCUSSION INSTRUMENTS.]

SONATA

The word *sonata* comes from the Italian *sonare,* an old form of *suonare,* which means "to sound," or "to play," as in "to play an instrument." A sonata is always an instrumental piece, and since about 1750 the term has most often referred to pieces that are written either for solo piano or for piano and one other instrument. Sonatas are often known by the name of the "other" instrument, so that a sonata for violin and piano is called a "violin sonata," and a sonata for flute and piano a "flute sonata." Sonatas for solo piano are called "piano sonatas."

The defining feature of a sonata is that it is composed of several distinct sections called "movements," each movement differing from the others in tempo and character. You might describe a symphony, concerto, or string quartet the same way, and in fact these forms are often considered sonatas for larger groups of instruments. They're just not *called* sonatas. [See CHAMBER MUSIC; CONCERTO; SYMPHONY.]

The classic, or Classical, sonata, as standardized by Joseph Haydn (1732–1809) and Wolfgang Amadeus Mozart (1756–1791), consists of three movements. The first movement is usually in a quick tempo (*allegro*), and written in "sonata form." (A movement in sonata form is organized in three sections, the exposition, development, and recapitulation. The form is not just for movements of sonatas, though. See SONATA FORM.) The second movement is slower (*andante,* or *adagio,* for example) and more lyrical, while the last movement is quick again, and often in the form of a rondo, which consists of a lively, catchy refrain that alternates with contrasting musical "episodes" [see CLASSICAL MUSIC~CLASSICAL ERA; LYRICAL~LYRICISM; RONDO]. Haydn wrote fifty or more keyboard sonatas (the earlier ones for harpsi-chord, the later ones for piano), while Mozart wrote more than twenty piano sonatas and almost forty violin sonatas.

In their symphonies and chamber music pieces, Haydn and Mozart often added a minuet after the slow movement, for a total of four movements. Ludwig van Beethoven (1770–1827) was one of the first to experiment with the four-movement form for the sonata itself, although when he chose to add a movement, it was usually a scherzo rather than a minuet [see MINUET; SCHERZO]. He varied the form in other ways, as well, changing the order of slow and fast movements, experimenting with long, slow intro-ductions that took on the character of independent movements, and, in two of his late piano sonatas, writing sonatas in just two extended movements. The fact that he wrote five cello sonatas was itself an innovation: neither Haydn nor Mozart had written any. Beethoven also wrote ten violin sonatas, a sonata for horn and piano, and thirty-two piano sonatas, among which are such famous pieces as the *Moonlight, Appassionata, Waldstein,* and *Pathétique* sonatas.

Indeed, Beethoven is the towering figure in the history of the sonata. He set extraordinary standards with the beauty, power, and variety of his music, and he influenced everyone who fol-lowed. The most important sonata composer among Beethoven's musical heirs was undoubtedly Johannes Brahms (1833–1897), who wrote three violin sonatas, two cello sonatas, two sonatas for clar-inet (or viola), and three piano sonatas. But the list of composers who have made significant contributions to the sonata literature would have to include most of the great names in instrumental music of the nineteenth and twentieth centuries. The sonata, like its compositional cousins the symphony, the concerto, and the string quartet, has never lost its appeal.

⁓

The term *sonata* didn't just appear out of thin air in the year 1750. With slight variations in spelling, in fact, it had been used as a title for various kinds of instrumental pieces since the Middle

Ages. During the Baroque era (ca. 1600–1750), the term was applied to pieces for single instruments ("unaccompanied sonatas," such as those for unaccompanied violin by J. S. Bach), pieces for one solo instrument plus accompaniment ("solo sonatas"), and pieces for two solo instruments plus accompaniment ("trio sonatas"). The trio sonata was the most popular chamber music form of the Baroque period. It's called "trio" because it has three "parts": two solo parts (played by two violins, for example, or a violin and oboe) plus the continuo part. The continuo part is generally played by two instruments, however, a keyboard instrument (harpsichord, for example) and either a cello or viola da gamba, which is why trio sonatas require four players, not three [see CONTINUO].

An interesting difference between Classical and Baroque sonatas is that in Baroque sonatas the keyboard parts were considered accompaniments — necessary, but secondary to the solo parts — while in Classical sonatas the piano parts were themselves solo parts, and the *other* instrumental parts were sometimes considered accompaniments. The great violin sonatas of Mozart and Beethoven were very much equal partnerships for the piano and the violin, but even so, like many Classical sonatas they often bore such titles as Sonata for Piano with the Accompaniment of a Violin. (After Beethoven's time, almost all sonatas were of the equal-partnership variety, and the old-fashioned titles disappeared.) Another distinction is that in Classical sonatas the piano parts were written out in their entirety by the composer, whereas in Baroque sonatas the keyboard parts included only the notes of the bass line, with numbers written below the notes to indicate the harmonies to be filled in by the performer. Not only was the Baroque keyboard part an accompaniment, it was a largely improvised accompaniment. [See ACCOMPANIMENT.]

First things first: sonata form and the musical form known as the sonata are not the same thing. A "sonata" is a piece (usually for piano or for piano and one other instrument) composed of several distinct sections called movements. "Sonata form" refers to the structure of an individual movement. To say that a movement of music is composed in sonata form means that the movement consists of three primary sections: an exposition, a development, and a recapitulation. Sonata form has its roots in various formal structures of the Baroque era (ca. 1600–1750), but it came to full flower in the works of the three composers who define the Classical era in music — Joseph Haydn, Wolfgang Amadeus Mozart, and Ludwig van Beethoven.

The first movements of Classical sonatas are, in fact, usually in sonata form. But sonata form is not restricted to movements of sonatas. The first movements of Classical symphonies and concertos — and of string quartets, piano trios, and other chamber music works — are usually in sonata form as well. (One-movement pieces like overtures may also be in sonata form.) Sonata form is sometimes called "sonata-allegro form," because the first movements of sonatas, symphonies, and so forth are usually in a fast (*allegro*) tempo, and it's also sometimes called "first-movement form." These names are probably best avoided, though, since not all movements in sonata form are either first or fast.

The opening section of a movement in sonata form is called the "exposition." (In fast movements, the exposition is sometimes preceded by a slow introduction.) The exposition is where the principal musical ideas are presented. These are the themes (melodies), rhythmic patterns, and chord progressions on which the movement will be built. Usually there's a first theme and a contrasting second theme: the first theme is often strong, assertive, or happy, while the second theme tends to be gentler, more reflective, or more lyrical. In Classical sonata form, the exposition is always repeated: you play it once and then you go back and play it again from the beginning.

After the repeat of the exposition, the music moves directly into the development. In the development, the themes and other musical elements of the exposition are put through a process of modification. They're still recognizable, but they're reworked and rearranged; they may be expanded, shrunk, chopped up into parts, or treated in various other interesting and clever ways. At the end of the development, there is typically some sort of transitional passage that leads into the recapitulation. The recapitulation is a restatement, sometimes with a few new twists, of the material of the exposition. Often the recapitulation ends with a coda, a musical extension that helps bring the movement to a close in a convincing manner. (*Coda* is Italian for "tail." See CODA.)

While it's tempting to think about sonata form just in terms of themes, the thematic functions of the exposition, development, and recapitulation are inseparable from their harmonic functions. The exposition establishes the key of the movement, the harmonic home base that's called the "tonic" harmony [see TONIC]. Next, the development journeys through harmonies far-removed and unrelated to the tonic, harmonies that create a sense of tension or musical instability. The development always eventually returns to the "dominant" harmony, however, which is the harmony that leads most strongly back to the tonic [see DOMINANT]. And with the recapitulation comes the return to the tonic, the final reestablishment and solidification of the home key and its reinforcement in the coda.

It should be emphasized that the descriptions above are based on generalizations, and that for every "rule" of sonata form in Classical works there are dozens of exceptions. Haydn, Mozart, and Beethoven were the great masters of sonata form, but none of them ever used the term itself — it was applied to their works by others, after the fact. If it suited Haydn to compose an exposition with a first theme and a second theme, he did so. If it didn't, he didn't, and in fact he wrote a number of works with just one principal theme in the exposition of the first movement. And Beethoven didn't hesitate to transform an expanded coda into a second development section, as in the first movement of the *Eroica* Symphony, or to turn what would ordinarily be a transition into a principal theme, or to include four or five principal themes in a movement instead of two. These great composers certainly established general patterns and principles, but they didn't follow recipes.

Sonata form remained an important element of musical composition throughout the nineteenth century, figuring prominently in the works of Franz Schubert, Robert Schumann, Felix Mendelssohn, Johannes Brahms, Antonín Dvořák, Max Bruch, Gabriel Fauré, Peter Ilyich Tchaikovsky, Anton Bruckner, and Gustav Mahler, among others. Various twentieth-century composers, including Igor Stravinsky, Béla Bartók, Ernest Bloch, Aaron Copland, Paul Hindemith, Sergei Prokofiev, and Dmitri Shostakovich, have also made use of sonata form in one way or another, and some contemporary composers are still tailoring sonata form to their individual styles.

Why has sonata form proved so enduring? The main reason is that the structure is so inherently satisfying. Exposition, development, and recapitulation: beginning, middle, and end. Sonata form provides all the time-tested elements of a good story — a clear beginning that establishes the principal characters and themes, a middle section that brings conflict and dramatic tension, and an end that provides a satisfying resolution. Sonata form does all this in purely musical terms, with melodic and rhythmic characters and character transformations, and with harmonic tension and resolution. It provides a context in which abstract musical elements take on clear identities, and in which we recognize direction and purpose in the progression of musical ideas.

[See SONATA; HARMONY~CHORD; KEY~TONALITY.]

SONG CYCLE

A song cycle is a set of songs whose poetic texts, often by a single poet, are linked by a common theme, mood, subject, or story. Though each is an individual entity, the songs of a song cycle are designed to be heard together as a unified musical piece. If the marriage of music and poetry in the song, or art song, represents a nineteenth-century Romantic ideal, the song cycle carries that ideal even further, allowing for an expanded range of expression, a deeper exploration of the individual psyche, and a more intense emotional effect [see ART SONG; ROMANTICISM]. Ludwig van Beethoven's *An die ferne Geliebte* (*To the Distant Beloved*), a set of six songs he wrote in 1816 to poetry by a young medical student friend, Alois Jeitteles, is generally considered the first modern song cycle.

Most of the great song composers have written song cycles. *Die schöne Müllerin* (*The Fair Maid of the Mill*) and *Winterreise* (*Winter's Journey*) of Franz Schubert (1797–1828) and *Dichterliebe* (*Poet's Love*) and *Frauenliebe und -leben* (*Woman's Love and Life*) of Robert Schumann (1810–1856) are among the most famous, and most beautiful. Hector Berlioz (1803–1869), Modest Mussorgsky (1839–1881), Gabriel Fauré (1845–1924), Claude Debussy (1862–1918), and Paul Hindemith (1895–1963) all wrote substantial and moving song cycles, as did Francis Poulenc (1899–1963), Benjamin Britten (1913–1976), Samuel Barber (1910–1981), and Aaron Copland (1900–1990), whose *Twelve Poems of Emily Dickinson* stands as a major contribution to the form. And it is a form that has not gone out of fashion: attracted and challenged by its expressive potential, contemporary composers such as Roger Ames, Dominick Argento, Seymour Barab, George Crumb, David Diamond, Ned Rorem, Bruce Saylor, and Hugo Weisgall, among many others, have continued to explore the possibilities of the song cycle.

SOPRANO

[See VOICE TYPES.]

The literal meaning of the Italian word *spiccato* is similar to that of *staccato* — "detached," or "distinct." In music, spiccato is a string-playing term, and specifically a bowing term: to play notes spiccato means to play them with a bouncing bow. *Spiccato* is also the name for the technique itself of playing with a bouncing bow.

Spiccato involves a controlled bouncing. The bow has to come off the string between each note, but the player must find a balance between making the bow bounce and letting the inherent springiness of the bow — with its stiff but flexible stick and tightened hair — do the work. String players use many kinds of spiccato strokes — soft, stiff, brushed, heavy, light, very bouncy — to produce a broad range of sounds, from soft and feathery to loud and harsh. One of the marks of a very accomplished string player, in fact, is the variety, flexibility, and control that he or she demonstrates with spiccato.

In musicians' Italian, the same term is often used as three different parts of speech. It's common, and correct, to say "Those notes should be spiccato, and light," or "Those notes should be played spiccato, and lightly," or "Those notes should be played with a light spiccato." When composers want notes to be played spiccato, they place little dots above them.

[See BOW~BOWING; STACCATO.]

SPINTO

[See VOICE TYPES.]

STACCATO

Staccato is Italian for "separated" or "detached." Staccato notes are not sustained for their full rhythmic value; they come to a short stop, which separates them from notes that follow. They usually have a clean, sharply articulated start as well. The opposite of *staccato* is *legato*, which means "connected" [see LEGATO].

Composers indicate staccato in written music by placing dots, dashes, or small inverted triangular wedges above the notes to be played staccato. String players play staccato by manipulating the bow so that it stops and starts cleanly between notes. Woodwind and brass players use a technique called "tonguing," which involves using the tongue to interrupt the flow of air into the instrument, and pianists vary their touch — by lifting their fingers quickly off the keys between notes, for example — and their use of the sustaining pedal.

In string playing, *staccato* is also the name for a specific kind of bow stroke, one in which a number of sharply articulated notes are all played with the bow going in one direction, up-bow or down-bow. The staccato stroke is usually "on the string"; when it's executed very rapidly, and in such a way that the bow bounces off the string, it's called "flying staccato." [See BOW~BOWING.]

STRADIVARIUS

Stradivarius is the Latinized last name of Antonio Stradivari (ca. 1644–1737), generally regarded as history's greatest violin maker. Stradivari was Italian — he lived and worked all his life in the northern Italian city of Cremona, not far from Milan — but the paper labels he glued inside his violins were in Latin:

Antonius Stradivarius Cremonensis
Faciebat Anno ———

(Antonio Stradivari of Cremona
Made in the year ———).

This is why a violin made by Stradivari is known as a Stradivarius. Musicians and instrument dealers often take the liberty of shortening the name to "Strad," as in, "She just bought a beautiful Strad."

Stradivari learned his craft as an apprentice to Nicolò Amati (1596–1684), whose paternal grandfather, Andrea Amati (ca. 1510–1580), is thought to have perfected the form of the modern violin, and whose family established the illustrious tradition that made Cremona the home of the world's finest violin makers for two and a half centuries. Working into his nineties, Stradivari probably made a thousand violins or more, of which about 650 survive. A Stradivarius today can cost a fortune: some of his instruments bring prices in the millions of dollars. (Grandfather's old violin in the attic is not likely to be a Strad, unfortunately, even if it has a label that says "Stradivarius." Such labels are found in mass-produced violins by the thousands, and they usually just indicate that the instruments are copies of Stradivarius models.) Stradivari also made cellos and violas, although in far smaller numbers than violins — somewhere upward of fifty-five cellos survive, and fewer than a dozen violas. He made other kinds of stringed instruments, as well, including guitars (only two survive) and most probably harps, lutes, and mandolins.

⌒

Why are Stradivarius instruments so highly prized? The most important reason by far is their sound. The best Strads have a rich, refined, resonant sound from the lowest notes to the highest. They're versatile: the same instrument can produce a dark, deep, velvety sound, or a stunningly brilliant sound. And they're powerful. A striking characteristic of Strads is that their sound seems to blossom, so that even over great distances they project clearly and beautifully. The power of a Strad, however, is not just a question of volume; true power depends on purity of sound, which is the quality that also enables a Strad to project beautifully in very soft passages, even in the largest concert halls. Lesser-quality instruments may seem quite loud "under the ear," but they don't project as well because there's more surface noise and less core to their sound.

A fine Stradivarius is also a joy to play. It's extremely responsive to the slightest changes in pressure and contact from the bow, and it feels *easy* to play. The violinist never has to force the sound from the instrument, and there always seems to be more sound available when needed. You might say that playing a Strad is like driving a high-performance automobile: it responds to the slightest touch, and there's always power in reserve.

Although there are many theories, there is no one secret to the sound of a Stradivarius and no simple explanation of Stradivari's genius. Many factors contribute to determining how a violin sounds, including the qualities of the wood, the shape of the instrument, the degree of arching and the precise variations in thickness of the wooden plates that form the belly and the back, and the qualities of the varnish, which seals and protects the wood but allows it to vibrate. The physical beauty of Stradivari's instruments attests to his excellent training, brilliant craftsmanship, and his eye for form and proportion. Beyond that, he must also have had a remarkable ear, along with an extraordinary knowledge of wood and a profound understanding of its acoustical properties and possibilities. Do Strads get better with age? Perhaps, but age itself is not responsible for their quality: Stradivari was famous during his own lifetime, and he made instruments on commission for kings, cardinals, and distinguished musicians and collectors all over Europe.

Not all Stradivarius instruments sound terrific, though. Each one has its individual characteristics, and although the general level is remarkably high, some are far better than others. The greatest Strads may be unsurpassed, but not every Strad sounds better than the best violins of less celebrated makers. There is even one violin maker whose instruments, far fewer in number, are considered by many concert violinists to be more desirable than those of Stradivari: Giuseppe Guarneri (1687–1744). Guarneri was a third-generation member of another of the great violin-making families of Cremona. The name he used on his labels was Joseph Guarnerius, but he's also known as Guarnerius *del Gesù* (of Jesus), or simply del Gesù, because his labels included a cross and the inscription IHS (for *Iesus Hominum Salvator*, Jesus, Savior of Men).

Guarneri's violins, while often less refined in appearance than those of Stradivari, are renowned for their tonal beauty and power. The nineteenth-century Italian virtuoso Niccolò Paganini played a del Gesù (his instrument was nicknamed "the Cannon" for its powerful sound) and did much to establish the Guarnerius reputation.

↜

A common question: In a blind test, could a nonmusician or "uneducated" listener tell the difference between a Stradivarius and some other violin? The answer is that it depends. If the other violin, whether old or modern, were an excellent one by a fine maker, the differences might not be readily apparent. But in a direct, side-by-side comparison of a great Stradivarius with a commercially produced instrument — or even with a handcrafted violin that was merely very good — the differences would be absolutely clear, even to the most inexperienced listener.

[See BOW~BOWING; STRINGED INSTRUMENTS; VIOLIN FAMILY.]

STRINGED INSTRUMENTS

Stringed instruments, also called string instruments, are instruments whose sound is produced by the vibrations of stretched strings. The pitch of a sound on a stringed instrument — the sound's highness or lowness — is determined by the frequency of vibrations of the vibrating string. The longer or thicker or looser the string, the lower the frequency and the lower the pitch. The shorter, thinner, or tighter the string, the higher the frequency and the higher the pitch [see PITCH]. On any stringed instrument, tuning a string is a matter of tightening or loosening the string, and playing different notes is a matter of playing on strings of different length or of altering the length of the strings with one's fingers (by "stopping" the strings against a fingerboard) while playing.

The principal kinds of modern stringed instruments are the

members of the violin family (violin, viola, cello, double bass), which are played with a bow and sometimes plucked; the harp and the guitar, which are only plucked; and stringed keyboard instruments such as the piano and harpsichord. When a musician says, "I'm a string player," however, it's usually understood that he or she plays violin, viola, cello, or double bass. In the same way, the string section of an orchestra consists of the violins, violas, cellos, and double basses.

All stringed instruments incorporate a wooden resonator or soundboard for amplifying the sound of the vibrating strings, which otherwise would be virtually inaudible. On the violin and the guitar, for example, the resonator is the body of the instrument itself. On most stringed instruments, including the stringed keyboard instruments, the strings are stretched parallel to the resonator, and they rest on a bridge of some sort that transmits their vibrations to the wood. On the harp, on the other hand, there's no bridge. The strings are more or less perpendicular to the soundboard, and are anchored to it directly.

Strings are made of a variety of materials. Piano strings are made of steel wire. On the lowest, thickest (and longest) piano strings, copper wire is wound around the steel. The strings of violins, violas, cellos, basses, guitars, and harps may be made of steel, nylon or a similar synthetic material, or of gut. Often the steel, nylon, or gut serves as the core of the string, and around the core is an extremely close and tight winding of very fine steel, aluminum, or silver wire.

A word about gut, also called catgut: it's not from cats. It's made by cleaning, pickling, and drying the intestines of sheep (or lambs) and twisting the fibers together under high tension. Synthetic strings are much more popular than gut nowadays because they're not as sensitive to changes in temperature and humidity, and they tend to last longer.

[See VIOLIN FAMILY; FIDDLE; GUITAR; HARP; KEYBOARD INSTRUMENTS; STRADIVARIUS; VIOL. See also BOW~BOWING; PIZZICATO.]

A suite is an instrumental piece that consists of a series of shorter pieces or sections. The sections of a suite are always related, but they're set off from each other by distinct changes in character, mood, and tempo.

The first pieces to be called suites were suites of dances [see DANCE]. The practice of pairing slow and fast dances had been common throughout Europe since the 1500s, but during the 1600s composers gradually added to the number of dances in their mixed sets, or suites, and eventually the full-length suite of contrasting dances became one of the most important instrumental forms of the Baroque period (ca. 1600–1750) [see BAROQUE]. As the Baroque suite developed, composers varied the selection and order of dances, but the arrangement that was more or less standard by the 1700s, especially in the works of Johann Sebastian Bach (1685–1750), is represented by the charming acronym PACSOG. This stands for prelude, allemande, courante, sarabande, optional, gigue. Since in any one suite all the dance movements are written in the same key, the contrasts in character and tempo are particularly important [see KEY~TONALITY; TEMPO]. The allemande tends to be of moderate tempo, the courante quick, the sarabande slow, and the gigue lively again. The "optional" section is most commonly a pair of bourrées (quick), minuets (moderate, graceful), or gavottes (moderate, stately), with other dances sometimes filling the bill. The prelude is a special case: it's freely invented, and isn't a dance at all [see PRELUDE]. Bach and his contemporaries wrote suites for solo instruments like the lute, harpsichord, violin, and cello, and also for orchestra. They didn't always call these pieces "suites," though. Another common title was "partita." Although *partita* originally meant "variation," by the end of the seventeenth century it had become a synonym for *suite*.

It's important to bear in mind that the Baroque suite was meant for listening, not dancing, and that the different sections, or movements, are mostly very stylized versions of the dances whose names they bear. In many cases they're hardly recognizable as dances at all. The exceptions are the optional dances, because they're the ones that were still in vogue as actual dances during the Baroque period. The others — allemande, courante, sarabande, and gigue — had evolved back in the 1500s and were already archaic. They were historical subjects, suitable for inspiring flights of musical fancy, not fancy footwork.

The Baroque suite essentially disappeared after 1750, displaced by other forms [see SYMPHONY; SONATA; CONCERTO]. In the nineteenth century, *suite* became a more broadly defined term, applied to pieces that were composed of extracts from larger works (works such as ballets, operas, and, later, film scores), and to other pieces with multiple sections, where the sections were related by musical type, subject matter, or story. The *Grand Canyon Suite*, by Ferde Grofé (1892–1972), is a twentieth-century example of this latter type, as is *The Planets*, by Gustav Holst (1874–1934), even though the "Neptune" section of *The Planets* includes women's voices. (So much for rules.) Good examples of the "extract" suite include the *Nutcracker Suite*, by Peter Ilyich Tchaikovsky (1840–1893), which contains only the overture, a march, and six of the dances from the complete ballet; the two *L'Arlésienne* suites, by Georges Bizet (1838–1875), and the two *Peer Gynt* suites, by Edvard Grieg (1843–1907), which are drawn from incidental music for plays; *Catfish Row*, an orchestral suite by George Gershwin (1898–1937) based on the music of his opera *Porgy and Bess;* and the suite by Sergei Prokofiev (1891–1953) from his music for the Soviet film *Lieutenant Kijé.*

When music is distilled from a larger work to make a suite, it is often reorchestrated, rearranged, or reconceived. Sometimes the original composer does the distilling, sometimes an arranger does it [see ARRANGEMENT]. Occasionally the transformation involves a complete change of scale. Igor Stravinsky (1882–1971), for example, took his ballet-theater piece, *A Soldier's Tale*, originally for seven instruments and three speakers, and turned it into a suite for clarinet, violin, and piano. The reasons for extracting a suite from a larger work are usually practical: it's a way to preserve and present the best or most popular sections of a work in a shorter, more economical (and often more profitable) form. There are fewer performers and no expensive costumes or staging, performances last fifteen to thirty minutes instead of two to three hours, and audiences get to hear music they love more often than they otherwise would.

SYMPHONIC POEM

A symphonic poem is a composition for orchestra, usually in one movement. It is a form of program music, which is music that attempts to tell a story, recreate a scene or picture, or convey impressions of a character, place, or event. Symphonic poems often take their subject, or program, from a work of literature. Both terms, *symphonic poem* and *program music,* were invented by the Hungarian composer Franz Liszt (1811–1886); among Liszt's better-known symphonic poems are such pieces as *Les Préludes* (1854), *Mazeppa* (1851), *Tasso* (1854), and *Die Hunnenschlacht* (*The Battle of the Huns,* 1857).

The ideal of the symphonic poem — a quintessentially Romantic ideal in its marriage of music, literature, and art — inspired many nineteenth-century composers, including Bedřich Smetana (1824–1884), Camille Saint-Saëns (1835–1921), Modest Mussorgsky (1838–1881), Peter Ilyich Tchaikovsky (1840–1893), Antonín Dvořák (1841–1904), Claude Debussy (1862–1918), Paul Dukas (1865–1935), and Alexander Scriabin (1872–1915). These composers didn't necessarily call their works "symphonic poems," however; instead, they often gave them descriptive or picturesque titles. Examples include *A Night on Bald Mountain* (Mussorgsky, 1867), *The Moldau* (Smetana, from a set of six symphonic poems called *My Country,* 1874–1879), *Prelude to the Afternoon of a Faun* (Debussy, 1894), and *The Sorcerer's Apprentice* (Dukas, 1897). Tchaikovsky called his *Romeo and Juliet* (1869) a "fantasy-overture" and his *Francesca da Rimini* (1876) a "fantasia," but by form and concept they fall squarely in the category of symphonic poems. In the late 1880s and 1890s, the German composer Richard Strauss (1864–1949) wrote a series of brilliantly orchestrated symphonic poems that he called "tone poems." Among his famous tone poems are such pieces as *Don Juan* (1889), *Tod und Verklärung* (*Death and Transfiguration,* 1889), *Till Eulenspiegels lustige Streiche* (*Till Eulenspiegel's Merry Pranks,* 1895), *Also Sprach Zarathustra* (*Thus Spake Zarathustra,* 1896), *Don Quixote* (1897), and *Ein Heldenleben* (*A Hero's Life,* 1898).

[See PROGRAM MUSIC; ROMANTICISM.]

SYMPHONY

A symphony is a large-scale work for orchestra, usually divided into four or more separate sections called "movements."

That's the technical definition. But just to mention the names of famous symphonies — Beethoven's Fifth, the *Eroica,* the Ninth, Mozart's Fortieth and the *Jupiter,* Schubert's *Unfinished,* Mendelssohn's *Italian,* the Brahms First, Dvořák's *New World,* Tchaikovsky's *Pathétique,* Mahler's *Resurrection* — is to conjure up whole worlds of musical beauty and grandeur. For more than two hundred years, the great symphonies by the great composers have been the cornerstones of the concert repertoire, and the very pieces that, for many people, symbolize classical music.

The direct precursor of the modern symphony was the Italian opera overture of the early eighteenth century. This form, called *sinfonia* in Italian, consisted of three separate movements, always in the order fast-slow-fast [see OVERTURE]. Toward the middle of the century, a number of composers started writing more elaborate sinfonias that were meant not for the opera house, but for concert performance. These were the first "symphonies," as we now use the term, and while many of them consisted of the traditional three movements, occasionally composers expanded the form to include four movements. The earliest symphony composers were mostly men whose names aren't terribly familiar today: an abbreviated list would include Giovanni Battista Sammartini (1698–1775), of Milan; Georg Matthias Monn (1717–1750), Georg Christoph Wagenseil (1715–1777), and Carl Ditters von Dittersdorf (1739–1799), of Vienna; Johann Christian Bach (1735–1782), J. S. Bach's youngest son, who settled in London; and Johann Stamitz (1717–1757), Ignaz Holzbauer (1711–1783), and Franz Xaver Richter (1709–1789), of Mannheim, Germany, the city that was home to the greatest orchestra in Europe at the time.

Joseph Haydn (1732–1809), who wrote 104 symphonies, is often called the father of the symphony. He was neither the first symphony composer nor even the most prolific (Dittersdorf wrote more than he), but he was the first to demonstrate what the symphony could become in the hands of a composer of genius. To put it simply, he made the symphony great by writing great symphonies. And his accomplishment was reinforced by the beautiful and brilliant works of his friend and admirer Wolfgang Amadeus Mozart (1756–1791), who wrote forty-one symphonies. (An interesting note: we naturally think of Haydn as an "earlier" composer than Mozart, since he was born much earlier; but Haydn wrote his last eight symphonies, which include the well-known *Military, Clock, Drumroll,* and *London* symphonies, after Mozart's death.)

Together, Haydn and Mozart established the standard for the four-movement structure of the Classical symphony. This structure included a lively first movement in sonata form (sometimes preceded by a slow introduction), a slower, more lyrical second movement, a minuet movement, and a fast last movement. (A movement in sonata form consists of three main sections — the exposition, development, and recapitulation — usually followed by a coda, which brings the movement to a close.) [See SONATA FORM. See also CLASSICAL MUSIC~CLASSICAL ERA; MINUET; SONATA.]

Ludwig van Beethoven (1770–1827) retained the four-movement model for his symphonies, and his musical language, especially his harmonic language, was substantially the same as that of Haydn and Mozart. But Beethoven expanded symphonic form and expression in countless ways, and in the symphony as in so many other musical forms, he led the way from the Classical era into the Romantic [see ROMANTICISM]. Beethoven wrote longer symphonies, with expanded slow introductions in some cases and greatly expanded development sections and codas, and he wrote bigger symphonies, more powerful, intense, and dramatic, for larger and more powerful orchestras [see ORCHESTRA]. He also replaced the minuet of the Classical symphony with the swifter and more dynamic scherzo [see SCHERZO], and in the final movement of his Ninth Symphony he took the remarkable step of augmenting the orchestra with vocal soloists and chorus. There's no denying the greatness of Haydn and Mozart, but as a symphonist Beethoven created a body of work that is unparalleled. To this day, his symphonies remain towering monuments, the standard against which all other symphonies are measured. Haydn and Mozart both wrote far more symphonies than Beethoven, but many of their early works are fairly slight, and only about fifteen of Haydn's symphonies and ten of Mozart's are performed regularly. Of Beethoven's nine symphonies, all are played frequently and all are wonderful and substantial pieces. At least four — the Third, Fifth, Seventh, and Ninth — are by common consent among the greatest masterpieces of Western music, and one, the Fifth, is probably the most famous piece in the history of classical music.

Among the great names in nineteenth-century symphonic composition after Beethoven are Franz Schubert (1797–1828), Hector Berlioz (1803–1869), Felix Mendelssohn (1809–1847), Robert Schumann (1810–1856), Anton Bruckner (1824–1896), Johannes Brahms (1833–1897), Peter Ilyich Tchaikovsky (1840–1893), and Antonín Dvořák (1841–1904). Gustav Mahler (1860–1911) straddles the divide between the nineteenth and twentieth centuries: he composed the first of his ten gigantic symphonies during the 1880s and the last (unfinished) in 1910. The most important symphonists of the twentieth century have been the Finnish composer Jean Sibelius (1865–1957), who wrote seven symphonies between 1899 and 1924; and three Russians, Igor Stravinsky (1882–1971), Sergei Prokofiev (1891–1953), and Dmitri Shostakovich (1906–1975).

The problem with making a list of important symphony composers is that the list must be either extremely long or annoyingly incomplete. With just a few scattered exceptions (Frédéric Chopin, Gabriel Fauré, Claude Debussy, and Maurice Ravel chief among them), and excluding those who have specialized in opera or other vocal music, virtually every major composer of the nineteenth and twentieth centuries has composed at least one symphony.

↩

Do orchestra musicians get tired of Beethoven's Fifth? Does it get boring to play the piece that's more familiar than any other? No and no. It's thrilling to play Beethoven's Fifth. And that's one of the reasons it's a masterpiece: no matter how many times you've played it — or heard it — there's no way to avoid being swept up by the first notes and carried along until the very end.

↩

SYMPHONIE CONCERTANTE: A *symphonie concertante* is not a symphony. The term is French, and was a common name during the Classical era (ca. 1775–1820) for a concerto featuring two or more soloists [see CONCERTO]. The Italian equivalent is *sinfonia concertante*. The solo instruments of a symphonie concertante may be strings or winds, or a combination of the two. Probably the most famous example of the form is the wonderful Sinfonia Concertante that Mozart wrote for violin and viola.

SYNCOPATION

Syncopation is a disturbance or interruption of the regular flow of rhythm. It's the placement of rhythmic stresses or accents where they wouldn't normally occur.

Music is divided into beats, and beats are grouped together in *measures* based on patterns of strong beats and weak beats. These patterns make up what is called the *meter* of a piece of music; they are "metrical patterns." In regular metrical patterns, or the regular flow of rhythm, the first beat of a measure — the downbeat — is the strongest beat, where the most rhythmic emphasis, or weight, is felt. Syncopation shifts this emphasis, or, to put it another way, it places the ac*cent* on the wrong syl*la*ble. A syncopated rhythm is one that places stress on a weak beat, or that creates a strong impulse on a subdivision of a beat, an in-between beat. Weak beats and in-between beats are also known collectively as "offbeats," and syncopated rhythm may be thought of as "offbeat rhythm."

Syncopation is a general term: there is no limit to the number or variety of possible syncopated rhythms, nor are there limits to the ways they may be used. A syncopated rhythm may occur just once in a piece or passage, or various syncopations may recur, regularly or irregularly, or syncopations may form repetitive patterns, with extended successions of stressed offbeats. Syncopation is one of the most powerful and versatile tools that composers can employ to create rhythmic interest and variety. And although some composers have certainly been more rhythmically inventive than others, syncopation has been an important element of musical composition for centuries. From the masters of the Middle Ages to Bach to Mozart to Beethoven to Tchaikovsky to Copland to Lennon and McCartney, there is no such thing as a composer who has not made extensive use of syncopation. Sometimes syncopation can even be a means to musical mischief or humor: many composers have enjoyed playing "Where's the beat?" and delighted in fooling us.

Some musical styles have built their character around syncopation. Syncopation is such an integral element of jazz and ragtime, for example, that for those styles the regular flow of rhythm is in fact a syncopated flow. "It don't mean a thing if it ain't got that swing," goes the Duke Ellington song, and it's syncopation that provides the swing.

[See BEAT; METER; RHYTHM.]

T

Tempo is the Italian word for "time." In English, however, *tempo* always refers to speed. "What's the tempo of this piece?" is a way of asking "How fast — or how slowly — does the music go?" This is a vital question, because how fast a piece passes in time — its tempo — is a fundamental element of its character and conception. Composers have various ways of providing tempo indications in their music, but even where those indications seem very precise, tempo remains a crucial area of interpretation for the performer.

[See TEMPO MARKINGS; METRONOME; RUBATO.]

TEMPO MARKINGS

Composers have a variety of ways to indicate what tempo they have in mind for a piece, how fast or slowly it should be played. One way is to give the piece a title that has associations with specific moods, movements, or dances. One would tend to perform a piece called "Funeral March of the Zombies," for example, in a tempo quite different from that of a piece called, say, "Crazed Tarantella of the Whirling Furies." Or, to pick slightly less extreme examples, if a piece from the 1700s is called "Sarabande," it will not be played at the same tempo as a "Gigue," because the sarabande of that period is a slow dance and the gigue a quick one.

Another way is to use words called "tempo markings," or

"tempo marks." Tempo markings are written above the music at the beginning of the piece, and later wherever the composer wants the tempo to change. They're usually in Italian, and the three primary ones are *allegro, andante,* and *adagio.* The original meaning of the word *allegro* is "cheerful," but it has come to mean "quick," or "fast," when used as a tempo marking. *Andante* is from the verb *andare,* "to walk," or "to go," and indicates a moderate tempo, what might be called a walking pace. *Adagio,* from the Italian for "at ease," means "slow."

There are a number of other standard tempo markings, and many modifiers to go along with them, although the modifiers often have more to do with the kind of expression or feeling the composer is looking for than with precise gradations of speed. The following lists offer a sampling of the most common tempo markings and modifiers.

Basic Tempo Markings

I.
adagio	slow
allegro	fast
andante	moderate
grave	slow, heavy
largo	very slow, broad
lento	slow
presto	very fast

II.
adagietto	"little adagio," a little faster than adagio
allegretto	"little allegro," somewhat slower than allegro
andantino	"little andante," an ambiguous term, meaning either slightly slower than andante or slightly faster, depending on your point of view
largamente	very slowly
larghetto	"little largo," slightly faster than very slow
meno mosso	"less moved," slower
più mosso	"more moved," faster
prestissimo	"very presto," extremely fast

agitato	excited
amabile	friendly
animato	animated, excited (also used by itself as a tempo marking, or to mean "faster")
appassionato	passionate
assai	quite, rather
cantabile	singing, lyrical
comodo	comfortable
con anima	with spirit
con brio	with verve
con fuoco	with fire, very energetically
con molto espressione	with much expression
con moto	with motion; moving along
con spirito	with spirit
giusto	right, reasonable
grazioso	graceful
ma non tanto	but not so much
ma non troppo	but not too much
maestoso	stately, majestic (also used by itself as a tempo marking)
meno	less
mesto	sad
moderato	moderate
molto	very
più	more
poco	a little
quasi	almost
risoluto	steady, resolute
sostenuto	sustained, held back (also used by itself as a tempo marking, or to mean "slower")
tranquillo	tranquil, peaceful (also used by itself to mean "slower")
vivace	lively (also used by itself as a tempo marking)
vivo	lively, quick

Indications of change of tempo

accelerando	getting faster
animando	getting faster, more animated
stringendo	getting faster ("squeezing")
allargando	getting slower, broader
calando	coming down, dropping away (actually applies to volume, but often means a simultaneous slowing down)
rallentando	getting slower
ritardando	getting slower (often abbreviated *rit.* or *ritard.*)
ritenuto	held back, slower
slentando	getting slower

Composers very often use the unadorned basic tempo markings — adagio, allegro, allegretto, and so forth. But when they choose to modify them, the modifier becomes part of the marking, as in the following examples:

allegro con brio, allegro molto, allegro vivace, allegro ma non troppo, allegro grazioso, allegretto quasi andante, andante cantabile, andante tranquillo, poco adagio, adagio con molto espressione.

Italian isn't *always* the language of tempo markings: a number of non-Italian composers have made a point of using their native language as well, or instead. Here are a few tempo markings in French and German:

French

animé	fast
lent	slow
modéré	moderate, medium tempo
vif	lively

German

bewegt	"moved," or lively (*bewegter* means "faster")
langsam	slow
schnell	fast
mässig	moderate

But indeed, since the 1600s, when tempo markings came into regular use, composers of all nationalities and linguistic backgrounds have mainly employed the Italian terms. This has to do first with the fact that most of the forms and practices of Western music — including the practice of using tempo markings — got their start in Italy and then spread throughout the other countries of Europe. The supremacy of Italian opera, for example, was unchallenged (except perhaps in France) from its beginnings in 1600 until the latter part of the 1700s, and Italian instrumental forms like the sonata and the concerto were known everywhere. Unchallenged, too, during this time was the supremacy of Italian musicians, who occupied many of the most important positions as composers and performers at royal courts and opera houses all over the continent. It was through the prestige and success of Italian music and musicians that the musical terms themselves took on prestige and currency. Musicians of all countries became familiar with them and adopted them. The continued use of Italian terms — for all facets of music, not just tempo markings — then became a matter of practicality, because with the common language came fewer possibilities for misunderstanding among musicians of different backgrounds. After a time, it also became a matter of tradition, and this is very important in itself, since musicians have always tended to have great respect and affection for tradition. To abandon the language used by Monteverdi, Bach, Handel, Haydn, Mozart, and Beethoven would be no small thing. Finally, the durability of the Italian terms undoubtedly owes a significant debt to the sheer beauty of the Italian language, a beauty that musicians have not been alone in appreciating.

Perhaps the most important thing to remember about tempo markings is that they are not exact, and are not meant to be. They must be interpreted by performers in light of the specific piece, individual taste and feeling, knowledge of style and tradition, the acoustics of the performing space, and the inspiration of the moment. Composers know this, and they count on it. They know that their notes on paper must be brought to life, and that the inevitable individual differences in interpretation are what make performances interesting and often illuminating. Three different pianists, for example, playing the same piece marked *Andante cantabile* — or the same pianist playing it on three different occasions — might choose three quite different tempos, but each performance might be completely convincing in its own way.

With the invention of the metronome around 1815, composers had at their disposal a means to be more precise in their tempo indications. In theory, a composer no longer had to rely on such inexact instructions as *Allegro ma non troppo*, but could specify exact tempos based on the number of metronome beats per minute [see METRONOME]. **METRONOME MARKS** are usually found at the top left corner of the music. The composer specifies a certain note value as the beat, say a quarter note, written like this, ♩, and then writes a number to indicate the number of beats he wants per minute: ♩= 60, for example, means the beat is the quarter note and there are sixty beats per minute. [See BEAT; METER; NOTATION.]

In practice, however, most composers continued (and continue) to use the Italian tempo markings even when they added metronome marks. A number, after all, cannot indicate spirit or expression, and even the most precise tempo indication is just a starting point, a helpful hint: it doesn't change the nature of the performer's interpretative responsibilities. Beethoven, for example, was the first major composer to use metronome marks, and he was quite careful in choosing them; yet there are many stories of Beethoven performing his own pieces at different times with very different tempos. As he himself wrote, "Feeling also has its tempo."

[See VOICE TYPES.]

TESSITURA

The literal meaning of the Italian word *tessitura* is "texture," or "weave," as in the weave of a fabric. In music for voice, the term refers to where a piece "lies" for the voice — how high or low the music is, not at its highest and lowest points, but in general. The tessitura of a piece determines what voice type should sing it. For example, a song or operatic role may contain notes that are singable by either a soprano or a mezzo-soprano: the lower-voiced mezzo can sing even the highest notes the role requires, and the soprano can reach the lowest. But does the role have a high tessitura, better suited to a soprano, or a low tessitura, suited to a mezzo? For whom would the role be a strain and for whom would it lie for the most part in a vocal comfort zone? Who would sound better singing it? It's not a matter of who can reach the notes, or of an occasional stretch in one direction or another, but rather of making sure that the person singing will be using the strongest and most beautiful part of her voice most of the time.

[See VOICE TYPES.]

THEME AND VARIATIONS

Theme and variations, also called "variation form," or simply "variations," is a musical form that's been common in instrumental music for the past four or five hundred years. The earliest variations were written for solo instruments such as the lute, organ, and harpsichord, but since the early 1500s composers have written variations for virtually every instrument and instrumental combination.

A theme is nothing more than a melody, or tune, or some sort of recognizable musical phrase. Most sets of variations start with what's called the "statement" of the theme. This is the theme in a basic, and usually quite simple, version. It may be an original theme, meaning one that's composed specifically for the piece at hand, or it may be a theme borrowed from another composer or from another piece by the same composer. After the statement of the theme come the variations, of which there may be just a few — or quite a few.

The variations are altered versions of the theme — musical sections or passages that are derived from the theme but that differ from it somehow. There are many ways to vary a theme. One way is to "decorate" it with added notes — the musical equivalent of wrapping it with ribbons and bows. Another is to change the tempo (speed), or to change the actual rhythms. Another way is to alter the harmonies, or chords, that go along with the theme. Altering the harmonies may include changing the key in which the melody is heard, sometimes even switching from a major key to a minor key, or vice versa. Yet another possibility is to change the musical figures that accompany the theme, to change the musical context or background, in other words. The overall sound or musical texture can be varied, as well, from a simple, spare sound, to a complex, dense sound, and in pieces that require more than one instrument, the instrumentation of the theme can be varied, too. A theme can also be chopped up, and its parts rearranged.

Not only are all these techniques, and more, available to the composer, but any of them can be combined with any of the others. In some sets of variations, you can easily pick out, or recognize, the theme in every variation despite the different treatments and settings. Some pieces, however, include variations in which the alterations are so extensive that they obscure the theme. In these sorts of variations, the theme functions as a kind of hidden musical scaffolding. Also, in some pieces the variations are part of a continuous fabric, each variation leading into the next without pause, while in others the variations are arranged as a series of separate musical sections, each with a clear beginning and end.

Sometimes the theme-and-variations form is used as the basis for an entire piece: the *Goldberg* Variations of J. S. Bach, the *Diabelli* Variations of Beethoven, and the Variations on a Theme by Handel of Johannes Brahms, for example, are all keyboard works that consist of a set of variations on a theme. Mozart's variations on the French song "Ah vous dirai-je, maman" (which more people know today as "Twinkle Twinkle, Little Star") is another such work. Brahms wrote a piece for two pianos called "Variations on a Theme by Haydn" (he later arranged the same piece for orchestra), and Tchaikovsky wrote a piece for solo cello and orchestra called "Variations on a Rococo Theme." Very often, though, just one movement of a piece will be in variation form: the *Trout* Quintet of Franz Schubert, for example, which is a quintet for strings and piano, takes its fishy nickname from the fourth movement of the work, a set of variations on Schubert's own song, "The Trout." Beethoven used variation form in the slow movements of his Fifth, Seventh, and Ninth symphonies and in the last movements of the Third (*Eroica*) and Ninth symphonies, as well as in movements of many of his other instrumental works.

Why have so many composers devoted themselves so extensively to the theme-and-variations form? Because the form itself has a built-in appeal. It provides a clear, coherent structure, it offers unlimited potential for variety of expression and for striking contrasts in mood and character, and it presents the composer with an exciting musical challenge: to build a substantial and compelling piece starting with just one simple melody.

[See ACCOMPANIMENT; CHACONNE~PASSACAGLIA; HARMONY~CHORD; KEY~TONALITY.]

TIMBRE

Timbre is another word for "tone color." It's the quality, or set of qualities, that gives a particular sound, voice, or musical instrument its individual character. There's no confusing a note played on the piano, for example, with a note played on the violin because the two instruments have completely different timbres. Even if the pitch of the two notes (the highness or lowness) is exactly the same, their timbre will distinguish them: a high C on the piano sounds different from a high C on the violin. For that matter, the timbre of a high C on one violin will be slightly different from that of a high C on a different violin.

❧

Differences in timbre often seem obvious to us: a trombone doesn't sound like a bassoon, a cello doesn't sound like a trumpet, and no two voices sound exactly alike. But what produces these differences? Explaining the "why" of timbre necessarily involves a little elementary acoustical physics.

When something vibrates at a certain frequency, measured in vibrations per second, it generates sound waves, or sound, of that frequency. Most sounds, or notes, however, are actually composed of a number of different frequencies. The tone of lowest frequency produced by the vibrating medium is usually the loudest. It is called the "fundamental," and it determines the pitch that is perceived for the sound — B-flat, for example, or C, or F-sharp [see PITCH]. The fundamental gives the note its name, in other words. The other, higher frequencies that are also part of the note (but that normally can't be detected separately by the ear) are called "harmonics," or "overtones." In sounds produced by different voices or instruments — with their different materials, shapes, weights, thicknesses, and so forth — the number and range of overtones is different, and the relative intensities of the various overtones differ as well. These differences in the distribution and relative intensities of overtones are what largely determine differences in timbre.

❧

A note on pronunciation: *timbre* is originally a French word, but it made its way into the English language long ago. You don't have to speak French, therefore, in order to pronounce it properly. Then again, the correct English pronunciation according to some dictionaries is "timber" (as in chopped trees), which sounds pretty strange, and which few people in the United States, at least, ever use. "Tamber" (rhymes with amber), which is also correct, seems like a better choice, and is in fact the more common pronunciation.

TIMPANI

[See PERCUSSION INSTRUMENTS.]

TOCCATA

A toccata is a type of keyboard composition, usually for organ or harpsichord. (*Toccare,* in Italian, means "to touch," or "to play," and *toccata* is the past tense.) The form developed in Italy in the 1500s and later spread to Germany. It became one of the important keyboard forms of the Baroque period (ca. 1600–1750), closely associated with such names as Girolamo Frescobaldi (1583–1643), Dietrich Buxtehude (1637–1707), and, especially, Johann Sebastian Bach (1685–1750).

The original toccatas were very free pieces; they had little formal structure and didn't adhere to any particular compositional rules. Mainly they featured rapid and difficult passages designed to show off the virtuosity of the performer. Many later toccatas, however, consist of a number of short sections, with sections in free style alternating with highly ordered contrapuntal sections or fugues [see COUNTERPOINT~POLYPHONY; FUGUE]. The dynamic equilibrium between freedom and order is in fact one of the fundamental principles of composition of the Baroque period.

Later composers, including Robert Schumann (1810–1856), Claude Debussy (1862–1918), Ferruccio Busoni (1866–1924), and Sergei Prokofiev (1891–1953), wrote pieces that they called toccatas, but these were gestures of affectionate, respectful nostalgia more than attempts to revive the form.

TONE POEM

[See SYMPHONIC POEM.]

TONIC

The tonic is the first note, or first "degree," of a major or minor scale; it's the note that gives the scale its name. The note C, for example, is the tonic of both the C-major and C-minor scales.

Tonic is also the name for the major or minor chord, or harmony, built on the first degree of the scale. And because all *keys* are based on scales, the tonic is the harmony that gives the key its name: in the key of C major, the C-major harmony is the tonic [see KEY~TONALITY]. A piece in C major may travel through a variety of different harmonies and keys, but in the end it always returns to C major. The tonic is the home base, in other words, the harmonic anchor of a piece.

[See DOMINANT; HARMONY~CHORD; SCALE.]

TRANSCRIPTION

[See ARRANGEMENT.]

TREMOLO ~ TRILL

Tremolo is from the Italian word *tremolare,* which means "to tremble," or "to quiver." A tremolo is either a very rapid repetition of a single note (or of simultaneously sounding notes) or a very rapid alternation between two different notes.

On a stringed instrument, a rapid-repetition tremolo is produced by moving the bow back and forth across a string (or strings, if two notes are being sounded at once). By definition it's not a measured repetition — the player doesn't count the bow strokes, but simply moves the bow back and forth as rapidly as possible. A rapid-alternation tremolo on a stringed instrument is called a "fingered" tremolo, because two fingers of the left hand must alternate rapidly to play the alternating notes. Sometimes, depending on what the composer indicates, a fingered tremolo is played all in one bow stroke, and sometimes with fast, back-and-forth strokes to match the fingers. (*Tremolo* can also be an adverb, as in "Please play those notes tremolo, not measured.")

On the piano, tremolos are usually of the rapid-alternation variety, but occasionally a composer will call for a tremolo on a single note, in which case the pianist must find a way to get the same key to go up and down as swiftly as possible. Wind players aren't called on to play tremolo very often, but they can play a single note tremolo by fluttering their tongues, and can also execute the equivalent of a fingered tremolo.

Two rapidly alternating notes that are right next to each other in pitch, that is, either a half step or whole step apart, constitute a TRILL [see HALF STEP]. On a stringed instrument, the alternating notes of a trill are always played in one continuous bow stroke, rather than by moving the bow back and forth for each note. To say that there's a trill "on" a certain note means that the note alternates with a note directly above it in pitch. A trill on the note A, for example, means that the two alternating notes are either A and B-flat or A and B.

The trill is what's known as a musical "ornament," and for several hundred years it's been the most common and most important of all ornaments. During the Baroque era (ca. 1600–1750), it was customary for performers (singers as well as instrumentalists) to add trills and other ornaments at their own discretion, but since the latter part of the eighteenth century, composers themselves have generally taken care to indicate where they want trills. Trills may occur anywhere in a piece, but they're used particularly often to embellish cadences, the passages that bring musical phrases, sections, or movements to a close. In concertos, especially concertos from the era of Haydn, Mozart, and Beethoven, it's common for the extended solo sections called cadenzas to finish with a trill just before the reentrance of the orchestra [see CA-DENCE~CADENZA].

While singers are usually proud to have "a good trill" — that is, to be able to execute trills well — they never want to hear that they have a tremolo. That's because in singing, the word *tremolo* is used to describe an overly fast, unattractive vibrato [see VI-BRATO].

TRIANGLE

[See PERCUSSION INSTRUMENTS.]

TRIO SONATA

[See SONATA.]

TROMBONE

[See BRASS INSTRUMENTS.]

TRUMPET

[See BRASS INSTRUMENTS.]

TUBA

[See BRASS INSTRUMENTS.]

In the early part of the twentieth century, the Viennese composer Arnold Schoenberg (1874–1951) developed a method of musical composition known as the twelve-tone technique, or twelve-tone system. In Schoenberg's view — a view not uncommon at the time — all the traditional compositional forms and techniques had been developed and expanded as far as they would go, and something new was needed. "Where do we go from here?" was the question, and the twelve-tone system was Schoenberg's revolutionary response.

The first step, as in all revolutions, was a negative one, the overthrow of the old order. Inasmuch as tonality, or tonal harmony — the system of writing music in major and minor keys, based on major and minor scales — had already been stretched to a point where it was hardly recognizable, Schoenberg felt it was time to reject it completely [see KEY~TONALITY]. It was also time, he felt, to discard traditional forms of melody, and indeed, to eliminate the repetition of all patterns, including rhythmic patterns. (Rhythmic regularity and continuity would be no more.) As a start, in other words, Schoenberg rejected all of the most familiar and dependable organizing factors in music as they had evolved over the preceding thousand years or so. [See HARMONY~CHORD; RHYTHM.]

He replaced them with the twelve tones. *Tone* is just another word for note, that is, a musical sound of specific pitch [see PITCH]. Imagine going up the scale on a piano and playing every note, black keys and white: there are always twelve separate notes before the next note repeats. Start on the note C, for example, and there are twelve notes before the next C. The distance from C to C (or from any note to the next note of the same name) is called an "octave," and the twelve notes that fill in an octave make up what's known as the "chromatic scale." Not counting the same notes heard in different registers (low C, middle C, high C), the twelve separate notes of the chromatic scale represent all the notes available in traditional Western music. [See OCTAVE; SCALE.]

To write a piece in Schoenberg's system, a composer takes the twelve notes of the chromatic scale and arranges them in an order of his or her choosing. This arrangement is called the "tone row," and it functions as the basis for the entire piece. No note of the row is more important than any other. There is no tonic, for example, and no dominant, and there are no implied harmonic relationships among the notes [see TONIC; DOMINANT]. All that counts is the order of the notes and the intervals between them — the distance in pitch from one note to the next.

In what might be called "orthodox" Schoenbergian technique, all twelve notes of the tone row must be heard in their original order before any one is repeated. Once the row has been stated, however, the composer is free to transform it in any number of ways. The row can be transposed, for example. To "transpose" a row is to shift it, in its entirety, up or down in pitch; to start on a different note, in other words, while maintaining the same sequence of intervals. The row can also be used in "retrograde," which simply means backward, going from the last note to the first; or in "inversion," meaning upside down: wherever the original row went up by a certain interval it now goes down by that same interval, and where the original went down it now goes up. Or it can be used in "retrograde inversion," which means upside down *and* backward. Because the tone row can be transposed so that it starts on any one of the twelve notes of the chromatic scale, and because it can be heard in any of four different sequences — original, retrograde, inversion, retrograde inversion — there are twelve times four, or forty-eight, different possible versions of the row. And it gets even more complicated in that the row can also be used in fragments, and notes of the row can be combined to make chords.

Twelve-tone music is atonal: it's not in a key. It also tends to be quite dissonant, because, unlike tonal music, it doesn't depend on consonant harmonies to provide stability or the resolution of tension [see ATONALITY~DISSONANCE]. In theory, the point in twelve-tone music is not that dissonance is good and consonance bad, but rather that they're both irrelevant. Schoenberg, however, especially in his early twelve-tone pieces, strongly embraced dissonance in order to eliminate even the faintest traces of tonality.

⌐

Twelve-tone music, and particularly Schoenberg's twelve-tone music, has never proved terribly popular among the concertgoing public. There are two main reasons. The first is indeed the pervasive dissonance of much twelve-tone music. Consonances, by definition, are "pleasing sounds," and although Schoenberg may have been willing to abandon them, most people aren't. The second is that to most listeners strict twelve-tone compositions just don't seem to make sense. Music is made up of the most abstract of building blocks — notes, sounds. In order for us to find meaning in those sounds, we must be able to perceive relationships between and among them. The forty-eight possible permutations of a tone row may make sense on paper, but to the ear they're mostly a mystery. And the elimination of pattern repetition in twelve-tone music is particularly problematic, because repetition is the very thing that makes patterns recognizable. Without recognizable patterns — old, familiar ones or newly established ones — we lose our bearings. We're not sure where we are or where we've been, and therefore it's hard to have an interest in where we're going.

This is not to say that there are no intelligible or moving twelve-tone pieces. A composer whose overriding goal is to write emotionally compelling music will find a way to do so, no matter the system or musical language in which he writes. The music of Alban Berg (1885–1935), for example, who, along with Anton Webern (1883–1945), was one of Schoenberg's two principal disciples, is remarkably powerful and expressive, and often quite lyrical. Berg probably achieved the broadest appeal of any of the twelve-tone composers, especially with his Violin Concerto and with his operas, *Wozzeck* and *Lulu*. Then again, Berg never adhered strictly to the rules of the system, and he usually managed to combine twelve-tone technique with traditional harmonies and melodies.

(In his later years, even Schoenberg relaxed the rules and included tonal elements in his music.)

❧

Twelve-tone music is also called "dodecaphonic" music, from the Greek word *dodeca*, "twelve." Because twelve-tone music is always based on a specific series of notes, it is also called "serial" music, and twelve-tone technique is considered a form of "serialism." Twelve-tone music was the first kind of serial music, but not all serial music is twelve-tone. Various twentieth-century composers have used series of different musical elements, including rhythms, dynamics, and groups of sounds, as the basis for their works. In all cases, however, serial music is atonal.

V

VARIATIONS

[See THEME AND VARIATIONS.]

VERISMO

[See OPERA.]

VIBRATO

When violinists play, their left hands always seem to shake. It can't be that violinists are always nervous, because their right hands don't shake (most of the time, anyway). The explanation is that they're using vibrato.

Vibrato, from the Italian word for "shaken," or "vibrated," is both a technique and an effect. The technique, used by violinists, violists, cellists, and double bass players, is to rock the fingers of the left hand rapidly back and forth on the strings as notes are played. The effect is a small, regular, up-and-down fluctuation in pitch for each vibrated note [see PITCH]. Vibrato is usually characterized by two factors: speed and width. The rocking motion can be fast or slow, wide or narrow. A wide vibrato causes the pitch to change more with each oscillation than it would with a narrow vibrato, because the wider rocking motion makes the fingertip cover more distance on the string. [See STRINGED INSTRUMENTS.]

Why do string players use vibrato? Because vibrato adds resonance to the sound of a stringed instrument. A vibrated note usually sounds richer or warmer than a nonvibrated note, and a passage played with vibrato has a completely different effect than one played without. It's not just a matter of flipping a switch, however, of turning the mechanism on or off. The accomplished string player has many types of vibrato at his or her command, covering an enormous range of fine gradations and possible combinations of speed and width. Vibrato is thus one of the string player's best tools for varying the sound, for changing tone quality and intensity from phrase to phrase or even from note to note within a phrase.

⌢

Singers also use vibrato, although *use* isn't exactly the right word. Vibrato happens, is more like it. For the string player, vibrato is a tool, something applied and varied by choice. But for the singer, vibrato is simply a by-product of proper breathing and tone production. Singers don't purposely produce vibrato, in other words, and, except for those who specifically try to sing without vibrato for expressive or stylistic reasons, they usually don't vary it on purpose. In the words of Mozart, "The human voice already vibrates of itself, but in such a degree that it is beautiful, that it is the nature of the voice." Studies of great singers have shown that the average speed of a beautiful vibrato is between six and seven oscillations per second, although in musical passages that increase in volume and excitement the vibrato generally speeds up and widens.

When a singer's vibrato is too fast to be considered pleasing, it's called a *tremolo,* Italian for "trembling." (*Tremolo* has a different meaning for instrumentalists. See TREMOLO~TRILL.) When it's too slow, too wide, or uneven in speed and/or width, it's usually called a "wobble." Ideally — in both singing and string playing — effective vibrato deceives the ear: we don't notice the actual oscillations in pitch, we just hear a beautiful, warm tone. Unpleasant vibratos make the vibrato noticeable, and it becomes a distraction. For singers, the culprit in tremolos or wobbles is usually vocal tension of some kind, caused by nervousness, fatigue, or improper technique, especially improper breathing technique (or in-

adequate "breath support," as it's called). Advancing age can play
a part, too, although older singers who sing "right" — in a relaxed, properly supported manner — have far fewer problems
than those who sing "tight."

Although woodwind and brass players can produce vibrato in
a variety of ways, they tend to use the effect very sparingly.
(Flutists are an exception. A certain amount of vibrato is an integral component of most flutists' sounds.) In general, jazz and pop
wind players make much greater use of vibrato than their classical
colleagues. [See WOODWIND INSTRUMENTS; BRASS INSTRU-
MENTS.]

VIOL

Viol is the name for a family of bowed stringed instruments
that were important throughout Europe during the 1500s and
1600s. Viols came in a variety of sizes and types, but the three
most common types were the treble viol, tenor viol, and bass viol.
Of the three, the treble viol was the smallest and highest-pitched,
and the bass viol was the largest (about the size of a cello) and
lowest-pitched. In seventeenth-century England, where music for
groups, or "consorts," of viols was especially popular, a mixed set
of treble, tenor, and bass viols was called a "chest of viols" — from
the chest, or cabinet, where they were kept.

Viols were always played either on the lap or held between
the knees, which is why the Italian name for viol was "viola da
gamba," or "leg viola." (In the 1500s and 1600s, *viola* was the
generic term in Italian for a bowed string instrument.) Although
viola da gamba started out as the family name, it came to refer almost exclusively to the bass viol. (The viola da gamba is not to be
confused with the modern double bass, however, which is also
sometimes called the bass viol. The double bass is indeed descended from the viol family, but its ancestor was an instrument
called the double-bass viol, which was much larger and lower-

pitched than the viola da gamba.) The revival of interest in early music and early instruments in the twentieth century has brought renewed attention to the viol family, and has encouraged contemporary instrument makers to make new viols modeled after the originals.

There are a number of important differences between viols and the members of the modern violin family (the violin, viola, cello, and double bass).

- ❖ Viols generally have six strings, as opposed to four for the members of the violin family.
- ❖ Viols have frets, while the instruments of the violin family don't. The frets on viols were originally just strings of gut (dried animal intestine) tied around the fingerboard. Frets provide a significant boost for the sound of stringed instruments [see GUITAR], and it's a particularly welcome boost for the viols, which have a much lighter construction and less powerful sound than the instruments of the violin family. As on the guitar, the frets are also helpful for playing chords in tune.
- ❖ Viols have flat backs, and shoulders that slope downward from the neck. The violin, viola, and cello have backs that arch outward and shoulders that are more square. (Although the double bass is considered a member of the violin family, it betrays its viol roots with its sloping shoulders and flat back.)
- ❖ Viol bows are different from violin bows, whose current design wasn't standardized until the late 1700s. (The members of the violin family all use bows of similar design, though the bows differ in length, thickness, and weight. See BOW~BOWING.) The stick of a viol bow curves away from the hair, while the stick of a violin bow curves in toward the hair, and the tension of the hair is much less on a viol bow than on a violin bow. Bowing technique is different, too: when playing an instrument of the violin family, the player holds the bow with the palm down (unless he's a double bass player using what's called the "German" bow), and he doesn't touch the hair. A

viol player, by contrast, holds the bow with the palm facing up and presses on the hair with the middle finger of the bowing hand in order to increase the hair's tension as needed.

By the 1700s, the viols had been largely supplanted by the sturdier, more powerful, and more brilliant instruments of the violin family. Except in the case of the double bass, however, the violin family didn't develop from the viol family. Indeed, the two families developed during roughly the same period, and, strangely enough, they're hardly even related. They may have had a common ancestor among the ancient Arabic stringed instruments, but the viols are closely linked to the guitar and the lute, while the violin family developed from various kinds of medieval fiddles [see LUTE; VIOLIN FAMILY].

During the seventeenth century, the viola da gamba was particularly important as a continuo instrument in instrumental groups of all types, from small chamber music ensembles to opera orchestras [see CONTINUO]. Eventually it ceded this role to the cello. Along with the cello, however, it also became a popular solo instrument, and composers continued to write solo pieces and sonatas for the viola da gamba long after they had left the other viols behind. The solo literature for viola da gamba extends to the middle of the eighteenth century, and includes, among many other works, three beautiful sonatas for viola da gamba and harpsichord by Johann Sebastian Bach.

VIOLA

[See VIOLIN FAMILY.]

VIOLA DA GAMBA

[See VIOL.]

VIOLIN

[See VIOLIN FAMILY.]

VIOLIN FAMILY

The members of the modern violin family are the VIOLIN, VIOLA, CELLO, and DOUBLE BASS. The violin, with the highest voice of the four, is the soprano of the family. The viola (to continue the vocal analogy) is the alto, the cello is a combination tenor-baritone-bass, and the double bass is the *basso profondo*, the "deep bass." As with real voice types, the actual ranges of notes overlap from one instrument to the other, but the sound qualities are quite different. The viola is a bigger instrument than the violin (anywhere from one to three inches longer), but like the violin it's played under the chin, held up with the left hand. The cello is always played sitting down, the instrument held between the legs and supported by a sharpened endpin that sticks in the floor. The double bass is so large that the player must either stand or lean against a high stool. All four instruments are played with a bow, but they can be plucked as well. (For discussions of some of the many terms and topics associated with the violin family, see the following: BOW~BOWING; CONCERTMASTER; FIDDLE; PIZZICATO; SECOND VIOLIN; SPICCATO; STRADIVARIUS; STRINGED INSTRUMENTS; VIBRATO; VIOL. See also CHAMBER MUSIC; CONCERTO; ORCHESTRA; SONATA.)

The viola, cello, and double bass share the basic features of the violin: four strings, a hollow wooden body, which acts as an amplifier for the vibrations of the strings, and a long, narrow neck with a fingerboard (not fretted) glued to it. The body consists of the top, or "table," which is made of spruce; the back, which is usually made of maple; and the sides, or "ribs," which are also made of maple. A slender maple bridge supports the strings and transmits their vibrations to the body. The fingerboard is made of ebony, and the tuning pegs, used to tighten and loosen the strings, are of ebony, rosewood, or boxwood. The modern double bass uses metal screws and a gear system to tune the strings.

Inside the body, not quite directly beneath the bridge, a narrow wooden dowel called the soundpost stands tightly wedged between the top and the back. The soundpost transmits vibrations from the top to the back, and also acts as a pillar to help support the top, which is subject to great stress from the pressure of the strings on the bridge. In French, the soundpost is called *l'âme*, "the soul," a pretty good indication of its importance. To reinforce low-frequency vibrations, a wooden strip called the bass bar is glued to the inside surface of the top on one side.

The members of the violin family are descendants of various kinds of medieval fiddles, bowed string instruments that were originally imported to Europe from the Middle East. Up until the early 1500s, the modern instruments were still evolving, but by the mid-1500s Italian craftsmen had created the models that, with minor modifications, have remained standard ever since. Quite a few four-hundred-year-old Italian instruments are still in use, in fact.

If the instruments themselves were standardized early on, however, their names weren't. It wasn't until the 1700s, for example, that the term *viola* was used to refer specifically to the instrument we now call the viola. From the fifteenth century until the eighteenth century, *viola* (plural: *viole*) served as the general term in Italian for any bowed string instrument. The members of what we now call the viol family were known as *viole da gamba* (leg violas), because they were always held on the lap or between the knees, and the members of the violin family, which had developed along very different lines from the viols, came to be called *viole da braccio* (arm violas), because at least some of them were held up with one arm. The word *violin* comes from the Italian *violino*, meaning "small viola."

The cello was originally called the *basso di viola da braccio*, or "bass arm viola," although it has always been played between the legs. The cello is related to the violin, however, and not to the viols; the purpose of the name *basso di viola da braccio* was to place it in the right family. The word *cello* itself has a curious derivation: it's a short form of the Italian *violoncello,* which means "small big viola." In Italian, the suffix *-one* means "big," and the suffix *-ello,* or *-cello,* means "small." A "big viola" would be a *violone,* and *violone* was in fact an early name for the double bass. Since the *basso di viola da braccio* was smaller than the *violone,* it became known, sometime during the 1600s, as the "small *violone,*" or *violoncello.* Violoncello is the instrument's original English name, too, but it's used less commonly now than *cello.*

The double bass is the one member of the modern violin family whose roots are in the viol family. Its back is flat, like a viol's (not arched, like a violin's) and it has the steeply sloped shoulders of a viol. Its name, too, comes from the viol family: its immediate forerunner was the "double-bass viol," the largest of the viols. The double bass is still sometimes called the bass viol, although it's known by many other names, too, including bass (the name most often used by musicians), contrabass, string bass, stand-up bass, bass fiddle, and bull fiddle. *Double* and *contra* are both terms that, when applied to an instrument, mean "lower octave"; they indicate the pitch range in which the instrument plays. Historically, the function of the double bass was often to play the same notes as the cello, but an octave lower [see OCTAVE].

The members of the violin family were sturdier, louder, and more brilliant than the somewhat older viols, and they gradually replaced the viols in most types of instrumental music. The violin, in particular, became the single most important solo instrument of the Baroque period (ca. 1600–1750), with a huge repertoire of unaccompanied sonatas, solo sonatas with keyboard, trio sonatas (for two violins and continuo), and concertos. Indeed, many of the important composers of the period were also virtuoso violinists, and they often used their works to expand the frontiers of violin-playing technique. Among the great violinist-composers of the Baroque were Salomone Rossi (ca. 1570–1630), Carlo Farina (ca. 1600–1640), Heinrich Biber (1644–1704), Giovanni Battista Vitali (ca. 1644–1692), Arcangelo Corelli (1653–1713), Giuseppe Torelli (1658–1709), Antonio Vivaldi (ca. 1675–1741), Francesco

Geminiani (1687–1762), Francesco Maria Veracini (1690–1750), Giuseppe Tartini (1692–1770), Pietro Locatelli (1695–1764), and Jean-Marie Leclair (1697–1764). The high point of Baroque violin music, however, was reached with the set of six Sonatas and Partitas for unaccompanied violin by Johann Sebastian Bach (1685–1750). The famous *Chaconne* for unaccompanied violin is from the second Partita.

Prior to 1700, the cello was used mostly as a continuo instrument [see CONTINUO], but during the latter part of the Baroque period it, too, blossomed as a solo instrument. Here again Bach outshone the rest: his six Suites for unaccompanied cello are the masterpieces of the Baroque cello repertoire. The viola and the double bass, meanwhile, were valued mainly for their role in opera orchestras and other large ensembles. During the Classical era (ca. 1775–1820), the viola gained greatly in importance, especially in chamber music. This was the era of Joseph Haydn (1732–1809), Wolfgang Amadeus Mozart (1756–1791), and Ludwig van Beethoven (1770–1827), and their writing for the viola reached new levels of sophistication and complexity. Mozart and Beethoven in particular gave the viola a much stronger individual voice in chamber music, and made ever-increasing demands on the skill of the performers. Double bassists, too, were faced with new technical challenges, especially in Beethoven's symphonies.

Prized for the beauty, brilliance, and clarity of its sound and for its extraordinary range of effects and expression, the violin has never lost its privileged position among instruments. The solo violin repertoire — concertos and sonatas — is virtually endless, and includes works by the vast majority of great instrumental composers up to the present day. The violin concertos of Beethoven, Felix Mendelssohn (1809–1847), Johannes Brahms (1833–1897), Max Bruch (1838–1920), and Peter Ilyich Tchaikovsky (1840–1893), just to name a handful, are among the most familiar and beloved works in all of classical music.

Next in size and scope of solo repertoire comes the cello. Haydn's two concertos are the most important of the Classical era, while in the nineteenth century the concertos of Robert Schumann (1810–1856), Tchaikovsky (Variations on a Rococo Theme), and Antonín Dvořák (1841–1904) stand out, along with the Double Concerto for violin and cello by Brahms. Important works for cello and piano include the five sonatas by Beethoven and two by Brahms, and various pieces by Mendelssohn, Schumann, and Frédéric Chopin (1810–1849). In the twentieth century, such composers as Gabriel Fauré (1845–1924), Claude Debussy (1862–1918), Sergei Rachmaninoff (1873–1943), Maurice Ravel (1875–1937), Ernest Bloch (1880–1959), Sergei Prokofiev (1891–1953), Dmitri Shostakovich (1906–1975), Samuel Barber (1910–1981), Benjamin Britten (1913–1976), and Krzysztof Penderecki (b. 1933) have contributed significant works for cello.

The viola's concerto repertoire, while considerably smaller than the cello's, is more extensive than many people realize. It includes Bach's Sixth Brandenburg Concerto (for two solo violas) and the wonderful Mozart Sinfonia Concertante for violin and viola, as well as concertos by Georg Philipp Telemann (1681–1767), Carl Stamitz (1745–1801), Ernest Bloch, Béla Bartók (1881–1945; an unfinished work), Darius Milhaud (1892–1924), Paul Hindemith (1895–1963), William Walton (1902–1983), Jean Françaix (b. 1912), and Krzysztof Penderecki. There are also works for viola and orchestra by Carl Maria von Weber (1786–1826), Hector Berlioz (1803–1869; *Harold in Italy*), and Max Bruch. A large portion of the repertoire for unaccompanied viola and for viola and piano consists of transcriptions of works that were originally written for other instruments [see ARRANGEMENT]. Violists play the six Bach Cello Suites, for example (an octave higher than written), and the two Brahms Clarinet Sonatas, which were published by Brahms himself in alternate versions for viola. The twentieth century, however, has seen a tremendous increase in the number of original pieces for viola, with Hindemith, Bloch, and Shostakovich leading the way.

Contemporary double bass players have commissioned or composed a number of solo works, and there are several interesting concertos for double bass by Domenico Dragonetti (1763–1846) and Giovanni Bottesini (1821–1889), both world-famous double bass virtuosos in their day. Nonetheless, the repertoire for solo double bass is quite limited. The double bass is simply not well suited for solo display — it's unwieldy, and its low sound doesn't project as clearly as that of higher-pitched instruments. It's not frequently used in chamber music, either, although it does figure prominently in three great works: the *Trout* Quintet and the Octet for winds and strings by Franz Schubert (1797–1828), and the Beethoven Septet for winds and strings. Dvořák's String Quintet, Op. 77, and Prokofiev's Quintet for winds and strings, Op. 39, also include double bass. It is in the orchestra that the double bass remains indispensable: the double bass section, eight to ten members strong, provides the powerful, deep foundation on which the orchestral sonority is built.

VIOLONCELLO

[See VIOLIN FAMILY.]

VIRGINAL

[See KEYBOARD INSTRUMENTS.]

VIRTUOSO

A virtuoso (from the Latin *virtus*, meaning "worth," or "excellence") is someone who is extremely good at what he or she does. In the world of music, the word *virtuoso* is generally applied to wonderful performers, and it may be used either as a noun or as an adjective: a person may be described as a "violin virtuoso," for example, or as a "virtuoso violinist." The term may also be used to describe a performance, as in, "She gave a virtuoso performance of the insanely difficult aria that closes Act II."

A basic requirement for a virtuoso is an extraordinary technical facility, the ability to perform very difficult music, especially fast music, with apparent ease. Indeed, one of the primary reasons virtuosos have always captivated audiences is that the speed of their physical movements is far beyond the scale of everyday human experience. Music involves more than physical challenges and stopwatches, however, and although speed is fascinating, as an artistic quality it doesn't really count for much by itself — or at least it shouldn't. A true virtuoso is someone who combines flash and dash with musical substance and understanding, someone who demonstrates not just the ability to play (or sing) fast and furiously, but the ability to play beautifully.

Virtuosos have played an extremely important role in the history of music. With their achievements over the centuries, they've regularly expanded our musical horizons, our ideas of what's possible with an instrument or with the voice. In so doing, they've set standards and lighted the way for other performers, but more importantly, they've inspired and influenced the work of countless composers. The history of music is literally filled with great pieces that were written for specific virtuosos. Often the virtuosos have been the composers' friends and colleagues, and they've requested or commissioned pieces to showcase their skills and add to their concert repertoire. There have also been many important composers who began their careers as virtuoso performers themselves, and who wrote pieces to display their own skills. To name just a few such composer-virtuosos: violinist Niccolò Paganini (1782–1840) and pianists Franz Liszt (1811–1886), Johannes Brahms (1833–1897), Sergei Rachmaninoff (1873–1943), and Béla Bartók (1881–1945).

[See CONCERTO.]

VOICE TYPES

There are three basic categories of singing voices for both men and women: high, medium, and low. For women, these categories, starting from the top, are SOPRANO, MEZZO-SOPRANO, and CONTRALTO. For men, they're TENOR, BARITONE, and

BASS. The terms refer not just to the voice types, however, but to the people who have them, or to the parts they sing: it's correct to say, "She sings soprano," or "She's a soprano," or "She's singing the soprano part." Mezzo-soprano (the Italian word *mezzo* means "middle") is often colloquially shortened to just plain mezzo, as in "She'd prefer to sing soprano roles, but she's really a mezzo."

Voice type isn't simply a matter of the actual range of notes that a person is able to sing; it has to do with the range in which the voice is strongest and the singer most comfortable, and with the quality of the voice. There are basses who can physically reach some of the high notes in "tenor range," for example, but even when they do, they don't sound anything like true tenors. (They mainly sound uncomfortable.) And it's the reverse for tenors who can reach low notes. They may be able to get down there somehow, but their voices don't have a "bass quality."

Within the basic categories of voice types, there are a number of specific classifications that are used primarily in the world of opera. Here are a few of them. (Again, the terms may refer either to the voice or to the person.)

COLORATURA SOPRANO (or simply COLORATURA): *Coloratura* (literally, "coloring") is the elaborate ornamentation or embroidery of a musical line. The term describes a style of vocal music — a style that usually includes plenty of swift, difficult passages designed to display the virtuosity of the singer — but also the voice type suited to that style. A coloratura soprano voice is extremely flexible and agile. It may be brilliant, but it is also most often "light," or slightly on the thin side. (With voices, lightness and agility usually go together.) In this case the classification implies both quality and pitch range: coloratura is the highest of the soprano voices.

LYRIC SOPRANO: The basic soprano voice. The term is almost a redundancy, as *lyric* means "singing," or "songlike." Lyric sopranos sing music in a wide range of styles, from sweet and light to powerful and demonstrative. The lyric soprano voice is generally quite agile, but also capable of sustained beauty and expressiveness.

DRAMATIC SOPRANO: The most powerful of soprano voices. The pitch range is no different from that of a lyric soprano, but the dramatic soprano is a "bigger," or "heavier," voice, capable of projecting over a large orchestra and singing music of the most demanding intensity.

SPINTO SOPRANO: *Spinto* ("pushed") is the short form of the Italian term *lirico spinto*, "pushed lyric." A spinto is a lyric soprano capable of the power of a dramatic soprano on occasion, but not on a regular basis.

COLORATURA MEZZO-SOPRANO, LYRIC MEZZO-SOPRANO, DRAMATIC MEZZO-SOPRANO: The distinctions are the same as for sopranos. The mezzo-soprano voice is generally somewhat "darker," mellower, or heavier than the soprano voice, even when singing the same notes. Some mezzo-sopranos possess voices of great agility and flexibility and are capable of brilliant coloratura, but in a pitch range somewhat lower than that of coloratura sopranos.

BOY SOPRANO: Before their voices change with puberty, young boys can sing in a very high soprano range. Generally, boy soprano voices are noted for their purity and sweetness.

LYRIC TENOR, DRAMATIC TENOR: The distinctions are the same as for the women's voices.

HELDENTENOR: A heldentenor is a dramatic tenor, but the term is usually reserved for tenors who sing certain lead roles in the operas of the German composer Richard Wagner. *Held* is German for hero, and *Heldentenor* means "heroic tenor." The heroic task for the heldentenor is to make himself heard over huge Wagnerian orchestras for hours at a time without dying before he's supposed to.

COUNTERTENOR: The highest of the male voices still heard [see CASTRATI], commonly defined as a male alto. A countertenor, in other words, is a man who sings in a range that is usually for women. The quality of the countertenor voice is hard to describe: it is produced mainly with what is called "falsetto" singing, but it can be quite rich and beautiful. Some would say that a woman's voice in the same range can sound fuller and more expressive, but that's a matter of taste, and of the capabilities of the individual singer. The countertenor is a voice type with a long and interesting history in both church music and opera, a history that runs from the Renaissance (ca. 1430–1600) through the 1600s and early 1700s, when women were still largely excluded from singing in public. Much music from those periods that is now commonly sung by women was originally written for countertenor.

BASSO PROFONDO: The lowest (*profondo* is Italian for "deep"), darkest, and heaviest of bass voices.

BASS-BARITONE: A bass, but a high bass, lighter and more flexible than the basso profondo, and generally of a more lyrical quality.

Voice type determines what operatic roles a person can — or should — sing. There are lyric soprano roles, for example, basso profondo roles, and so forth [see TESSITURA]. Indeed, composers generally have specific voice types (or specific singers) in mind when they create operatic roles. (This doesn't mean that a certain role is always sung by the same voice type. The title role of Georges Bizet's *Carmen,* for example, is usually sung by a mezzo-soprano, but over the years many sopranos have sung the role, as well.) Not surprisingly, voice type in opera is usually linked with character: lighter and higher voices tend to be associated with youth, innocence, and gaiety, while fuller, darker, and lower voices carry the burdens of age, wisdom, sexuality, tragedy, and evil.

With all this cataloguing, it's important to keep in mind that the distinctions among various categories and subcategories of voice types are not rigid, and that few singers fit neatly and precisely into just one slot. For one thing, the pitch ranges of the categories often overlap significantly. Many mezzo-sopranos, for example, can comfortably sing all but the highest notes in soprano range. And singers are always interested in expanding their possibilities and their repertoire. A lyric tenor, for example, might decide to try dramatic tenor roles, and a mezzo-soprano who usually sings coloratura roles might find herself perfectly at home in certain lyric roles. And interestingly, people's voices change, either with age or training, sometimes enough to switch voice types completely.

⌐

Choirs and choruses are traditionally divided into two sections apiece for women and men — soprano and alto for women, tenor and bass for men. Within these sections some people may be called upon to sing higher or lower than others, which is why there are often such additional divisions as first sopranos (higher) and second sopranos, and first tenors and second tenors.

W

WIND INSTRUMENTS

A wind instrument is any instrument whose sound is produced by the vibrations of a column of air inside a tube, or pipe. Wind players don't actually try to blow air into or through their instruments, however. They don't have to: because wind instruments are open to the air, the air column that fills the instrument is already there. It's always there. Wind players use their breath only to produce vibrations. And the vibrations that they produce — whether in a reed, their lips, or in the air of a mouthpiece — are what cause the column of air inside the instrument to vibrate.

The *pitch* of the sound on a wind instrument — its highness or lowness — is determined by the length of the vibrating air column: the longer the column, the lower the pitch; the shorter the column, the higher the pitch [see PITCH]. All wind instruments have some way to vary the length of the vibrating air column in order to produce different notes.

There are two principal families of wind instruments: the woodwind instruments, which include flute, oboe, bassoon, clarinet, and saxophone, and the brass instruments, which include trumpet, French horn, trombone, and tuba. The organ is also a wind instrument, but it has a whole set of pipes, not just one; it's by far the most massive and complex wind instrument.

[See BRASS INSTRUMENTS; REED INSTRUMENTS; WOOD-WIND INSTRUMENTS; ORGAN.]

The principal woodwind instruments of the modern symphony orchestra are the FLUTE, CLARINET, OBOE, and BASSOON. Each of these instruments is the head of a family, or section. The flute family includes the flute and piccolo; the clarinet family includes the clarinet, bass clarinet, and E-flat clarinet; the oboe family includes the oboe and English horn; and the bassoon family includes the bassoon and contrabassoon. The saxophone is also considered a woodwind instrument.

A woodwind instrument is essentially a long tube, or pipe. In order for the instrument to sound, something must make the column of air inside the tube vibrate [see WIND INSTRUMENTS]. The members of the clarinet, oboe, and bassoon families depend on reeds to set the air column vibrating; the player's breath makes the reed itself vibrate. The clarinet uses a single reed, which vibrates against the mouthpiece in which it's set, and the oboe and bassoon both use a double reed, whose split ends vibrate against each other between the player's lips [see REED INSTRUMENTS]. The members of the flute family are the only woodwind instruments that are not reed instruments. The mouthpiece of a flute is just an oval-shaped hole cut into the side of the instrument near one end. The player blows across (not *into*) the hole, and the stream of breath strikes the sharp, far edge of the hole, setting up localized air vibrations. These localized vibrations are what set the air column in the instrument vibrating. The same principle applies when blowing across the opening of a bottle to produce a sound.

On woodwind instruments, as on all wind instruments, playing different notes (that is, varying the pitch of notes) is a matter of changing the length of the vibrating air column. The longer the air column, the lower the frequency at which it vibrates and the lower the note; the shorter the air column, the higher the frequency and the higher the note [see PITCH]. While brass players can change the actual length of their instrument's tubing, using either valves or a slide (as on the trombone), woodwind players can't — the length of tubing they have to work with is fixed.

Woodwind players depend instead on a series of holes drilled into the sides of their instrument. By covering or uncovering the holes, the player changes the *effective* length of the tube: when all the holes are covered, for instance, the length of the air column is the same as the full length of the tube, but when a hole is open, it's as if the tube ended right at that hole. Uncovering a hole, in other words, shortens the length of the vibrating air column. (When a number of holes are uncovered, the one that determines the pitch of the note is the one closest to the vibration source, that is, the one that makes the air column the shortest.) While the air column can be shortened to varying degrees, there's no way to make it longer than the full length of the tube. This means that the lowest possible note on a woodwind instrument is the note that sounds when all the holes are covered.

Covering and uncovering holes is not the only way woodwind players can play different notes, however. Like brass players, woodwind players can increase their lip tension and breath pressure to produce changes in pressure within the air column. This technique is called "overblowing." (Woodwind players and brass players both use the term *overblowing*, but the specific playing techniques are completely different. Overblowing is also different from one woodwind instrument to the next.) Overblowing causes the air column to vibrate in partial lengths, meaning at higher frequencies, and the result is higher pitches. When used in combination with covering and uncovering holes, overblowing greatly expands the range of possible pitches on a woodwind instrument.

Since there are far more holes on a woodwind instrument than a player has fingers, woodwind players must cover and uncover the necessary holes by using an array of metal keys, which are part of a system of levers, rods, and springs, all connected to felt-padded hole covers. The key mechanisms for the various instruments are quite elaborate and sophisticated, and the fingering systems can be extremely complex. The modern bassoon, for example, has between seventeen and twenty-two keys, and a look at a fingering chart for the bassoon — a chart that indicates which fingers must press which keys to play all the different notes — is enough to make a nonbassoonist dizzy.

Despite their name, not all woodwind instruments are made of wood. Most modern flutes, for example, are metal. Among professional players, silver flutes are the most common, but many professionals use fourteen-karat gold flutes, and some use flutes made of platinum. Oboes, clarinets, and bassoons *are* made of wood. Bassoons are made of maple, while oboes and clarinets are usually made of African blackwood (sometimes called grenadilla), a kind of rosewood that grows in Mozambique and Tanzania and that's so dense it doesn't float. Piccolos, too, are often made of African blackwood. Student model woodwind instruments are sometimes made of plastic.

The FLUTE is one of mankind's oldest instruments, and in one form or another it's been known to virtually every culture around the world. The modern flute used in Western classical music is known technically as a transverse flute because the player holds it out to one side and blows across a hole in the side of the instrument. Other flutes, such as the recorder, are "end-blown" — the player blows directly into an opening in one end of the instrument. Transverse flutes were known in Europe from medieval times, but up until the late 1600s their tonal and technical capabilities were quite limited. Most composers preferred to write for the recorder, which had a sweeter sound and more accurate pitch. French instrument makers made great improvements in the transverse flute, however, and by the mid-1700s it had generally replaced the recorder. Johann Sebastian Bach (1685–1750) and George Frideric Handel (1685–1759) wrote for both recorder and flute. The instrument they called *flauto* (Italian for "flute") was actually the recorder. When they wrote for what we now call flute, they specified *flauto traverso*. The flute parts in Bach's Second and Fourth Brandenburg Concertos, for example, were originally intended for recorder, while his various sonatas for solo or accompanied flute, the trio sonatas with flute, and the Suite in B Minor for flute, strings, and basso continuo were composed for the transverse flute.

By the late 1700s, the time of Haydn and Mozart, most orchestras included at least a pair of flutes. The PICCOLO found its place somewhat later: Ludwig van Beethoven (1770–1827) became the first to give the instrument an important role in symphonic music by including piccolo parts in his Fifth (1808), Sixth (1808), and Ninth (1824) symphonies. *Piccolo* means "small" in Italian, and the piccolo is a small flute. It's half the length of a regular flute, in fact, and sounds an octave higher [see OCTAVE]. It's the highest of the woodwind instruments, and its sound can "cut through" even the loudest and thickest orchestral sonorities.

In the 1830s and 1840s, a German flute virtuoso and flute maker (and goldsmith) named Theobald Boehm (1794–1881) revolutionized flute playing. Even with the improvements that had come before, the flute was still awkward to play, and its pitch remained unreliable. Boehm essentially reinvented the instrument, spacing and shaping the holes differently and developing an entirely new key mechanism and fingering system (used on the piccolo, as well). With only minor modifications, the Boehm flute has remained the standard ever since.

The chamber music repertoire for flute is extensive. It includes, in addition to an enormous quantity of Baroque music and a steadily growing body of contemporary work, the four quartets for flute and strings by Mozart, the Beethoven Serenade for flute, violin, and viola, Op. 25, the Sonata for flute, viola, and harp (1915) by Claude Debussy, and sonatas for flute and piano by Joseph Haydn (1732–1809), Bohuslav Martinů (1890–1959), Sergei Prokofiev (1891–1953), Darius Milhaud, (1892–1924), Paul Hindemith (1895–1963), and Francis Poulenc (1899–1963). Solo works include Debussy's *Syrinx* (1912) for unaccompanied flute, and concertos by Antonio Vivaldi (ca. 1675–1741), George Frideric Handel, C.P.E. Bach (1714–1788), Wolfgang Amadeus Mozart (1756–1791), Carl Nielsen (1865–1931), Jacques Ibert (1890–1962), and Walter Piston (1894–1976). A person who plays the flute may be called either a "flutist" or a "flautist," although in the United States, flutist is now the more common designation.

↜

The modern OBOE most likely originated in France during the 1600s. The word *oboe*, which is the instrument's name in both English and Italian, comes from the French name, *hautbois* (pronounced "oh-bwah"), meaning "high wood," or "loud wood." Early English versions included *hautboy, howboie, hoyboye,* and *hoboy.* The double-reed forerunner of the oboe was an instrument called the "shawm." Shawms in various sizes had been known in Europe since at least the thirteenth century, and in fact the French originally used the word *hautbois* as a name for small shawms.

The sound of the "new and improved" *hautbois* — the oboe — was more pleasing and varied than the shawm's, and easier for the player to control because of certain differences in the way the reed was held between the lips. The oboe very quickly became popular throughout Europe, and by 1700 most orchestras included a pair of oboes. Oboes predated flutes in the orchestra, in other words, and for much of the eighteenth century oboes were the primary high woodwind instruments of the orchestra. Since 1700, there's hardly been an orchestral composition that has not included oboes.

In addition to countless Baroque works, important chamber music works featuring the oboe include the following: Mozart's Quartet for oboe and strings, K. 370; Robert Schumann's Three Romances for oboe and piano, Op. 94; a trio for oboe, bassoon, and piano by Poulenc; the *Fantasy Quartet* for oboe and strings by Benjamin Britten (1913–1976); Prokofiev's Quintet for oboe, clarinet, violin, viola, and bass, Op. 39; and sonatas for oboe and piano by Hindemith, Poulenc, Milhaud, and Camille Saint-Saëns (1835–1921). Solo works include Britten's *Six Metamorphoses* for unaccompanied oboe, J. S. Bach's Double Concerto for oboe and violin, two concertos by Handel, eight by Georg Philipp Telemann (1681–1767), two dozen by Tomaso Albinoni (1671–1751), and concertos by Richard Strauss (1864–1949) and Ralph Vaughan Williams (1872–1958).

Some consider the ENGLISH HORN a "tenor" oboe, though most think of it as an "alto" oboe. Either way, it's a longer, lower, and mellower instrument than the regular oboe, which all agree is the "soprano" of the family. Besides the difference in length (about 31½ inches for the English horn compared to just over 23 inches for the oboe), the most noticeable physical difference between the two is that the oboe has a slightly flared bottom end, or bell, while the English horn has a bulb-shaped bell. The English horn has been in existence, in various forms, since the late 1600s, but it's been a standard member of the orchestra only since the 1830s. It acquired its present shape in about 1839, thanks to a French instrument maker named Henri Brod, but strangely enough, nobody really knows when or how it acquired its name. Famous solo passages for the English horn are found in the *Roman Carnival Overture* (1844) by Hector Berlioz, César Franck's Symphony in D Minor (1886–1888), Antonín Dvořák's Ninth Symphony (*From the New World*, 1893), and *The Swan of Tuonela* (1893) by Jean Sibelius.

If the oboe is the soprano and the English horn is the alto or tenor, the BASSOON is the bass of the double-reed family. It consists of a long wooden tube constructed with a tight bend so that it doubles back on itself, forming two parallel columns. If it weren't doubled, it would extend to a length of about eight and a half feet and would be impossible to play. The reed isn't inserted directly in the instrument, as on the oboe, but fits on the end of a long, curved metal tube called the crook, or bocal. (The English horn also uses a bocal, but a much shorter one.)

The bassoon's family tree has a number of very old branches, all of them fairly twisted, but the modern bassoon seems to have originated among the same group of seventeenth-century French instrument makers who improved the flute and created the oboe. The bassoon joined the orchestra around the same time as the oboe, the two instruments forming the foundation of what would develop into the modern woodwind section. One of the important figures in the early history of music for the bassoon was Jean-

Baptiste Lully (1632–1687), court composer to King Louis XIV of France. In his ballets and operas, Lully often paired one bassoon with two oboes for the "trio" sections of his minuets [see MIN-UET]. During the Baroque period (ca. 1600–1750), many composers wrote sonatas and trio sonatas with bassoon, and many also wrote bassoon concertos [see SONATA]. Antonio Vivaldi alone wrote thirty-eight bassoon concertos.

The greatest of bassoon concertos is the Mozart Bassoon Concerto, composed in 1774, when Mozart was eighteen. Mozart also wrote a delightful Duo for bassoon and cello. Carl Maria von Weber (1786–1826) wrote a Concerto and also an Andante and Hungarian Rondo for bassoon and orchestra, and about a hundred years later Edward Elgar (1857–1934) wrote a Romance for bassoon and orchestra. The post-Baroque chamber music repertoire with bassoon as the featured instrument is unfortunately neither extensive nor terribly distinguished. The Poulenc Trio for oboe, bassoon, and piano is worth mentioning again, and there are also sonatas for bassoon and piano by Saint-Saëns and Hindemith.

The "sub-bass" of the double-reed family is the CONTRA-BASSOON, also called the double bassoon. *Contra* is Latin for "against," but in this context *contra* and *double* both mean "lower octave," which describes the pitch range of the contrabassoon as compared to the bassoon. It's a range in which the sound vibrations can often be felt as well as heard. Double also refers to the instrument's length, however, for the only way the contrabassoon can produce such low sounds is for the tube to be twice as long as that of the bassoon. The contrabassoon is tremendously heavy and cumbersome, with four parallel wooden columns as opposed to the bassoon's two, and a metal bell. Contrabassoonists always play sitting down, with the weight of the instrument supported by the floor.

Both Handel and Haydn wrote occasional parts for an early form of the double bassoon, and Beethoven called for double bassoon in his Fifth and Ninth symphonies. The modern contrabassoon did not appear until the 1870s, however, when a completely new design was developed by the Heckel company of Wiesbaden, Germany. Pieces with prominent parts for the contrabassoon include *The Sorcerer's Apprentice* (1897), by Paul Dukas, Maurice Ravel's *Mother Goose* (1911), and Ravel's Piano Concerto for the left hand (1930). The contrabassoon is about the furthest thing imaginable from a flashy solo instrument, but there is one excellent concerto for contrabassoon and orchestra, written in 1978 by the American composer Gunther Schuller.

The CLARINET was the last of the principal woodwind instruments to join the orchestra. The modern clarinet evolved from earlier forms in the early 1700s — later than the oboe, bassoon, and flute — and it wasn't until quite late in the century that orchestral composers included it in their scores with any regularity. Of Mozart's forty-one symphonies, for example, only four, Nos. 31 (1778), 35 (1782), 39 (1788), and 40 (1788), include parts for clarinet. All of Beethoven's symphonies, on the other hand, call for a pair of clarinets: by 1800, the clarinet was in the orchestra to stay.

The flute, oboe, and bassoon all have characteristic tone qualities that give them strong and very appealing individual identities, or "personalities." Of all the woodwinds, though, the clarinet is the one with the *widest* range of tone qualities. The sound of the very low register of the clarinet, for example, is worlds apart from the sound of the high register, and the clarinet can go from the smoothest and gentlest of singing sounds — in *any* register — to all manner of boisterous exclamation and flourishes, not to mention honks and shrieks [see REGISTER].

Mozart was the first major composer to recognize and exploit the clarinet's potential, and his Clarinet Concerto remains the jewel of the solo clarinet literature (although it was originally intended for a hybrid instrument called the "basset-clarinet," a cross between the clarinet and an older, slightly lower clarinetlike instrument called the "basset horn"). Other composers who have written important clarinet concertos include Weber (two concertos), Gioacchino Rossini (1792–1868; Variations for clarinet and orchestra), Debussy (First Rhapsody for clarinet and orchestra), Hindemith, Carl Nielsen, and Aaron Copland (1900–1990). Igor Stravinsky (1882–1971) wrote a piece called *Ebony Concerto,* for clarinet and jazz band.

The clarinet has by far the richest post-Baroque chamber music repertoire of all the woodwind instruments. Among the masterpieces of this repertoire are the Quintet for clarinet and strings, K. 581, and the Trio for clarinet, viola, and piano, K. 498, by Mozart, the Beethoven Trio for clarinet, cello, and piano, Op. 11, Schumann's *Fairy Tales* for clarinet, viola, and piano, Op. 132, and *Fantasy Pieces* for clarinet and piano, Op. 73, and four works by Johannes Brahms (1833–1897): the Trio for clarinet, cello, and piano, Op. 114, the Quintet for clarinet and strings, Op. 115, and the two Sonatas for clarinet and piano, Op. 120, Nos. 1 and 2. Other composers who have written substantial chamber works featuring the clarinet include Johann Nepomuk Hummel (1778–1837), Felix Mendelssohn (1809–1847), Saint Saëns, Vincent d'Indy (1851–1931), Max Reger (1873–1916), Stravinsky, Olivier Messiaen (1908–1992; *Quartet for the End of Time*), and Béla Bartók (1881–1945), whose *Contrasts* for clarinet, violin, and piano (1938) was commissioned by the jazz great Benny Goodman. Contemporary composers who have made significant contributions include Seymour Barab, John Harbison, Robert Muczynski, Max Raimi, Bruce Saylor, and Paul Schoenfield, among many others.

Two other members of the clarinet family, the BASS CLAR-INET and the E-FLAT CLARINET, are employed fairly often in the modern symphony orchestra. The E-flat clarinet is a small, high-pitched clarinet. It was originally a military band instrument, and was first used in the orchestra by Hector Berlioz in his *Symphonie Fantastique* (1830). The bass clarinet sounds an octave lower than the clarinet. To make its greater length manageable for the player, it curves upward at the lower end and downward at the upper end. The instrument was invented near the end of the eighteenth century, and Berlioz was one of the first to write for it. It's often found in the large-scale works of Richard Wagner (1813–1883), Gustav Mahler (1860–1911), Arnold Schoenberg (1874–1951), and Igor Stravinsky.

⌒

The SAXOPHONE was invented by the Belgian instrument maker Adolphe Sax (1814–1894) in about 1840. It uses a clarinet-style mouthpiece with a single reed and is generally considered a

woodwind instrument, but it's made of brass. It comes in a variety

of sizes, the most common of which are the soprano saxophone,

instrument for use in military bands, and it became well known in

the United States starting in the late 1800s largely through the ef-

The saxophone is used only occasionally in the orchestra.

Among the composers who have written significant orchestral

Ravel, in *Bolero* and in his orchestration of Mussorgsky's *Pictures

at an Exhibition;* Prokofiev, in the *Lieutenant Kijé Suite* and the

ballet *Romeo and Juliet;* Alban Berg (1885–1935) in the opera *Lulu,*

and Britten in the opera *Billy Budd.* Important solo works include

(1865–1936), and Ibert's *Concertino da camera* for saxophone and

There are a number of well-known chamber music pieces that

least one other instrument. Among the great works in this cate-

gory are the Mozart Quintet for piano and winds (clarinet, oboe,

piano and winds, Op. 16, the Beethoven Septet for violin, viola,

cello, double bass, clarinet, bassoon, and French horn, Op. 20, and

Septet combination. There is also a substantial repertoire for the

bles. The French horn is a brass instrument, but its sound blends

very well with the woodwinds, and it often joins forces with

[See ORCHESTRA.]

X–Z

XYLOPHONE

[See PERCUSSION INSTRUMENTS.]

ZARZUELA

Zarzuela is the national opera of Spain. Like comic opera, operetta, and musical comedy, it features appealing melodies interspersed with spoken dialogue.

Zarzuela takes its name from the Palace of the Zarzuela (*Palacio de la Zarzuela,* in Spanish), a royal retreat near Madrid that was the site of lavish dramatic productions in the mid-1600s. (Zarzuela is one of two musical forms — the other being oratorio — named after a building.) The plays performed at the palace featured ballet and popular dances, extravagant scenery and staging, and musical numbers in the form of recitatives, solo songs, duets, and choruses [see RECITATIVE]. At first the plays were known as *fiestas de la Zarzuela* to identify them specifically with the palace, but by the end of the century similar productions had been mounted successfully in various locations, and the well-established form was simply called *zarzuela.*

In the early 1700s, Italian serious opera (*opera seria*) conquered Spain (as it conquered England and Germany), and zarzuela, which had become very popular, was completely eclipsed. It had a brief revival toward the end of the eighteenth century, but it couldn't compete with the tremendous success of the *tonadilla,* a very light comic form that was essentially the Spanish equivalent of Italian comic opera (*opera buffa*). [See OPERA.]

A nationalistic movement in Spanish musical circles in the 1830s and 1840s brought about the real revival of zarzuela. The composer Francisco A. Barbieri (1823–1894), who wrote more than seventy zarzuelas, was the most important figure in this revival, which saw the development of two distinct types of zarzuelas. The *zarzuela grande,* or "big zarzuela," has three acts, and its subjects are generally serious, even tragic. The *género chico,* meaning "small type," also called *zarzuelita,* is the comic version, and it has only one act. Both the big and the small types retain the tradition of mixing music with spoken dialogue.

A particularly significant event in the history of zarzuela was the founding of the Teatro de la Zarzuela in Madrid in 1857. This theater was the artistic home for Barbieri, and for such major zarzuela composers as Joaquín Gaztambide (1822–1870), Pascual Arrieta y Corera (1823–1894), Cristóbal Oudrid y Segura (1829–1877), Manuel Fernández Caballero (1835–1906), Federico Chueca (1846–1908), Tomás Bretón y Hernández (1850–1923), and Ruperto Chapí (1851–1909). These composers may not be exactly household names among non-Spaniards, but in Spain their music is extraordinarily well known and well loved. Composers of comparable stature in the United States, for example, would include Broadway greats like Irving Berlin, George Gershwin, and Richard Rodgers. In recent years, touring companies from Spain have done much to raise zarzuela's international profile, as have individuals such as the famous Spanish tenor Placido Domingo.

INDEX

Page numbers in boldface type denote main entries and key words.

MILES HOFFMAN is music commentator for National Public Radio's *Morning Edition*®. Previously, Hoffman entertained and enlightened the nationwide audience of NPR's *Performance Today* with his sparkling musical commentary, "Coming to Terms," which aired weekly from 1989 to 2002.

Hoffman is violist and artistic director of the American Chamber Players, with whom he regularly tours. A graduate of Yale University and the Juilliard School, he is a nationally renowned violist who has appeared as a soloist with many orchestras around the country. He frequently speaks as a featured lecturer for orchestras, universities, chamber music series, festivals, and other organizations.